RM

-

김남준

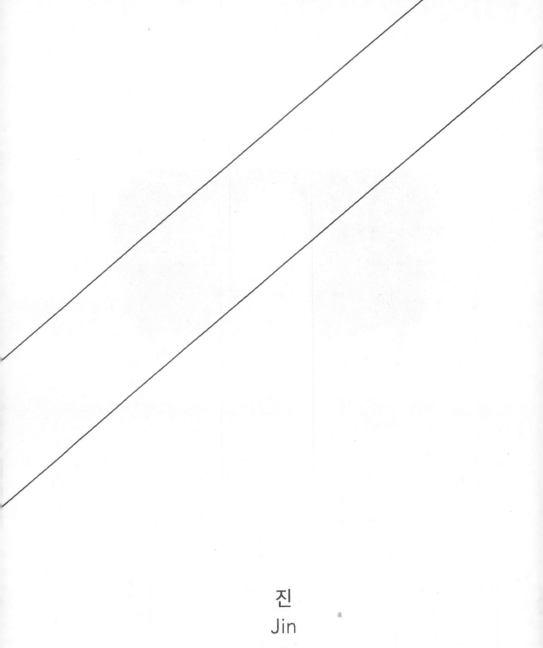

진
Jin
-
김석진

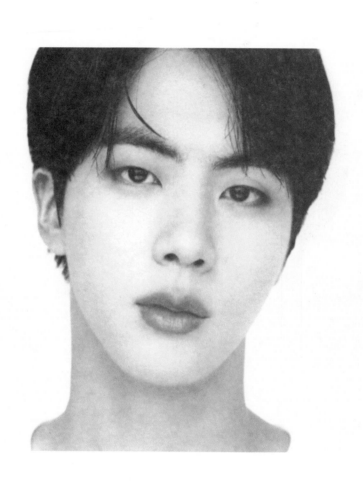

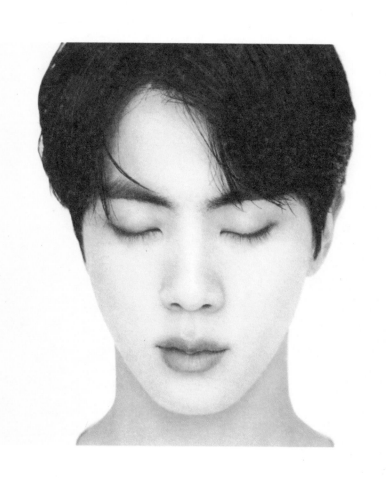

슈가
SUGA
-
민윤기

제이홉
j-hope
-
정호석

지민
Jimin
-
박지민

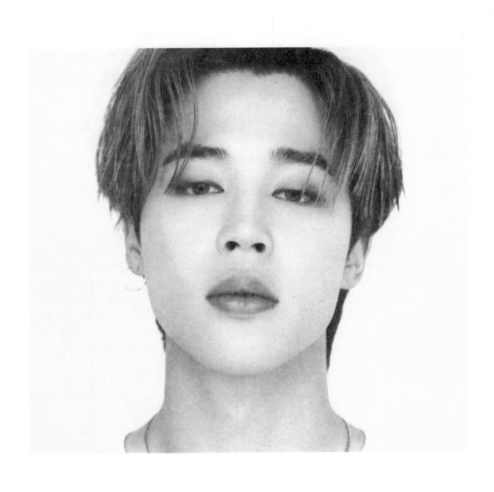

뷔
V
-
김태형

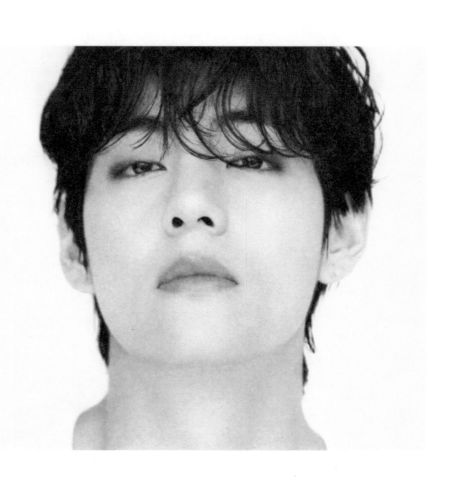

정국
Jung Kook
-
전정국

BEYOND THE STORY

10-YEAR RECORD OF BTS

Myeongseok Kang

BTS

Translated from the Korean by

Anton Hur, Slin Jung, and Clare Richards

MACMILLAN

CONTENTS

CHAPTER 1

SEOUL

1

CHAPTER 2

WHY WE EXIST

45

BEYOND THE STORY

SEOUL

‖‖ ‖ ‖ ‖ ‖   SEOUL   ‖ ‖ ‖ ‖ ‖‖

Korea's busiest crossroads is in Seoul's district of Gangnam, near Sinsa Station. Those driving down the Hannam Bridge over the Han River into Gangnam will pass through this crossroads before heading to different parts of the district, like Nonhyeon, Cheongdam, or Apgujeong. When there's a lot of traffic, drivers might be staring up at the traffic lights for tens of minutes, waiting for their turn, which is why the subway is probably the best way to get to Sinsa Station, if that's your destination.

But if your destination is specifically somewhere near Exit 1 of Sinsa Station, that's a slightly different story—for example, if you happen to be heading for the Cheonggu Building, which in 2010 housed Big Hit Entertainment, later known as HYBE.

Seoul, Gangnam-gu, Dosandaero 16-gil 13–20. Even with the address, it's not easy to find the Cheonggu Building if you have never been to Gangnam or the Sinsa Station crossroads. According to the KakaoMap app, the distance between this building and Exit 1 is 568 meters. But it's impossible to tell from the map that the building is near the end of a steep incline. Nor that several pivots along the way are necessary in order to reach it. Unless you're driving there with the aid of GPS navigation, it could be a bit of an effort and wandering around to find Cheonggu Building.

——I was at a loss.

Such was the case for Jung Ho-seok, who would debut three years later as j-hope of BTS. After signing a trainee contract with Big Hit Entertainment in April 2010, he was undergoing training in his native city of Gwangju when the company ordered him to move into the Big

Hit Entertainment trainee dormitory near the Cheonggu Building in Seoul. He arrived on December 24, 2010.

———I was so scared. It was Christmas Eve and the streets were full of cheerful people, but I couldn't get my bearings at all.

Never had he ridden the Seoul subway or experienced Christmas Eve in trendy Sinsa-dong. This was an area with high foot traffic, even for Seoul, but the elusive location of the dormitory was as intimidating to j-hope as the crowded subway or the unfamiliar vista of the Sinsa neighborhood.

———I kept saying, "This is frustrating!" and ended up calling the then head of A&R. "So, how do I get there?"

After his call, he "kept going straight, and like, somehow and somehow" to use his words, and finally arrived at the dorm. This was the beginning of his dorm life, which he had been looking forward to since the day before and which he still remembered vividly ten years later. On that day, however, he was in for a shock.

———SUGA was there in his underwear (laughs). There were leftover trotters in the sink, laundry strewn on the floor, and everyone walking around in their underwear. 'I guess this is dorm life?' I thought.

Big Hit Entertainment

About a month and a half before this, in the beginning of November, Min Yoon-gi—who would debut as SUGA of BTS—had arrived at Sinsa Station Exit 1, just as j-hope would, and was looking for the dorm.

————My parents dropped me off. There's a practice studio in the basement of Yujeong Restaurant near the Cheonggu Building. I stood there until Pdogg came out and took me inside. My parents told me later that I looked like I was being dragged off somewhere (laughs).

SUGA was seventeen years old at the time. He was a bit too young to leave his hometown of Daegu to come up to Seoul just because he wanted a career in music. But in Korea, it is difficult to grow into a mainstream artist if one doesn't happen to be in Seoul.

————I was in a dance crew in Daegu, and there was a studio I worked in. But the pie was just too small. We might have an event gig from time to time? Sometimes we were paid in tickets for our performances, not money. Not that we were doing it for the money necessarily, but I wonder if we should've at least been paid enough to buy a meal, and a lot of times we weren't paid even that.

By the time SUGA entered Big Hit Entertainment, he was already a paid songwriter working in Daegu. He attended music hagwons to learn MIDI, was introduced to composers, and went from studio to studio doing all kinds of work. Back then, there was no arts high school that taught mainstream music in Daegu, which was why for a time he studied classical music with an eye on entering arts high school that way. He learned different kinds of music from various musicians, composing everything from school songs to trot. But for a teenager dreaming of a career as a professional musician, especially a teenager obsessed with hip-hop, his prospects outside of Seoul were slim.

————Hip-hop wasn't very mainstream in Daegu at the time. This was when people made fun of rappers, calling them "hip-hop warriors," and when the hyoungs I made music with did cyphers[1] in the park, we'd get maybe twenty people as an audience. And our first one had two people.

It was a fairly reasonable choice for SUGA to head to Seoul, in retrospect. Indeed, SUGA and j-hope had deliberately made the decision to enter the idol audition process before joining Big Hit Entertainment as trainees; j-hope had undertaken auditions with other companies and already had specific dreams of debuting as a singer by the time his dance hagwon recommended him for an audition with Big Hit.

As Korean idol groups became explosively popular in the 2000s, not only domestically but internationally, teenagers aspiring to stardom flocked to famous dance hagwons that not only taught dance but also introduced promising students to entertainment companies in Seoul. This was also how j-hope's initial training was outsourced to Gwangju before he entered the dorm in Seoul.

———The Big Hit A&R people came to Gwangju and sat in on the auditions in person. I danced for them, and then did eight months of outsourced training after I succeeded in the audition. Once a month during this training, I made videos of myself dancing and singing to send to the company.

Meanwhile, SUGA, who was already a professional songwriter, became interested in a particular person at Big Hit Entertainment.

———I always liked the songwriter Bang Si-Hyuk. I really liked the T-ara song "Like the First Time," and learned that Bang had

---

1 A hip-hop term for rappers gathering in a circle and taking turns making up verses to the same beat.

written that song. He wasn't on television or anything back then, but he was already famous as a songwriter among people in the know.

For teenagers with limited insider knowledge of the entertainment industry, trusting a company recommended by one's dance hagwon or taking an audition because a favorite songwriter happened to work there was the best course of action.

Even before the incredible success of today's BTS, Big Hit Entertainment in 2010 was already a well-respected company, more than worthy to be a young musician's dream company. Bang Si-Hyuk—the current chair of HYBE—established Big Hit in 2005, and by the time j-hope and SUGA had signed on, he had raised a string of successful artists like 8Eight, J-Lim, and 2AM to stardom. 2AM's "Can't Let You Go Even if I Die" in particular, composed by Bang, was a massive hit that rocketed the team to supremacy. Big Hit Entertainment was hardly small fry in the scheme of things, with a stable of successful artists and the owner and main producer of the company well-known for his ability to consistently crank out hits.

But the team Big Hit was trying to build at the time with trainees like SUGA and j-hope, the team that would become BTS, was proving to be something of a new challenge for Bang Si-Hyuk.

The making of a K-pop idol group is like the production of a Hollywood blockbuster. Everything converges into a single effort, including capital, planning, advertising and PR, and even the brand value of the company itself. In spite of this, the industry was so competitive that only about five boy groups and five girl groups in a decade could be considered successful. Most of these popular groups came from what was known as "the big three": SM Entertainment,

YG Entertainment, and JYP Entertainment. These companies, like Hollywood's major studios, had the lion's share of capital and industry know-how.

Big Hit, of course, had 2AM. But co-label JYP was the one that led the effort from training to launch. That was why for Big Hit Entertainment, the process of casting, training, and launching was a whole new venture.

And it went without saying that this whole process was much more difficult and costly than simply launching a balladeer. Idol groups need simultaneous mastery of song and dance on stage, and all that singing and dancing need to be trained into them, which means enough practice space is needed to teach scores of trainees vocals and dance. For those, like SUGA and j-hope, who moved away from home, as well as whoever happens to show high potential and is therefore deemed closer to debuting, room and board need to be provided. To prepare an idol group for their debut requires not only offices for the company itself but literal "spaces" for all of the above.

This was why j-hope could only be taken aback by what he saw that Christmas Eve when he first entered the dorm. Big Hit Entertainment was a major company in the entertainment industry, one that a budding artist like j-hope could trust to nurture his talent. But in some ways, the company was arguably closer to being a kind of start-up, with administrative offices and recording studios in cramped quarters on the second floor.

Bang Si-Hyuk used one of those tiny rooms for his artistic and administrative work, including meetings. It was so small that there was room for no more than three people, and that third person would have to sit on the floor. Instead of bringing all the trainees into the same building, Bang rented practice space and accommodations around the Cheonggu Building.

These spaces, like their offices, were only just enough for their most basic functions, which is apparent when contrasting Jung Kook's practice footage from February 2013˙ with the BTS dance footage filmed in HYBE HQ.˙˙ In 2013, Big Hit clearly had everything they needed and more for a company of their size. But compared to "the big three," they might as well have had nothing.

One thing Big Hit had a disproportionate abundance of was people. Take the trainees, for instance. There were about fifteen male trainees vying to become BTS. At one point, there had been twenty trainees competing to join the girl group Glam, which debuted a year before BTS. And importantly, Big Hit also had the producer and content creator Bang Si-Hyuk, the producer Pdogg, and the performance director Son Sungdeuk.

But for the two teenagers who had come up to Seoul from Daegu and Gwangju, the first thing that made a big impression, like SUGA's comment about moving into the dorm, was the fact that there were a whole lot of other teens their age with similar interests. SUGA remembers:

———I went to the recording studio and RM and Supreme Boi were there, and other trainees, and we got all excited just talking about music.

RM,[2] who would become the leader of BTS, spent his teens as Kim Nam-joon in the city of Ilsan, Gyeonggi Province. He remembers the municipality as "a city where everything was satisfying."

———The city was so well-planned when it was built, and all the green
spaces had an emotionally calming effect.

The city was home to the Ilsan Lake Park, which was easily accessible to anyone who lived in the vicinity. The residential areas were mostly apartment complexes, and there were the two large commercial zones: La Festa and Western Dom. The city was indeed planned out from its very founding, with impeccably arranged roads and facilities. The entire city was spacious and peaceful for most of the week, with the two commercial districts becoming busier and more festive from Friday night through the weekend.

———It's a place where there's a certain feeling of comfort. There's a
little of that city gray and the bored faces of pedestrians, but
there are no tall buildings or big corporate offices, which makes
the sky easier to see. It has an excellent environment for con-
centrating on your studies. It's not the countryside, but it feels
like that to me.

While near Seoul, Ilsan wasn't as large or bustling as the capital, which became a factor in RM discovering hip-hop. He started going online in first grade and learned about rap through Nas and interviews and documentaries of hip-hop artists on YouTube, while picking up English along the way.

---

2 RM's moniker since 2012 was initially "Rap Monster" until he changed it to "RM" on November
13, 2017, in the spirit of embracing a wider variety of music.

But offline, the life of middle-schooler Kim Nam-joon was at somewhat of a distance from hip-hop. It was about as far as the distance between Ilsan and Seoul's Hongik University neighborhood.

———If Ilsan offered any advantage to hip-hop, it was the fact that Sinchon and Hongdae were so close. Just a bus ride away. It was my dream to perform in places like Drug or Geek Live House, which don't exist anymore, and maybe in a bigger place like Rollinghall later on.[3] That place could hold 500 people.

A bus ride from Ilsan to Hongdae took a little less than an hour. But if a weekend in Ilsan meant a family of three or four taking a stroll around the lake in the park, a weekend in Hongdae and Sinchon meant rappers and aspiring rappers and their audiences gathering in clubs.

When RM made the decision to audition with hip-hop label Big Deal Records in 2009 to become a professional rapper, it didn't mean he would simply be going back and forth on a bus between Ilsan and Hongdae. It meant jumping into a world he had only seen online, a world completely different from the city he had loved so much that he said, "It's a privilege to have been born in Ilsan." Not only that, but the place where he ended up arriving wasn't Hongdae but Gangnam.

———I made the first cut, so in my second audition I got to perform with artists who had debuted, but I messed up the words. I thought it was over for me.

But interestingly enough, a friend of the rapper Sleepy of the hip-hop duo Untouchable happened to come to the afterparty for the audition,

---

3 In 2022, a few days after the December 2 release of his solo album *Indigo*, RM would hold a small concert for two hundred fans at Rollinghall on December 5.

and he mentioned that Sleepy had been interested in RM's work recently and took his phone number.

————Sleepy said he'd seen me at an audition. He must've been impressed because he talked about me and asked for me. So I gave my phone number to his friend to pass on to him. That's how we wrote emails to each other. Sleepy happened to be old friends with Pdogg. And when Pdogg asked him, "Do you know any rappers who are young?" he recommended me.

Then came the call featured in "A Common Trainee's Christmas"˙ posted on the BTS blog[4]˙˙ pre-debut: "A bumpkin from Ilsan / who made the top 1% nationwide / suddenly gets a call during midterms." Sleepy called RM and asked, "Hey, do you know this guy named Bang Si-Hyuk?"

RM, who had made the top percentile in his national mock exams. SUGA, who had been writing songs since he was twelve and was already a professional musician in high school. And the other trainees in the dorm, who had auditioned for Big Hit Entertainment as rappers and hip-hop fanatics. For all of them, dorm life was crucial to their development in a musical sense, especially if their music happened to be hip-hop and rap. According to j-hope:

————It was a rap den, a den of rap.

---

4 In December 2012, approximately six months before their debut, BTS launched their official blog—which they themselves managed—and their Twitter account.

At the time of his audition, j-hope did not know how to rap at all. He did Yoonmirae's "Black Happiness" for the rap portion, but he felt so dissatisfied with it that he feared he had failed his audition. To j-hope, the happenings in the dorm must've come as quite a culture shock. He recalls:

———Wow, as soon as you walk into that dorm, the kids just started freestyle rapping at you. I couldn't do any of that! Every weekend, the company filmed us rapping freestyle. But then they'd come back to the dorm and keep putting on beats and doing rap.

The dorm overflowed with hip-hop, with impromptu singalongs to songs like Wiz Khalifa's "Black and Yellow" going on in the middle of the night.

Those dormitory days where hip-hop was work, play, and life all rolled into one for a bunch of teenagers would play an important part in the formation of BTS's identity in the coming years. On hip-hop, and the group's special bond, j-hope would say:

———You couldn't *not* rap in that environment. And everyone was so encouraging to me there. I asked them all sorts of stuff about rap and studied up on it and just learned a lot.

Although j-hope was a rap newbie, the beats-filled life at the dorm made him quickly fall in love with hip-hop, which also allowed him to forge new friendships with his fellow trainees. A place where rappers and this dancer who now rapped had gathered to train as professional musicians—this was what j-hope refers to as "Season 1" of their dorm life.

"Season 2" began with the arrival of Jung Kook.[5]

---

5 This narrative follows the order of the members entering the trainee dorms, which is RM, SUGA, j-hope, Jung Kook, V, Jimin, and Jin. The order of BTS members entering Big Hit Entertainment as trainees is j-hope, RM, SUGA, Jin, Jung Kook, V, and Jimin. RM would go on to become the first trainee confirmed to debut as BTS.

Season 2

As BTS's debut began shaping up, the trainees at Big Hit Entertainment were divided into two groups. One was the high-potential group of trainees who seemed ready for their debut, and the other group was made up of trainees whose debut wasn't yet confirmed. RM, SUGA, and j-hope were in the first group.

————I thought, 'Wow, I want to be there, too.' Because I'd come here because of Rap Monster.

Jung Kook was famously brought on by Big Hit Entertainment in 2011 at one of the auditions for *Superstar K3*, a TV audition program on Mnet. But the story of how a Busan middle schooler named Jeon Jung-kook decided to come to Cheonggu Building in Seoul is a bit more complicated than that. Jung Kook had already received business cards from seven different entertainment companies during the *Superstar K3* auditions.

————None of them really told me why they wanted to sign me. I remember one of the companies wanted me to come to a hotel room near the *Superstar K3* audition site for an audition. They wanted to get a video of me singing.

The first reason Big Hit managed to beat the odds and secure Jung Kook was, oddly enough, MBC's *Star Audition: The Great Birth*, a direct competitor to *Superstar K*. On that show, Bang Si-Hyuk was featured as a mentor for the auditioning hopefuls. Jung Kook says:

————Bang Si-Hyuk was famous, according to my dad, and he suggested I try going into his company.

Just as RM used the Internet to learn about rap artists, Jung Kook searched the Internet for more information on Big Hit Entertainment and learned of the rapper trainees there who were preparing for their debut, including RM, whose rap videos were available on YouTube. Jung Kook says:

———Hyoung's rap was great and his English was so impressive, I said, "This is where I'll go!"

But when he auditioned for *Superstar K3*, Jung Kook wasn't sure he wanted to be a singer necessarily.

———Sports, art, music . . . I was pretty good at arts and sports, which made me think, 'Maybe this is where my aptitude is.' So as I was wondering whether to do sports or art, I thought why not try becoming a singer. That was a job a lot of people would appreciate, so I auditioned. It wasn't exactly a joke, but I wasn't worrying myself going, 'What if I fail?' either.

Meeting Rap Monster, whom Jung Kook had gotten to know through an Internet search, as well as a host of other rappers at the dorm he eventually entered, was like seeing a new world open before him. From his first day there in June 2011, it was like getting several older brothers all at once. Jung Kook remembers:

———j-hope would come back to the dorm really late and take out a meal from the fridge and eat it, while going, "Do you want some?" to me.

And the "hyoungs" would take their new little brother everywhere. Jung Kook laughs as he remembers:

———Not long after I entered the dorm, one of the hyoungs played a prank on me. He claimed anyone who just moved in had to buy everyone bingsu. So I did, and we all ate it together.

The three hyoungs who had gone to auditions to achieve their dreams. The little brother who went to an audition program and became a trainee after being inspired by such hyoungs. This slight generational difference foreshadowed that the world was about to change not only for Jung Kook but for the rapper trainees as well.

This "Season 2," as referred to by j-hope, was a prelude to "Idol Season." To the future members of BTS, idols—along with hip-hop and their bond with each other—became another cornerstone of their identity.

Each in Their Position

V also had a less-than-smooth journey from his hometown of Daegu to the Cheonggu Building in the fall of 2011.

————We were ripped off by the cab driver. My dad and I got on and paid 38,000 won to go from Express Bus Terminal to Sinsa Station. I remember clearly that we passed three tunnels.[6] I still remember what the cabbie said as we got off: "Be careful, lots of people here try to force customers into premium taxis to rip you off."

The moment V first entered the dorm was like arriving at a new and mysterious world. V remembers:

————Jung Kook was at a lesson so he wasn't home, and j-hope, RM, and SUGA were there.

V didn't think his expectations from before he arrived in Seoul would change. He says:

---

6 The two points are only about two kilometers apart and there is no need to enter any tunnels. Even in 2023, more than ten years since this incident, the cab ride would cost about 6,000 won on an ordinary taxi during the daytime.

————I figured I would not be in the same team as them. 'The three of them love music and do hip-hop, and I guess I'm just someone who's only living here with them.'

V, a high school fresher, had become a trainee at Big Hit only six months after he had begun taking dance classes. Ever since he had sung onstage at his elementary talent show, he had wanted to become a performer, and he had played the saxophone since his first year in middle school with the goal of entering an arts high school. But K-pop dance was something he had learned in a hagwon over a period of six months. This was why he'd had no intention of auditioning when the A&R team at Big Hit had come down to Daegu to his dance hagwon to find new trainees.

————Just the fact that an entertainment company would come down from Seoul was a novelty to me, so I went just to watch. They had auditioned only the kids who had gone to the hagwon for two, three years when at the end, one of the A&R people pointed at me and said, "Can we see that kid dance, too?" and then I got in.

Around the time V entered the dorm, RM, SUGA, and j-hope were already working at a recording studio provided by Big Hit Entertainment. The three were already posting songs on the BTS blog before their debut, having built up enough expertise in rap, composing, and dance to hold long discussions on these subjects. SUGA in particular was desperate to debut:

————Father used to hate people in music. But . . . once I passed my audition and began showing up on posters, he would brag about me a lot. Which made me think I'd better debut soon. Even if I'd fail to make a mark, I wanted to have debuted.

In contrast, Jung Kook and V only began training in vocals and dance in earnest when they joined the dorm in 2011. To V, the trio of RM, SUGA, and j-hope were already artists. V recalls:

———The three hyoungs were so good at music, so dedicated to their work, and they seemed like experts to me. I was just happy to be a trainee by their side.

Having just started as a trainee, the prospect of a debut seemed very far away to V.

But just six months later, when Jimin came up from Busan in May 2012, the others—including V—struck him as being ready to debut immediately. Jimin recalls:

———I'm very shy and I was nervous . . . I was trembling. I came to the dorm and there were so many shoes in the foyer . . . The shoes overflowed into the apartment. But even that was really cool. The hyoungs came out, and they were trainees but already looked like celebrities to me. RM in particular looked exactly as a celebrity should. And V was such a classic idol. Really handsome and wearing a red snapback cap.

The older boys who did hip-hop and the boy who was the same age and looked as good as any idol. The trainees, as seen through Jimin's eyes, were already entering their "Idol Season." Rappers who lived and died by hip-hop, the dancer who was influenced by them to write his own rap lyrics, the vocalist who was just learning to dance, and the youngest who showed potential in both song and dance. Jimin found it difficult to imagine such disparate talents ever coming together as one team.

———I was convinced the hyoungs would debut first as a hip-hop group.

—

— I figured I would not be in the same
team as them. 'The three of them
love music and do hip-hop, and I
guess I'm just someone who's only
living here with them.'

—V

—

—

But Jimin's arrival was a preview of how the planning for their group would go in a different direction. If they were to become an idol group together, Jimin would join j-hope as one of the main dancers but bring a completely different sort of flair to the team.

Before he came to Seoul, Jimin had already been spending his teenage years in dance.

———We had an afterschool break-dance club, and I remember a bunch of boys just got together and said, "Hey, do you want to try this?" Which became, "Should I really?" We gathered to practice on Saturdays when we didn't have school, and then did an actual performance . . . That's when I felt it, the thrill. I completely fell for dance.

Jimin's main criterion for choosing a high school was also "a place I can learn dance," and, hoping to become acquainted with a larger variety of dance, he specialized in contemporary dance at the Busan High School of Arts. To his parents, he explained his goals of learning dance in Busan, auditioning, and moving to Seoul. He remembers his first impressions of the capital:

———I thought, 'Well, Seoul is the same as Busan.' Like, 'That's it?' (laughs). I had come with my father because I was transferring schools.

Unfortunately, Jimin, like V, also fell victim to a taxi scammer.[7]

———It might take as little as fifteen minutes to get from Express Bus Terminal to the company offices, but it took over half an hour. I'd taken a taxi because I wasn't familiar with the subway lines,

---

7 Because taxi apps are more common now, such scams are less likely to occur.

and the fee came out very high. My father had gone down with me to Busan, but the day I went into the dorm, I came to Seoul alone. And that's when I first met j-hope, who had come out to get me.

———Are you Mr. Park Ji-min? (laughs).

j-hope still recalls the moment he first met Jimin.

———That's how we first said hello. "Ji-min? Mr. Park Ji-min?" Like that. We said hello and talked on the way up to the dorm. I asked him if he danced and he said, "Yes, I did Popping," and I said, "Hey, I did street dancing, too." "I hope we'll be able to help each other!" That kind of thing. It was a somewhat awkward conversation (laughs).

It's not easy to imagine a rapper from the Hongdae stage and a contemporary dance major who started out as a break-dancer making music in the same team. But approximately eight years later in early 2020, BTS would combine elements of both disciplines in "Black Swan." This melding of contrasting talents occurs sometimes in the K-pop industry, where idol groups are normally composed of a variety of positions such as rapper, dancer, and vocalist. And the members' even more diverse personalities and backgrounds become a touchstone that allows their fans to emotionally immerse themselves in their characters and music, as long as a harmonious team was formed in the first place.

A team spearheaded by a group of underground rappers that included a middle schooler who had just started lessons needed more than just cohabitation to cohere into a group—they needed some form of alchemy.

———I was fooled (laughs).

Jin laughs, thinking back to his casting at Big Hit Entertainment in the spring of 2011. What the worker in charge of signing him had promised him back then technically hasn't come to fruition. Jin continues:

———"Look at how idols these days go into acting, we'll let you become an actor eventually." That's how they convinced me. They were very persuasive.

Indeed, around that time, it wasn't uncommon for a member of an idol group to also be working as an actor at the same time. While some members specialized in singing and dancing, others were more known for appearing in variety shows or dramas on television, pulling in audiences from outside the idol market.

As Korea's idol market expanded with the rise of BTS's popularity and more acts began performing overseas, fewer idols ventured into acting. Jin, for one, became too busy doing stadium tours around the world with BTS, which naturally made him focus on his work as a musician.

But many idols, to this day, continue to sing and act at the same time. Jin had entered university as an acting major. His interest in idol music sprung from his curiosity about artistic activities in general.

———I do like to try different things. I figured I'd be able to have a variety of experiences if I were an idol and an actor at the same time.

Laughing, he adds:

———Reality had other plans.

Until he became a Big Hit Entertainment trainee, Jin had a happy, fairly relaxed upbringing. Jin himself describes his childhood in Gwacheon, Gyeonggi Province

———I could just go down to the playground and my friends would be hanging out, and if I ever wanted to talk to anyone I'd just call them up and say, "Hello, I'm such-and-such." All the kids in the neighborhood were friends with each other, and our parents would befriend each other as well. Walking down the street, you'd run into someone you'd say hello to every five or ten minutes.

Even moving from Gwacheon to Seoul didn't change his life much. Jin's parents once suggested he go to the country and try out the farm life.

———My parents said, "Let's try different things to see what you have an aptitude for." And that my granddad, grandma, and uncle were farmers, so why not try farming for a bit? That's how I ended up growing strawberries and melons for a month. I did so much pruning for the melons that I didn't want to eat melons for a long time after that (laughs).

Jin is the oldest member of BTS. When he signed with Big Hit Entertainment, he was eighteen and in his first year of university, at the age when most Korean youth begin thinking about what they want to do with their lives. Jin says

———Since becoming a trainee, I worked hard during practice hours.

But I didn't exactly stake my life on it, as they say.

The future he had vaguely imagined for himself was to keep training, debut as an idol, and at some point, incorporate acting into his schedule. And so, Jin continued to go back and forth from his home to training sessions at Big Hit.

But in the summer of 2012 when he entered dorm life, Jin had no choice but to change his entire lifestyle. By the time he joined the other boys at the dorm, the lineup for BTS had been decided, and that meant the content and quantity of Jin's training would change drastically. Jin thinks back to those days

———The company did not tell us we were going to debut, in so many words. But we were almost the only trainees left at the dorm at this point, which made me think, 'I guess it's going to happen soon.'

Jin also remembers his first impressions of the dorm.

———(Sigh) . . . Clothes strewn everywhere, cereal scattered on the floor, the dishes hadn't been done . . .

On January 27, 2013, Jin made a posting on the BTS blog titled "How Trainees Usually Make Tteokgguk."* His ambition had been to create a proper meal he could share with the other members.

———For example, SUGA would basically just "eat to live." He ate chicken breasts for protein but even eating them was too much of a hassle for him so he would blend it with some grape juice and a banana and gulp that down straight from the blender. I had a taste of it and thought, 'Nope, this isn't it,' and cooked up some things that I sprinkled with hot sauce or steak sauce.

Before staff was hired some months later to help with the cooking and cleaning, Jin managed to coordinate the other members into taking turns with chores. As with many other people, cooking and cleaning were key activities for Jin in maintaining a semblance of a normal life. The problem was, Jin himself had to admit that they were simply getting too busy for normality.

—————After about three months there . . . I finally realized why they had come to live the way they did. On days when we had a lot of rehearsals, we'd be working fourteen hours out of a twenty-four-hour day.

School of Hip-Hop

Dewey Finn (played by Jack Black), the main character in the movie *School of Rock*, is a nameless musician who under false pretenses gets a job at an elementary school in place of a friend who is a licensed teacher. When he realizes how talented the students are, he tries to put them together into a rock band. The students, however, know nothing of rock music, and Dewey ends up teaching them the history of rock-and-roll during class instead of the usual curriculum.

If one were to switch rock music with hip-hop, this "School of Hip-Hop" was what went on in the BTS dorm. RM created a playlist of artists including Drake, Nas, the Notorious B.I.G., and Tupac Shakur for his fellow members who were less familiar with the genre. RM says

—————I made a list out of about fifty acts whom we could listen to together. We did cyphers to develop our rapping sensibilities and deliberately watched videos together.

That RM had took it upon himself to be the Jack Black of the dorm was because BTS was mired in a uniquely terrible situation in the world of idol music.

Big Hit Entertainment had debuted a girl group called Glam a year before BTS, with a docuseries of their formation shown around that time on SBS MTV (now known as SBS M). Teaser trailers for their debut were also released on YouTube.

But unfortunately, Glam never caught on in popularity, and Big Hit Entertainment was saddled with a sizable financial burden. When a small-to-medium-sized entertainment company fails at an idol project, the consequences are more treacherous than anything that can be described in words. As SUGA describes the mood back then

——I thought the company was going to go under.

But to RM, the biggest problem they were facing was that their group, which was about to debut, didn't seem to know in what direction they were supposed to go musically. RM says

——Bang Si-Hyuk and I would have the members listen to artists like A$AP Rocky or Lil Wayne. But the members who joined later on knew Big Hit as a company created by the Bang Si-Hyuk who had made 2AM and 8Eight and had worked at JYP Entertainment. But now they were being asked to do hip-hop and rap, which must have presented for them some confusion.

The best RM could do was to talk to the debut-imminent group about hip-hop as much as possible. Right until their debut, RM, SUGA, and j-hope's School of Hip-Hop was holding nonstop classes. Some nights, they would come home after rehearsals ended at 11 P.M. and talk about music until 6 A.M. with no sleep.

Thankfully, the students of this school were very diligent. V recalls

——There was a time when RM, SUGA, and j-hope would sit us four vocalists down and very seriously say, "I really think you should listen to this song," or "Let me teach this to you." RM put so much care into putting together the best songs in hip-hop history that I couldn't possibly say no to him. His care was so palpable that I felt I absolutely had to listen to these songs a lot, even if I happened to dislike them.

The classes were slowly paying off. V says

——Since then, I've come to a point where I'm proud of saying I listen to music the most among all the members. Listening to all that hip-hop back then made me fall in love with it. I would ask the hyoungs to recommend more music, and I would find my own tracks to listen to as well.

V's response has something to do with how the classes were taught. This is how Jimin remembers RM, SUGA, and j-hope's teaching:

——The hyoungs would say things like, "Isn't this the coolest?" and show us all the gestures the artists would make themselves as they played us the songs. At first it was just fun and laughter, but there came a point where I saw how it really was the coolest. I thought, 'This music these hyoungs are into, this is real music.'

Jimin adds:

——That's how we were indoctrinated into the hip-hop mindset (laughs).

The Battle for Razor-Sharp Dance

——Arrrrrrrgh!

When asked about BTS's training process before their debut, j-hope playfully lets out an exaggerated groan before elaborating.

———The alarm goes off at 10 A.M. and we grab a salad, some bread, and chicken breast and go to the practice studio. Then we practice and review ourselves as we keep screaming "Argh!" and start all over again and then it's "Arrrgh!" again and all of a sudden, it's 10 P.M. Then we go back to the dorm and sleep. Ad nauseum.

As previously mentioned, Big Hit Entertainment had more trainees than one would expect from a company of their size. Any entertainment company just starting out with thirty trainees would inevitably need to prioritize resources. The practice studios were always crowded, and the trainees had to take turns with lessons. Jin says:

———When I got to rehearsals after school, there would be four studios and the boy trainees would be gathered in one studio. The other studios were being used to prepare Glam for their debut.

But with the tepid reception of Glam by mainstream audiences, the company reallocated their resources to BTS. Except this time, the resources were being reallocated under a greater financial strain.

Which was why, once the BTS members were confirmed to debut, Big Hit Entertainment was forced to release all their other trainees from their contracts. This was how the time and space to train the seven boys who would become BTS was procured. Their rehearsal times also increased. Significantly.

If RM, SUGA, and j-hope were running a hip-hop school in the dorm after hours, the practice studios were a war zone of dance. It would be fair to say that the members had more trouble getting used to dancing than getting used to hip-hop.

With hip-hop, the trio of RM, SUGA, and j-hope at least had

similar sensibilities, and the younger members only had to follow the example of the older ones. But the only members back then who were used to dancing were j-hope and Jimin. RM and SUGA hadn't even imagined they would need to learn dance. j-hope explains:

———SUGA and RM told me once that they thought we were going to become a group like 1TYM and wouldn't have to dance at all.

1TYM was a hip-hop group that included Teddy, who had also produced BIGBANG, 2NE1, and BLACKPINK. They became popular in the late 1990s and early 2000s during the rise of hip-hop in Korea, and it seems RM and SUGA had assumed BTS would follow in their footsteps as a hip-hop group with mainstream appeal.

Of course, 1TYM, like BTS, emphasized the role of vocalists as well as rappers, and they had some choreographed movement in their acts. But according to Jin, BTS reset their mandate to become an "overperformance group." Of the mood in the training sessions at the time, Jin says:

———The proportion of our training taken up by dance actually wasn't that big in the beginning. But suddenly dance became important and our training time for it went up a lot. We trained really hard especially in the two months before our debut, and there were days when we would be dancing for twelve hours.

Anyone reading this book is sure to understand what "overperformance" means. Not long after, in their performances for their debut song "No More Dream," Jimin would execute a move where he would, with a boost from Jung Kook, fly into the air and walk across the backs of the other members standing in a line.

But the acrobatics was not all that made the overperformance training so arduous. Jin adds:

———Bang Si-Hyuk asked for a little too much back then (laughs). He would be watching playback of our performances on a PC and press spacebar to pause. Then he would critique every angle of our bodies and even our finger placements. He watched our dancing frame by frame. We danced the same choreography for two months.

As Jin described, BTS practiced the choreography for "No More Dream" to the point where they were in sync right down to every single frame.

2AM, Glam, and the four years it took for Big Hit Entertainment to debut BTS was basically the company catching up to the past twenty years of the industry. It was an endeavor that required much research. The company analyzed the factors that made successful idol groups into hits, and regularly consulted industry experts for their advice. Occasionally, Big Hit would post a reward for anyone in the company who could come up with the best proposal for the production of a successful artist.

What Bang Si-Hyuk learned in this process was that idols moved to a completely different beat compared to the music industry that came before. Idol music exploded onto the scene with the debut of Seo Taiji and Boys in 1992, and with the 1996 debut of H.O.T., an industrialized production system was put in place. BTS debuted as the idol system approached the twentieth year of its golden age. Its first teenage fans were now in their thirties, and as fandom culture developed over the years, the content and standards the fans demanded also became clearer.

Kalgunmu, or "razor-sharp group dancing," was such content. Fans wanted their favorite groups to create awe-inspiring moments of perfect synchronized dancing. Not only did such perfection bring a visual joy to their fans but it also served as proof of how hard the members had worked on their teamwork in order to achieve it. But to Bang Si-Hyuk, who was part of Korea's first generation of hip-hop and R&B producers at JYP Entertainment, kalgunmu was not something he was even considering. In hip-hop, dancing was more about emphasizing the personalities of each performer, which led to less pressure for perfectly synchronized movements.

But in the world of idol music, kalgunmu was the law of the land. And while there was an absolute need to follow this law, Jin remembers that even for idol singers, BTS had ended up in the "overperformance" category of artists.

———Sure, group dancing is essential for idols, but our dancing was more intense than the usual.

As their mandate for reconciling the genre characteristics between hip-hop and idol music became clearer, BTS was required to practice even harder. At night there was the School of Hip-Hop convened by RM and SUGA, who became students during the day at the "School of Dance" alongside the others who were not used to dancing. j-hope was the teacher in this latter school. He talks of those days:

———Jimin and I were the only members who had learned dance before we entered the company. I felt like the first thing we needed to do was to help the other members find dancing fun. Outside of our regular training sessions, we occasionally practiced at dawn. It was kind of like the "den of rap" where we would put on a beat and try freestyling. Rap had become fun for me during those sessions, and I wanted the same thing to happen with dance for the others. I'd just put on music and go, "Now dance, just dance however way you want," that kind of thing.

Fortunately, the members were very diligent about their studies in this school. j-hope continues:

——We came together a lot better in training than expected. When SUGA became obsessed with dance he would even joke, "I don't want to rap anymore, let's dance." It's hard to believe I bet, but he and I once went to Hongdae to learn breaking (laughs).

Worlds Collide

But even j-hope, who had opened his own ad hoc dance school in the practice studios, had become completely exhausted six months before their debut. He recalls:

——It was probably the beginning of January, 2013. We were so tired, even when we should've been at our most motivated. There was a practice studio where they filmed our dance moves, and we basically lived in there. Which was why we would stop talking when we entered there, became really prickly about things . . .

In their quest to become an "overperformance group," the members practiced their choreography and took lessons at the same time. In the midst of it all, they also went on specific diets to be at their best possible physical states when on stage, to the point where they were obsessive about the amount of salt they would put on the chicken breasts that they ate for protein.

But suffering and worry had more to do with their mental than their physical states. To be affiliated with Big Hit Entertainment, which was not as well-known as SM Entertainment, invited a kind of gaze j-hope felt was overwhelming.

——When people kept asking us when we were debuting, to a trainee that's really . . . That question is like a knife to the heart.

j-hope was truly desperate. The fraught journey to his debut reads like a series of desperate moments. He recalls his life's story up to his move to Seoul:

——I didn't learn a lot at the hagwon where I learned to dance, because of the tuition fees. So for the most part during lessons, I would just sit on the hagwon sofa. Because I loved dance so much . . . After the lessons, I would keep practicing on my own in the practice studios. The hyoungs who taught me, especially this one dancer named Bangster, became a kind of teacher to me.[8] He said to me, "Hey, do you want to come to our practice studio and practice with us?" And that's how I joined the dance team Neuron.[9] That's where I first came in contact with street dancing. Later, when I signed my contract with Big Hit Entertainment as a trainee, there was no place for me to practice. That was why despite signing the contract, I stayed behind at the Gwangju hagwon where my dance training was outsourced to. And that's when the A&R team contacted me. Telling me it was time to come up to Seoul.

j-hope, RM, and SUGA had to wait two years until their debut, and Big Hit Entertainment was barely scraping by at the time due to

---

8 Bangster, or Lee ByungEun, is currently a performance director at HYBE.
9 The line "entered Neuron" appears in j-hope's song "Chicken Noodle Soup" (Feat. Becky G).

Glam's failure. The practice spaces were so cramped that someone's singing in one room would carry over to trainees in the room three doors down. These circumstances, to the seven boys who were about to debut, were a source of great anxiety.

SUGA especially had reasons to be anxious. He was preparing for his debut despite the aftereffects of a shoulder injury incurred from a traffic accident. He explains:

———I did all kinds of part-time jobs in 2012, right before our debut was set. My family needed money, so I would teach MIDI, work in a convenience store, and do deliveries, and it was on a delivery where I injured myself on a motorcycle.

SUGA's voice turns a shade quieter as he recounts the turmoil of those days:

———The company was in dire straits, and I was worrying my head off as to whether I could continue my life as a trainee. It was really hard for me, the act of living itself. I'd left home pinning all my hopes on debuting, I'd managed to enter this company . . . I felt so desperate.

Jimin had his own issues concerning his debut. He recalls:

———I had given up a perfectly good life learning dance in high school to come up to Seoul, but no one cared . . . You could be eliminated after any of the tests they would put us through time to time, which was scary. I was really putting the pedal to the metal then.

As Big Hit Entertainment let go of all their trainees save the ones earmarked for BTS, Jimin became more and more anxious that the company could let go of him as well at any time. Unlike RM, SUGA, and j-hope, the vocalist-position members including Jimin had no assurance they would be allowed to debut in BTS. The lack of time for proper training and the obligation to train even harder after his debut was decided put more pressure on Jimin.

———I wanted desperately to find the reason why I was in this scene. That I wasn't here only because I was forcing it or out of sheer luck. Which was why I tried to make one more person like me, to show one more person how much better I was doing . . . Maybe I was a little impatient.

Jimin's desperation at the time resulted in the following episode, a serious one at the time but somewhat cute looking back.

———I didn't know how to dance like a member of an idol group. I'd never dealt with dancing like this until I became a trainee. So whenever the movements changed, I would pause and memorize the position. You know that Zolaman character, that stick figure with the big head and sticks for a body? I drew every single move and position in that character and memorized them. It made everyone around me laugh.

Meanwhile, Jung Kook, who was still quite young, was in the process of learning about himself while experiencing dorm life for the first time and undergoing copious amounts of training.

———My personality completely changed. Being tossed into a place full of strangers made me very shy all of a sudden. I would try to avoid everyone else's shower times when using the bathroom, and I slept in the upper bunk of a bunkbed, but even as I sweated from the heat at night, I wouldn't go down from my bed in case I woke up the hyoung sleeping in the lower bunk . . . I realized then, 'Ah, I'm just very shy.'

His particular situation was a perfect storm of the combined realities of K-pop, the upcoming debut of BTS, and Big Hit Entertainment's corporate situation.

Korean idols normally debut in their late teens, or at the latest, their early twenties. Many of them begin as trainees in their mid-teens under contract with entertainment companies. Jung Kook, who would debut at the age of fifteen, is considered a younger case in terms of both entering an entertainment company dorm and debuting as an idol. On top of his age, there was also the prospect of debuting with older boys like RM and SUGA, who had already been active on the hip-hop scene and were obsessed with that genre of music. This meant at the same time as he was training and worrying leading up to his debut, Jung Kook had to discover just what kind of person he was deep down. He says:

———To tell you how bad it was, you know how once you reach middle school, you learn how to use the formal register with your upper-classmen? I didn't even know how to do that. Informal Korean felt natural to me, and I didn't pay much attention to the people around me. But then I entered the dorm and saw how I was coming off. That's when I started using formal Korean. How do I say this . . . I think I was lacking in my attitude toward other people, in understanding and deference and empathy. And then I met the other members and thought, 'Oh I see, this is how you're supposed to act with others' or 'I should speak like this, too' and learned how to express my feelings by seeing how it was done.

To Jung Kook, RM was especially the reason he had decided to sign with Big Hit Entertainment, and j-hope and SUGA were his role models. Jung Kook adds:

———Those hyoungs were on a higher level among the trainees, which made me think, 'Wow, I want to be like them, too' or 'The hyoungs are dressed so cool" and I would buy the same clothes (laughs). Back then, I think I was having these trivial thoughts more than worrying over whether I was going to debut or not.

On the other hand, the three hyoungs he looked up to were burning up with anxiety as their debut was pushed later and later. The day they would finally get to stand onstage seemed further away than ever, and the group seemed to be going in a direction they hadn't expected. Amid all this, they had to teach hip-hop to the others in the dorm and set the tone for the younger members they were living with.

In addition to this, RM, who had become the team leader, had the task of receiving from Bang Si-Hyuk the big picture about their group. RM remembers:

————The company never pressured me into doing things. But they did remind me that the smallest things could create big risks and say things like, "You have to do well as a leader" or even, "You have to wake up the members of your group."

This was where worlds were colliding in the dorm. To RM, SUGA, and j-hope, debuting was an immediate problem, whereas the four vocalists who were debuting faster than they had anticipated were still grappling with what it meant to be put out into the world. Jin says:

————I hadn't really understood what it meant to be an idol. If I'd known beforehand, it would have been easier to get used to that reality. But once I'd debuted, I was just so busy, and also so happy . . .

Once their debut was set, Jin had to readjust to a trainee life that was very different from the one he had been used to until then. Jin and RM went as far as to have a serious conversation about it at one point. Jin says:

————The both of us were in agreement that the team had to go up. But the difference between us was that I was wondering if we could pursue our happiness a little first and then think about what was going to happen, while he believed we had to give our all now for the sake of later happiness.

While thinking in a slightly different direction, V says as well that he thought differently from the three rapper hyoungs.

————Most people train for years before debuting, so I hadn't even considered that my time would come only after a few months of training. I made sure I attended all the practices, but outside of practice times, I hung out with my school friends a lot.

To V, debuting was still far away, and he wanted to experience being a teenager properly as well as working as a trainee.

But V's life abruptly changed once he heard the following from the company:

"It's time for your debut. You, you're BTS now."

And What about You Guys?

The more you look back on BTS's preparation for their debut, the more surprising it is that none of them quit in the process, despite being seven boys from different hometowns and with different values, musical tastes, and time spent in training, coming together to train in less than a year for their debut as a team.

j-hope has some candid thoughts regarding this:

————We didn't fuse together well at first. Our backgrounds were just so different, and we wanted different things. One would go, "I want to become a musician," and another would be like, "I just like being onstage." It was hard to calibrate our sense of objectives toward a single goal.

But ironically, their debut as BTS being decided also became a decisive factor in their becoming closer to each other. V remembers:

——While I argued a lot with Jimin, who is my age, and with the other members as well, we worked together so much and talked with each other so much that little by little, we really did feel we were becoming a team.

RM making his hip-hop playlists and j-hope teaching dance were acts stemming from their desperation for their debut. Of how this goal affected them, j-hope explains:

——The moment it was decided the seven of us would debut as a group, that's when our concept as a group fell into place. We knew what we needed to do, what kind of dance and songs we would do. And we talked among ourselves a lot. "We have, I have this goal. What about you guys? Shall we do this together?" That kind of thing.

Their cohesiveness went beyond sincere conversations, spilling over to every aspect of their lives. V says he became closer to the other members through commonalities in their daily lives:

——We all needed to be on diets, but me and RM weren't very good at it. And since being of "kindred spirit" is serious business, RM and I would often go off to eat something nice together. Or hide things to eat and secretly share them with each other . . .

V's team-building methods were also handy when it came to the younger members.

———I would sneak outside the dorm with Jimin and we'd eat together and talk together. Or go to the jjimjilbang spa with Jung Kook or ride sleds when it snowed. And then pretend nothing had happened when the manager would check up on us at the dorm (laughs).

Meanwhile, Jin got closer to V by looking for things they had in common.

———By the time V and later Jimin entered the company, all the trainees I had been close to had left. Except for about ten who were thought to have potential . . . I thought it would be too sad if more trainees left, which made me wonder a lot if I should make the effort to get closer. But V liked old manhwa and anime, just like me. So I would go up to him and go, "Hey, have you seen this one?" and that's how we became friends.

RM and SUGA taught the members hip-hop, j-hope taught dance, and Jin used whatever ingredients available in the dorm to cook up meals for everyone. In this process, the older members began to understand the young members and the younger members learned from the older ones.

Jim speaks of the musical influences and encouragement he received from the other members:

———The hyoungs felt very "raw" to me. The way they were like, "I just like listening to music," so unpretentiously. SUGA is a bit stoic and would say things simply and firmly, but then he would also come up to me and say things like, "I hope you work hard and do well . . ." I couldn't *not* like the hyoungs, and that's how I became interested in their music.

SUGA, on the other hand, was learning how to communicate with the world through his conversations with the other members.

The moment it was decided the seven of us would debut as a group, that's when our concept as a group fell into place.

And we talked among ourselves a lot.

"We have, I have this goal. What about you guys? Shall we do this together?" That kind of thing.

—j-hope

————It was really hard to respect the fact that we were all different people. I used to be very extreme and trapped in a black-and-white mindset. My immature mind would think, 'Why is he thinking that way? Shouldn't a normal human being think this way?' And eventually I went beyond thinking, 'That guy is different from me,' to accepting, 'That person is just being themselves.' It did take a bit of time.

The answer to the question of why none of the members of BTS quit during that time may be found in the words of some of the members.

Jin sums up the situation back then:

————"Adjusting" seems to be the right word. Because once I entered the dorm, I realized, 'Ah, I guess this is how I should live from now on.'

SUGA speaks of his pride as a musician:

————If it weren't for the music, maybe I would've quit partway through? Or if it had been at some other company with a different culture? I released a lot of things in me making music. I don't know how I had so much confidence back then, making all those songs. A lot of them I get embarrassed about, listening to them now. But the people who are obsessed with hip-hop, they have this attitude, 'I'm the best in the world!' you know? (laughs).

And of course, we need to hear from the leader of the team:

————The members were just good people. Very good people . . .

RM continues:

————The only thing I know how to do is music. I came into this company to make music, and because I believed my work was fundamentally to make music. And because I've been here the longest, I did have the most say in things. To be honest, this made it much easier for me as the leader. And I received so much respect from the other members. It makes me think they've been very good with recognizing and accepting each other. They really treated me well.

The long time it took for them to debut was well spent in training and building their trust in each other through much conversation and exchange. And so, the seven members who had differed in every way began to transform into a team, just like in the lyrics of the song "Paldo Gangsan," revealed four months after their debut, in the video˙ taken in that very practice studio where they had sung and danced so ceaselessly.

> *In the end it's all Korean*
> *Look above, it's the same sky we face*
> *It could be a big cringey, but we're the best*
> *We understand each other, right?*

CHAPTER 2

2 COOL 4 SKOOL

O!RUL8,2?

Skool Luv Affair

DARK&WILD

WHY
WE EXIST

2 COOL 4 SKOOL | THE 1ST SINGLE ALBUM

Skool Luv Affair | THE 2ND MINI ALBUM

DARK&WILD | THE 1ST FULL-LENGTH ALBUM

WHY WE EXIST

We Will Survive

BTS Debut: "Our Role Model Is BIGBANG, We Will Survive"

On June 12, 2013, just one day before the official debut of BTS, an article on Korean portal site Naver's news section reported on the BTS debut showcase that took place at Ilchi Art Hall in the Cheongdam-dong neighborhood of Seoul's Gangnam District. Until Naver took down the comment function on celebrity news articles, thousands upon thousands of comments were left on this historic page.

The highly sanitized versions of the earliest comments are: "They're probably not going to last long," and "'Bulletproof Boy Scouts' is a stupid name." But as time passed and BTS gained popularity, more supportive comments were added to the article. By the time BTS became an international sensation, the article had become an internet pilgrimage destination, with visitors posting wishes like "Please let me get into the university I want" in the comments section—an online phenomenon reserved for the sites of the most spectacular miracles.

The changes in these comments show the past and present of BTS: their past as a team derided from the starting line, and their present as an unbelievably successful group of artists. There were many reasons behind the abusive comments from the early days, but ultimately, they boiled down to this (again, highly sanitized) message: BTS wouldn't last long after their debut and were clearly bound for failure.

Indeed, the deck seemed to be stacked against them. In 2012, the year before BTS's debut, SM Entertainment had debuted EXO. In the

100 days leading up to D-day, they released twenty-three teaser videos introducing the character of the team and the individual members. In 2014, the year after BTS's debut, YG Entertainment debuted WINNER, who had already made a name for themselves in August 2013 through Mnet's survival program *WIN: Who Is Next*.

These pre-debut promotional blitzes were the perfect opportunities to attract idol fans, and were built on a strong foundation of planning and funding. Success seemed to be assured for EXO and WINNER, and these premonitions turned out to be correct. Like their SM Entertainment predecessors H.O.T. and TVXQ, EXO quickly built up a fan following, while WINNER's debut song "Empty" topped the real-time charts on every Korean music streaming platform.

BTS, meanwhile, ran a blog. The very first entry was posted by RM on December 21, 2012, showcasing his mixtape song[10] "Vote."* The post received its first comment on December 24, three days after the posting. The fifth comment was posted on January 5, 2013. The sixth? More than a month later, on February 16.

Compared to SM and YG, Big Hit Entertainment was positively tiny. And this tiny company was debuting a team whose role model was YG's BIGBANG.

---

10 An unofficial free album or song. The term first came into use in the days of cassette tapes and has multiple other meanings that are rarely used today. As mixtape songs are not as strongly developed for marketability, artists are at liberty to showcase more of their personal values and emotions.

There was nothing wrong with being from a small company or looking to BIGBANG as role models. But many comments on BTS's debut article accused them of "trying to capitalize on BIGBANG's success." In the Korean idol industry, it was considered almost underhanded for idols from a smaller company to name popular groups from bigger companies as role models; and these groups had no fans of their own to defend them until they built up popularity and established a fandom of their own.

This mindset was rooted in the preconception that idols from smaller companies never find explosive success. BTS was far from the only male idol group to consider BIGBANG a role model. Around this time, BIG-BANG members G-Dragon and Taeyang were on Mnet's *WIN: Who Is Next* and mentored trainees who would form WINNER, which allowed YG to showcase their up-and-coming talent to existing BIGBANG fans. It is easier for idol groups under established management companies to quickly build a consumer following thanks to the know-how, resources, and existing fandoms at their companies' disposal. BTS was at a massive disadvantage, and it seemed all but impossible to close the gap.

The Big Picture

Although not backed by as much capital as EXO or WINNER, BTS's blog was a strong promotional effort in its own right. Just like the YG Entertainment trainees on *WIN: Who Is Next*, BTS members released their music before their official debut. And just like EXO's individual member teasers, BTS also began to introduce new members, starting on January 12, 2013, with a video of Jimin dancing in the practice studio.* Other content included videos of the members spending Christmas together and individual vlogs in which they spoke candidly into the camera.

The reality of BTS and Big Hit Entertainment's position was clear from shots of the practice studio: the space barely seemed big enough for Jimin alone, and the studio where they recorded their vlogs was positively tiny. And yet the blog contained everything an idol fan could want to see from their favorite stars. BTS members showcased their rap, singing, and dance skills—with Jin even posting photographs of himself cooking at the dormitory—and were honest with themselves and their fans in their vlogs. Jin recalls:

———One of the staff members at the company said this was the fad these days so we should give it a try, and it sounded fun, so we started it. We were using a really tiny laptop, and it was tough because I hadn't done it before. But I did as much as I possibly could.

Jin's comment offers a look into the context of the blog. At the time, pre-debut promotional initiatives for K-pop idol groups generally meant publicizing the audition process through music channels on cable TV, or having members feature on reality shows. But instead of appearing on television, BTS members expressed their genuine selves to audiences through vlogs posted on YouTube.

If not for Glam's failure, the BTS blog might have been backed by more resources. But a budget crisis was not the only reason BTS members made their own pre-debut promos. The experience with Glam had taught Big Hit Entertainment a critical lesson: before bringing a new artist to the public, it was important to secure even just one more fan who would listen to their music.

As YouTube was the biggest hub for video content among teenagers at the time, Big Hit Entertainment started a YouTube channel titled BANGTANTV* for video uploads, which would be posted on the blog. Soon, the blog and the Twitter** accounts run independently by the BTS members-in-training became the go-to platforms for fans to learn more about their lives. Meanwhile, Big Hit Entertainment made plans for an official social media presence on platforms used commonly by fandoms—such as Twitter,*** Daum cafés, and KakaoStory—and established tailored goals and content styles for each platform. For instance, one of Big Hit's goals after BTS's debut was to attain a specific number of new followers on days BTS featured in a music program.

This new approach to promoting an up-and-coming idol group played an important role in establishing a unique identity for BTS. Videos on the blog showcased unpolished compositions by the trainees, choreography practice in tiny practice studios, and glimpses into members' genuine trepidations as they spoke into the camera without any airbrushing.

It was a complete rejection of genre norms in Korea's idol industry, where every frame of every video was perfectly produced for public consumption. BTS members were not just idols. They were rappers who released mixtapes and YouTubers who gave tutorials on music production and dance. Jimin reminisces about posting his dance practice video, showing how the BTS members felt about this unprecedented promotional strategy:

———I didn't know if something like that had been done (already). I just made a video for the first time to say, "This is what I look like." That opportunity was in itself so precious.

While at the time this was the most ambitious strategy that was still feasible for Big Hit Entertainment, the members themselves did not think too deeply about the reasoning behind it, instead focusing on being genuine to their audiences. They poured their hearts out.

Limitations

Looking back on the production of "No More Dream"* in their debut album *2 COOL 4 SKOOL*, SUGA recalls:

———When we were working on that song, I sat in Pdogg's room in the Cheonggu Building and thought, 'Aw, I really want to go back to the dorms,' thousands of times a day. We should be going to the dorms to sleep by seven or eight in the morning, right? But we had to finish our work by the end of the day, for days on end . . . That was the hardest part."

I pick up my pen every night
And close my eyes after the sun rises

These lines from "We are bulletproof PT.2"* were a perfect encapsulation of RM, SUGA, and j-hope's reality as they composed the lyrics for the songs in *2 COOL 4 SKOOL*. They would practice all day to polish their razor-sharp choreography until they were in frame-by-frame sync while also working on the songs for the album. In the little time they had in between, they would shoot their vlogs and other videos and manage the blog.

"No More Dream," the title song of the album, loomed ahead like the final boss at the gates of BTS's debut. Jimin describes what the song was to them:

———It's not difficult now, but back then, the choreography . . . We could barely breathe.

The dance accompanying "No More Dream" is made up of big, wild moves, which had to be performed in perfect sync. Each member had to start and stop each movement with military precision, tense and ready throughout the entirety of the performance—and make sure to jump up to exactly the same height. And as mentioned earlier, even their diet was under strict control. Jin discusses the team's vibe at the time:

———In "We are bulletproof PT.2," we all had to show off our abs, so we worked out, and we couldn't eat what we wanted because of the prescribed diet . . . Everyone was cranky.

While the members pushed their physical limits in the practice studio and the dormitory, RM, SUGA, and j-hope also pushed the limits of their souls in the studio, struggling with the lyrics to "No More

Dream." RM had to compose a staggering twenty-nine versions of the rap lyrics for this particular song.

———I once went up to Hakdong Park near the Cheonggu Building and screamed out loud. The rap just wasn't coming, and I felt like I was suffocating.

Producer Bang Si-Hyuk had the final say on which version of the lyrics would be chosen, and, at the time, he and RM had different perspectives on the rap lyrics to the title song. RM explains:

———Bang Si-Hyuk thought we should reflect the latest trends. But I'm from the generation that grew up with Nas and Eminem, so there was a point of conflict. It was about whether or not I could accept what we call "trap flow," and it was hard for me to accept. Our big issue with the debut album was how we could quickly reflect new hip-hop trends, and that's where Bang PD and I had trouble coming to a compromise.

A common misconception outside the idol industry was that management companies were in charge of everything about the music, taking the lead in musical creativity. But even the most finely produced songs cannot shine if the idols performing them are untalented or unwilling.

The idea of "giving voice to teenage realities through lyrics" sounded great in a vacuum, but someone had to go about composing those lyrics. Bang Si-Hyuk's decision was to have the composers in the group—RM, SUGA, and j-hope—also take leading roles as lyricists from the very first album.

But as the differences in RM and Bang's perspectives showed, it was extremely difficult to produce lyrics that would satisfy both the hip-hop scene and the idol industry. No one would have been surprised if this gambit had failed. RM, too, confesses that accepting the musical direction of their first album was no easy task.

———I listened to a lot of music, almost as if I was studying. I got these contemporary-style songs and listened to them, analyzed them. It actually took more than a year, I think, before I started to genuinely love those trends and internalize them.

These were just some of the many things BTS did to challenge their own experiences and values. The lyrics to "A Typical Trainee's Christmas,"* uploaded on the blog on December 23, 2012, and January 11, 2013—before the production of "No More Dream"—illustrate the difficulties they faced:

> *(Even this year) I pulled all-nighters practicing*
> *(Cry) I'm still a trainee*
> *I really wanna debut next year*

The blog post "A Typical Trainee's Christmas: Review,"** posted around the same time, shows the members practicing their choreography, holding recording sessions, and celebrating the holiday late at night over a tiny cake. When asked how he endured that period, Jin, who uploaded the post, answers:

———I was a trainee for almost two years, so it naturally became a part of my life. I thought it was about time for me to debut as an idol, but I didn't really want to look for another company, so I thought

I should do it here (laughs). So I decided to do the dances I learned at this company . . . It was just that kind of feeling.

And the Edge

The blog post "A Typical Trainee's Christmas: Review" also includes complaints like "I thought we might get a Christmas holiday, but we all ended up going on vacation to the Bangtan Room," and "The Boss is terrible / Won't take us out to dinner once, even after we made that song asking for a company dinner . . ."

Even in the most liberal of countries and cultures, it is not easy for a pre-debut trainee to publicly voice his complaints about the label's CEO. And Korea is a country where idol groups cannot be launched without significant capital, time, and planning know-how.

In spite of this, Bang Si-Hyuk had the members write their own blog posts and publicly share their thoughts and feelings as trainees alongside their mixtapes and journal entries. Once training had become part of daily life, as it had for Jin, the trainees began to talk about themselves in a candid and genuine manner.

This was the beginning of the team that would become Beyond The Scene.[11] Jimin reminisces:

———When the hyoungs were writing the lyrics, they kept asking me for input too. "What do you think about this kind of content?"

---

11 In July 2017, about four years after BTS's debut, Big Hit Entertainment unveiled the group's new brand identity and added a new meaning to their name. In addition to the original meaning of "Boys who protect teenagers from oppression and prejudice" in "Bulletproof Boy Scouts," "Beyond The Scene" indicates the group's mission to always aim for the horizon, reaching for their dreams without resigning themselves to reality.

"What are kids around you like?" "Aren't any of your school friends chasing their dreams?" Stuff like that. I was really thankful.

RM, SUGA, and j-hope's lyrics in *2 COOL 4 SKOOL* reflected the stories of all the BTS members. This is the reason "We are bulletproof PT.2" discusses the anguish of rappers crossing from the hip-hop scene to the idol industry and writing rap lyrics all night, while also including Jung Kook's personal experience as a teenager with an atypical student life, in the lyrics "Instead of going to school, I sang and danced all night in the practice rooms." When this song was written, BTS members were neither rappers on the hip-hop scene nor idols on the public stage. Rather than covering up the realities of the precarious trainee's life in hip-hop swag or idol fantasies, they used hip-hop techniques to showcase their experiences exactly as they were.

This was the unique position BTS took from the beginning of their career, and the perspective they continue to take in telling their stories. Rather than follow the grammar of either hip-hop or idol music, they used the languages of both genres to talk about themselves.

In that sense, *2 COOL 4 SKOOL* is almost a log of their journey: how a group of nameless trainees who could neither take center stage nor live ordinary lives finally made their debut.

The album begins with "Intro : 2 COOL 4 SKOOL" (Feat. DJ Friz) with the rap lyrics "We're simply telling our stories on behalf of teens and twentysomethings." In "Skit : Circle Room Talk," the members talk about their childhood dreams. "Outro : Circle room cypher" has each member tell his own story in cypher form. Finally, the lyrics of the CD-exclusive hidden track "Skit : On the start line" clearly describes their pre-debut life: "Trainee / In a way, it's exactly who I am / But a difficult word to define / Not belonging anywhere / Not really doing anything either /

2 COOL 4 SKOOL

THE 1ST SINGLE ALBUM
2013. 06. 12

TRACK

01 Intro : 2 COOL 4 SKOOL
   (Feat. DJ Friz)
02 We are bulletproof PT.2
03 Skit : Circle Room Talk
04 No More Dream
05 Interlude

06 Like
07 Outro : Circle room cypher
08 Skit : On the start line
   (Hidden Track)
09 Path (Hidden Track)

VIDEO

 DEBUT TRAILER

 "No More Dream"
MV

 "No More Dream"
MV TEASER 1

 "We are bulletproof
PT.2"
MV

 "No More Dream"
MV TEASER 2

That kind of stage / A transition period." Most importantly, this track ends with the following lyrics:

> *Because I'm a trainee*

This was their self-definition: trainees in the Korean idol industry. But not just any trainees: ones who poured their trainee lives into hip-hop form and turned their debut album into a record of their experiences.

From the beginning, BTS's music reflected the lives of the members. The B-side tracks in 2 COOL 4 SKOOL, "Intro," "Interlude," "Outro," and "Skit," became a template on which later albums would be formatted.

It was a time when only the tiniest minority knew of the Bulletproof Boy Scouts. But BTS were already forging their own identity, one they hold on to today.

Teamwork!

——"Hyoung, how do I get that cool vibe like you?" (laughs).

Before their debut, Jimin admired RM to the point of asking how he could be like him. And not just because RM was the leader, or because he had the talent to work on songs without any help. The seven trainees developed a powerful bond during their time in the dormitory, and by the time the debut members had been finalized and their schedule set, they had deeply influential roles in one another's lives. Jung Kook even says:

——Until now, the biggest blessing of my life is meeting these hyoungs.

He goes on to say,

———When I compare the "me" who had a normal student life with the "me" who grew up at this company with the hyoungs, the "me" right now learned a lot more and gained a lot more. I don't know what exactly, but I learned so much. For example, I was actually ridiculously greedy. I hated losing, I was proud, and I was stubborn. I used to get in a lot of trouble because of that, and although my temper still flares up sometimes, I learned to be understanding of other people first.

Having been a junior high student during his time as a trainee, the management company was Jung Kook's home and school, and his fellow members were his family and teachers. He adds,

———We lived together, so the hyoungs naturally influenced me, and I naturally accepted it. From the way the hyoungs spoke, to their personalities. And with music, too.

The time the members spent together at the dormitory and the practice studios, rubbing off on one another, gave rise to a unique team vibe. This spirit of support and encouragement paid off when BTS's debut was finalized and the team entered a period of seemingly endless training sessions. With a shared goal in mind, they carried one another to their goal. "Dope" from the later album *THE MOST BEAUTIFUL MOMENT IN LIFE PT.1* contains the lyrics "Everyday hustle life," an attitude that was engraved into the members from the very beginning. Jung Kook elaborates:

———We all challenged one another. There was something like that among us vocalist members, so we'd ask each other about our singing or talk about things like "This is how I've been practicing recently." If one of the members sang a cover song, we'd encourage him, like "Wow, your singing's gotten way better."

In that respect, everything from the beginning of 2013 in the lead-up to their debut served as a powerful source of momentum for their future. BTS's debut was set, the members had a clear goal, and the disparate perspectives stemming from differences in age, hometown, and musical background slowly converged.

V looks back on his time as a trainee:

———Well, I wasn't normally a "practice buff." So people did have to tell me to practice more (laughs). When I suddenly got in the mood, I'd think, 'Maybe I should do some practice,' and I think I just did what I felt like.

But this was only V's outlook on the sudden new life he'd found himself in, never having expected to become a trainee but now only months from an official debut. He was slowly revving his engines. A little more firmly than before, V explains,

———I got a lot of criticism when I was a trainee, but I actually have pride because of that. Because I was criticized, I could really feel that I grew afterwards, and nothing that happened after our debut could faze me. Because I'd been through a lot already.

V smiles about the other BTS members, but says with a serious look in his eye:

———The way I see it, all of us members are ridiculous. We're quite feral and therefore stubborn to the end. I love it because in this group, no matter how much our hearts break, we only love the stage even more. 'So I fell down, no big deal,' that kind of sentiment.

While the members pushed themselves beyond their physical and mental limits with their growing teamwork, Big Hit Entertainment's debut plans were unfolding on schedule. The blog revealed the members one by one, and the vlogs let the members communicate with their fans.

The mixtape song "A Typical Trainee's Christmas" was followed by "Graduation Song,"* complete with an MV, by j-hope, Jimin, and Jung Kook. It was uploaded on both the blog and YouTube on February 8, 2013.

The blog, launched on December 21, 2012, with a posting of RM's mixtape song "Vote," had turned into a BTS media channel packed with glimpses into the members' lives, pictures, music, and dance moves. It was the prototype of the social media format that is now used on many HYBE artists' social media channels.

On March 22, 2013, about three months before the official debut, the blog was updated with a video of j-hope, Jimin, and Jung Kook at dance practice.** The final pre-debut blog post, titled "130517 Bangtan Vlog"*** included vlog entries from all the members except V. These posts are still on the blog today, allowing even the newest of BTS fans to look back at how the team members transformed themselves as they prepared for their debut.

Big Hit's debut plan for BTS had not attracted the attention of many at the time, but that did not mean the plan was a failure. People were leaving comments on the blog even before the official debut, and the members were beginning to develop a fandom. And though the debut showcase venue was not the largest, these early fans packed the seats on that fateful day.

Just like the members, the budget and resource limitations at the time were also pushed to their limits. This meant the debut plans were meticulous and tight, leading to a small episode that only the members still recall. Jimin explains:

———This was before V's reveal. Us six were revealed up to Jung Kook, but the company said, "V is our secret weapon."

V was revealed to the public on a visual concept photo teaser for the BTS debut album on June 3, 2013. Hiding the presence of an attractive member until the last minute, then making a surprise reveal to add a new dynamic to the team is a strategy with a proven track record. However, at this point, the other members had already been communicating with their burgeoning fans in the months leading up to the debut. Jimin recalls,

———We got fan letters and presents. Each and every one of us. But V was the only one who didn't get anything.

It could have been a disheartening situation for a trainee still in his teens. But the other members showered V with encouragement. Jimin adds:

———I remember we all got together in our room and encouraged V. Like, "It's only because you didn't get an official reveal yet, don't get too down."

June 13, 2013

A little before D-day, the team was practicing the choreography for "We are bulletproof PT.2,"* which alongside the title song "No More Dream" would be performed on Mnet's *M Countdown* on their debut day of

CHAPTER 2

June 13.[12] During this session, j-hope sustained an injury that caused synovitis in his right thigh.

The choreography of the second half of "We are bulletproof PT.2" involves a solo by j-hope where he falls to his knees on the stage while simultaneously bending backward until his back touches the ground. Repeating this move caused significant strain on his leg, and the synovial fluid causing the swelling had to be removed via syringe. But before he could be asked why he went so far, j-hope, recalling the incident, responds firmly:

——If I have to do something, I have to make sure I do it. Me, I hate putting out things that "stink."

Debut prep is a long, complicated, and difficult road, especially for trainees in smaller companies. But in most cases, D-day comes so quickly that no one has time to feel empty. And although the first performance is not usually the last, it is the most important performance for the vast majority of idol groups.

The K-pop idol industry emphasizes performance and style almost as much as musical ability, which makes the weekly music programs on both broadcast and cable TV some of the most important publicity channels for talent. As a result, countless idol groups clamor for limited broadcast slots each week. Groups that fail to develop a significant following at their debut performance, or at least the first week of their debut, are unlikely to attract further attention. Slots on next week's episode are never guaranteed, and some performances must be shortened to fit the show's runtime, meaning artists may not always

---

12 June 13, which is the day after the release of the debut album *2 COOL 4 SKOOL*, and the day BTS first performed in public, is now recognized as BTS's debut anniversary and is celebrated each year in as a fan event titled BTS Festa.

have the chance to show all they have to offer. This is not a problem for established artists, but for newly debuting idols—even ones backed by major management companies—music show appearances could make or break their careers. BTS's very future, in other words, hung on their very first performance. Jin still remembers the tension of that stage:

────There's a part in the "No More Dream"* choreography where I have to jump with the lyrics "It's a lie," but unlike in practice, we have mic packs and in-ear monitors hooked up to our pants since we're actually onstage. Because of the extra weight, every time I landed from a jump, my pants got pulled down bit by bit. My mind went blank, and since I was a newbie, I couldn't just shout, "Let's do one more take!" So I thought I made a mess of my first performance and cried.

But Jin's fears proved unfounded, as BTS had a superweapon ready to capture audiences in a single stroke: the dance break in the second half of "We are bulletproof PT.2." In this sequence, j-hope makes the jump with the knee landing (the move that led to his injury), and Jimin flips over him. Jimin then turns around and throws his hat, which Jung Kook catches before starting his own dance. j-hope recalls how the sequence came about:

────We were practicing, when Son Sungdeuk-seonsaengnim suggested, "Wanna each show off a specialty in the second half of the song?" So we each developed choreography, and the three of us stayed behind in the practice studio, laid out the mats, and practiced over and over again.

Their backbreaking efforts paid off. The combination of eye-catching moves, complete with flip, enraptured audiences and got the team the attention they sought. Jung Kook describes how he felt:

———The thing is, I'm not actually catching the hat. It only looks that way from the seats. But anyway, the second I caught the hat, the people there were like, "Whoa!" I got goosebumps.

j-hope also felt that his efforts leading up to the debut were rewarded.

———Before the performance, all we heard from the seats were, "Who are those guys?" But they saw our moves and started reacting, like "Wow!" It was exhilarating. And I felt like, I'm really glad I danced.

The in-person audiences were not the only ones impressed by BTS. As soon as BTS's stage ended, then head of business operations at Big Hit Entertainment, Lenzo Yoon, received more than thirty phone calls, with callers from around the industry praising the performance and even proposing business opportunities.

The first broadcast performance showed the BTS members what they could gain from the stage. Jung Kook learned that being in the spotlight made him "nervous, excited, tense, and happy." Jimin recognized the existence of their fans. He explains,

———Even now, I remember that one row next to the broadcast cameras during our first performance.

The "one row" refers to the fans who came out in person to watch BTS live. Fans of artists who feature on music shows can come to performances as a group through the management companies, and the number of fans that companies can gather depends heavily on the artists' popularity and recognition. At the time, BTS only drew about a dozen fans, who took up about one row in front of that small stage. Jimin goes on to say,

————If you think about it, we're total strangers, but they came all that way just because they liked us, and stood there for us . . . They wanted to see us onstage, so they woke up early, couldn't even get proper sleep, and waited. And we prepared our performance so we could show those people.

Their preparations led up to a debut with a small happy ending.

Outsiders

A trainee on the cusp of debut is, naturally, the subject of everyone's attention. Company staff members are responsive to their every move, and even seemingly unapproachable CEOs and company owners have encouragement to spare. And of course, support and expectations from friends and family are at an all-time high.

But when the trainee finally makes their debut and appears on a music show, they see the cold, hard reality: the world is not that interested.

Each episode of a typical Korean music ranking program, which essentially plays all week long, features about twenty artist teams ranging from freshly debuted newbies to veteran performers who have been onstage for decades. The finale is always performed by the most popular artist of the episode.

During the filming, most of the artists featured that day wait in

Even now, I remember that one row
next to the broadcast cameras during
our first performance.

—Jimin

the green room with the other artists. In this teeming crowd, up-and-coming idols—even ones from the biggest management companies—are practically anonymous in a sea of new faces. They are lucky if no one happens to hear a bad word out of their mouths and spreads awful rumors about them in the industry.

Even among new artists, BTS were outsiders, practically stranded on an island of their own. And this was not just because Big Hit Entertainment was such a small company. Jin looks back on their plight as they waited in the green room for their performance:

———I was so curious that I asked another artist, "How do you have so many friends here?" And they said, "Oh, this person was at my management company before." "What about that person?" I asked, and they'd say, "Oh, we used to be trainees together at my old management company." It was like that with most people. They didn't become friends after their debut, they were already friends before that. But our company was the very first for all of us. So at that point, we stopped leaving the green room altogether.

Just as many trainees left Big Hit Entertainment before BTS's debut, it is common for idols-in-training to change management companies multiple times. And due to the sheer size of the biggest management companies, a significant number of trainees develop friendships with contemporaries from other companies.

But the members of BTS had never been associated with other companies, and they had no particular cause to interact with other trainees. RM and SUGA had switched from hip-hop to the idol industry, and the other members had no time to turn their gaze outward because they were always listening to hip-hop at the dorms with RM and SUGA and perfecting their choreography in the practice studio.

Jimin describes how it felt to be in the same space as other artists at the very beginning of BTS's career:

————I still have no idea why, but we seriously only ever stuck with one another. And I think it must have been hard for other people to approach us, too. We were all clearly on edge because we were determined to do hip-hop, not meeting other people's eyes . . . (laughs)

They were the outsiders in the green room—or, to be completely blunt, they were just seven people no one cared about.

But at the same time, the members found their attention naturally drifting to the outside world. Even if they were clustered together in one corner of the green room, they could not avoid the music from the show. The TV in the green room showed real-time footage from the performances taking place outside, and the in-ear monitors they'd put on provided a live feed of other artists. These audio feeds in particular were a huge shock to BTS, because for the first time, they were comparing themselves to their fellow artists. Jimin explains,

————There was a clear difference in our team's and the other singers' vocals. I was a newbie, and I didn't know my own voice clearly or what my own weapons were, so I just thought, 'Oh, why am I so awful?' and 'Everyone's so good.' I finally realized that I was a small fish in a big pond.

He adds,

————If I wanted to improve somehow, I had to practice my singing, but I didn't know how to practice. So I just kept singing blindly. Every time I made a mistake, I went to the bathroom to cry.

V also criticizes his own early performances:

————Sometimes I'm browsing YouTube and one of our team's older videos shows up, but I always skip those. I'm not ashamed of them. They're precious memories, and they're always in my mind, so when I see them after a long time has passed, I think, 'That's what things were like back then,' but at the same time, I feel like, 'Why did I do that at the time?'

V continues,

———I like my old self too. It's because I went through all that that I'm the person I am today.

BTS's debut exposed them to a flood of outside influences that heavily impacted their early activities. Jung Kook began to sing everywhere, to the point that he thought, 'All the time I spend singing in the twenty-four hours I have is practice time.' Jimin describes the mood in the team at the time:

———It wasn't just me, I think V and Jin also felt an inadequacy in their respective vocal skills. I had a bit of an inferiority complex too, so I thought, 'I have to do better.' If one of our members was practicing his singing, I did too.

And so, the members went on practicing even after their debut. SUGA discusses how he felt at the time:

———I felt like a trainee throughout all of 2013. I didn't really feel like I'd debuted. Because nothing changed. The only difference was that we had TV appearances, but the things we practiced were the same. That was when I realized debuting wasn't the end. 'It all repeats itself,' I thought.

SUGA's intuition proved correct. The BTS members learned that their goal of debuting was only the first step in a long journey—a journey that would take them back to their practice studio.

The Sad Rookie Kings

Just as they declared at their debut showcase, BTS managed to survive 2013. Their first album *2 COOL 4 SKOOL* (released in June 2013) and their follow-up album *O!RUL8,2?* (released in September of that year) ranked 65 and 55, respectively, on the Gaon Chart's[13] 2013 album rankings.[14] It was the best showing among all idol groups that debuted that year.

BTS also swept the Best New Artist awards at all the major Korean music awards at the end of 2013, including the Melon Music Awards (MMA), the Golden Disc Awards, the Seoul Music Awards, and the Gaon Chart Music Awards,[15] but not Mnet's MAMA.[16]

However, the award shows they attended to accept their prizes only served to show the members the reality they faced. Jin recalls:

——When we won the New Artists Prize at the MMA, I think it was SHINee-seonbae who won Artist of the Year. Who in Korea back then didn't know SHINee? Everyone knew about BEAST and Infinite, too. But as for us, it was a time when people used to call us, "Those bulletproof vest guys."

BTS was given no attention at the award shows. They were dwarfed by countless established artists who were already beloved by the public, and because BTS was the only group from Big Hit Entertainment to attend, they did not have older colleagues from the company to introduce them to other artists.

---

13 South Korea's official music chart, launched by the Korea Music Content Association. The system was relaunched as the Circle Chart in July 2022.
14 Net unit shipments, minus units returned.
15 The Gaon Chart Music Awards was renamed the Circle Chart Music Awards in 2023.
16 Mnet Asian Music Awards, renamed MAMA Awards in 2022.

O!RUL8,2?

THE 1ST MINI ALBUM
2013. 09. 11

VIDEO

COMEBACK TRAILER

ALBUM PREVIEW

CONCEPT TRAILER

"N.O"
MV TEASER 2

"N.O"
MV TEASER 1

"N.O"
MV

No one spoke to them, and they could not approach anyone. All they could do was attend the award shows, step onto the stage to give brief comments and thanks, and return straight to the dormitory.

In the year 2013, when the aforementioned BTS albums ranked 65 and 55 on the Gaon Chart, EXO had six albums in the top ten, ranked at 1, 3, 4, 6, 7, and 10. This is one reason BTS is the only Korean male idol group to debut in 2013 that is still discussed today. It was a time when one team had a powerful hold on the market, making it nearly impossible for newcomers to survive.

It is no exaggeration to say that the industry's attention was focused entirely on EXO and the debut of the YG Entertainment trainees who appeared on *WIN: Who Is Next*. BTS's accomplishments at the award shows proved only that they had survived, for now. There was no guarantee they would still be around in 2014 and 2015. If TVXQ and BIGBANG were the icons of the Korean idol industry's second-generation male idol groups, EXO and the upcoming YG group were almost certain to be the kings of the third generation.

This context is part of the reason that the response to BTS's second album *O!RUL8,2?* came across as such a shock.

According to the Hanteo Chart, which gathers data on physical and digital music sales, BTS's debut album *2 COOL 4 SKOOL* sold 772 units in the first week of release, while the second album *O!RUL8,2?* sold 2,679 units in the first week of release: more than triple the sales of the first album. Week 1 sales for follow-up albums released by idol groups generally reflect the expectations of the fandom built up by the previous album, meaning that *2 COOL 4 SKOOL* had been received well by audiences. However, shipping data was not so optimistic. According to the Gaon Chart, *O!RUL8,2?* shipped 34,030 units in

2013—only a 9,589-unit increase over *2 COOL 4 SKOOL*, which shipped 24,221 units.

Although no one had expected shipping numbers to also have tripled, it was true that growth had failed to meet expectations. An increase from 20,000 to 30,000 units, as opposed to an increase from 200,000 to 300,000, was not a particularly significant achievement in the industry.

In the "ARMY Corner Store"* video released in June 2021 to commemorate BTS's eighth anniversary, RM describes the four albums they released prior to *THE MOST BEAUTIFUL MOMENT IN LIFE* series as a cycle of "sweet, bitter, sweet, bitter." *O!RUL8,2?* was the first of the "bitters."

j-hope looks back on the confusion:

———When we debuted with "No More Dream" and "We are bulletproof PT.2," we got a great stage response, so I think we were honestly a little buoyed. But then in the next album, with "N.O,"** it felt kind of like . . . being smacked around a bunch?

Diss

Shockingly, the disappointing response to *O!RUL8,2?* was only one of many tribulations waiting in the wings.

Few artists can keep up a streak of successes, and BTS, having made a memorable debut, had a few more chances ahead of them. Both the team and Big Hit Entertainment already had a roadmap planned out for the future: the final song in *O!RUL8,2?*, "OUTRO : LUV IN SKOOL," was a preview for the next album. *Skool Luv Affair* would deal with the theme of love, an ambitious step to propel the team further into the industry. The team also managed a turnaround with *O!RUL8,2?* by focusing on "Attack on Bangtan" as the follow-up song.

"Attack on Bangtan" carries over the confidence and energy BTS built up after their debut, adding speed to the explosive power of "No More Dream" from the first album. The team was running ahead with a momentum all their own, refusing to slow even after the disappointment of "N.O."

j-hope remembers how the members had no intention of letting their circumstances get them down:

———Back then in those circumstances, giving up wasn't even an option. Everyone was like, "You worked hard to debut, but you're just going to quit?" and "We have to do this." We had a "Ugh!" moment with "N.O," but with "Attack on Bangtan," it felt like we were finding our groove again.

Jin also injected the team with a sense of calm.

———There's steps to everything. Sometimes you have to climb slowly. And we knew that all the other people who succeeded climbed up slowly, little by little.

But the real "smack-around" came from an unexpected place several days afterward on November 21 at music critic Kim Bong-hyun's podcast *Kim Bong-hyun's Hip-Hop Invitational.*

RM and SUGA made an appearance on the podcast's one-year anniversary episode, with rapper B-Free also in attendance. What unfolded next is already widely known to the public. As the recording may be found with a quick YouTube search, it will not be reproduced here. To summarize, B-Free dissed BTS.

———Looking back, it feels like we went through something everyone has to go through once in their lives.

RM continues calmly,

———Taking an insult (Translator's note: RM uses the English word "insult" rather than the Korean equivalent) like that to our faces, and from someone in the same industry . . . the Korean word "moyok," feels too flat, I can't think of a word more suitable than "insult." Anyway, that was when I learned "how to respond when you're walking down the street and you get slapped in the face out of nowhere."

RM gives a hollow laugh. Indeed, B-Free's diss was even more shocking than a slap in the face, because he passed judgment on BTS's musical identity without even listening to their album.

It is difficult to imagine a K-pop idol making an ad hominem statement to an artist in another genre. But the opposite continues to be a regular occurrence on the Korean entertainment scene, having started from the very first generation of idol singers. This stems from a widespread stereotype that idol music is inferior in quality and professionalism.

However, some people—like B-Free—act as if they are judges at an audition, publicly passing judgment on idol groups' musical identities in spite of not having that authority.

Idols by nature anyway,
They shush me and look down on me

The lyrics from "BTS Cypher PT.1"* in *O!RUL8,2?*, released before RM and SUGA's encounter with B-Free, contains the team's answer to all such criticism. BTS knew what the public thought of them and responded to such people with a cypher, which is a hip-hop technique. "We On"'s lyrics go even further with the ambitious declaration, "Fans, the public, maniacs / Yeah I'm makin' 'em mine." "INTRO : O!RUL8,2?"'s question "What was my dream?" and "N.O"'s "It really is now or never / We still haven't accomplished anything yet" show clearly why the members chose to be part of BTS.

BTS's music documents the journey of its members: from not knowing their own dreams, to understanding their ambitions, to fighting to make their goals a reality, and finally to developing their own perspectives on the way the public perceived them.

Different people will respond differently to BTS's music, as musical taste is completely subjective. However, no one can deny that the BTS members filled their songs with their genuine emotions and experiences from this time. In "Skit : R U Happy Now?," the members express how happy they are in spite of how busy they are, and in the following song, "If I Ruled The World," they muse on what they might do if they find success, in a humorous tone. These songs show BTS's response to their small taste of success from the debut album.

If *2 COOL 4 SKOOL* is BTS's autobiographical record of the uncertainty of trainee life, *O!RUL8,2?* is their rallying cry as they march into the spotlight, telling the story of BTS's idol life in a hip-hop package—a unique storytelling style that would go on to define the team.

"N.O"'s theme of wavering between dreams and reality could be realized in any genre. But for BTS, this was not just one small, disparate motif standing apart from the rest of their music. Throughout *O!RUL8,2?*, and even their debut album *2 COOL 4 SKOOL*, the members poured out genuine, personal stories into their music, giving concrete form to their determination with lyrics like, "It really is now or never / We still haven't accomplished anything yet" and delivering the message with passionate performances onstage.

SUGA meant it when he stated on *Kim Bong-hyun's Hip-Hop Invitational* that he wanted BTS to act as a bridge between idol music and hip-hop. As their music up to that point showed clearly, that had been their aim from the very beginning. "Paldo Gangsan"' in particular encapsulates BTS's early-debut identity. j-hope explains how the song was made:

———Because we came from such different backgrounds, there was a suggestion that it would be really fun if we could talk about one another's hometowns and rap in dialects. We said, "I'm from Gwangju, you (SUGA) come from Daegu, and you (RM) come from Ilsan in Gyeonggi Province, so let's each talk about our hometowns and take this song someplace."

"Paldo Gangsan" was only possible because all of the members had come from outside Seoul. Though they began their musical pursuits elsewhere, each member made his way to the capital in order to make his idol debut: a phenomenon that occurs in all industries, because so much of Korean infrastructure is based in Seoul. Not only that, K-pop idol industry norms had the seven young men grouped into a team that shared a dormitory together.

In spite of adhering to industry standards in some ways, BTS charted new territory by conveying the origins of each member and describing how they came together as a team, in musical format. This process of talking about one another through music, says j-hope, served to strengthen their bonds:

———I don't know how to describe this in words, but . . . I don't think we had prejudices about one another's hometowns. So the conversations were easygoing and we could just laugh together and enjoy hometown stories, and that's how the song developed. It was born because we had respect for one another's origins.

However, when *O!RUL8,2?* was first released, very few people appreciated BTS's novel use of music. BTS were loners in the idol industry, and rappers from the hip-hop scene like B-Free had dissed them without even listening to their work. And no one had batted an eye at such attitudes. In the conversation with RM and SUGA, B-Free had insulted not only their music but also the group's name and SUGA's stage name. And when the episode was made public, some even took B-Free's side online and made hateful comments about BTS.

At the time, that was the reality of the industry for BTS and the majority of idol groups. It was an era when people online felt free to make degrading comments about artists' names, looks, and actions—not even their music—for no reason other than the fact that they were idols.

Several years later, RM looks back on this moment:

——It's exactly that. "The history of the struggle for recognition." We wanted to be recognized. To prove ourselves.

For RM and the others, it was inevitable that they would seek out a reason for doing what they did. RM adds,

——I looked up and studied so much about insults and hurts, and I got even more passionate. 'Oh, I really have to do better.' Do what better, I wasn't sure, but I'd already made my debut, and already got dissed, so I wanted to somehow do something that was within my scope, and really empty myself out.

It was not long before RM's determination was realized, at least in part. A crew member from Mnet who watched the *Kim Bong-hyun's Hip-Hop Invitational* clip contacted Big Hit Entertainment, and RM made an appearance on the May 13, 2014, episode of the *4 Things Show*, an interview program that looks at the subject of the episode from four different angles, in a deeper and more nuanced way than many programs today, not to mention 2014. It was the perfect opportunity for RM to clarify his own thoughts as he struggled between his identities as a hip-hop artist and an idol.

——It was extremely important to me, having unloaded something like that. The hurt was still there, but [the interview] comforted my heart in some ways . . . Bad things have to happen for there to be good things. And I thought at the time, 'Oh, something like that happened, but thanks to that, people are coming to reach out to us.'

Their struggles continued, and BTS would face unimaginable challenges. But those difficulties ironically helped the members renew their determination and even opened up new opportunities. This was only the beginning of their early career. Concerning this period, SUGA simply says:

——I try not to think about those times if I can help it. Because ultimately, we're the ones who won and ended it.

Someone's Strength

Skool Luv Affair, BTS's third album, was released in February 2014. To use RM's expression, it was the second "sweet" in the "sweet, bitter, sweet, bitter" cycle that was their first four albums. Public reception to title song "Boy In Luv"* was explosive, propelling the team to their first top-rank candidacy on a TV music show. The album recorded 86,004 shipments on the 2014 Gaon Chart album rankings, a 250% increase over the previous album *O!RUL8,2?*.

Unlike previous title songs "No More Dream" and "N.O," which were darker takes on teenagers with dreams facing down reality, "Boy In Luv" explored teenage romance and injected a cheerful tone to their previously rough image. By refining the wildness they showcased in "Attack on Bangtan," they developed a unique, BTS-style love song. Though the dance choreography remained powerful and energetic, it included more lighthearted motions and school uniform-style costumes that made the team even more approachable to teenagers. "Just One Day,"*** a later song in the same album, also centers on young love, cementing the theme "the way we love" as defined by the first track "Intro : Skool Luv Affair."

This new direction was the first step in BTS's musical expansion. Where previous albums were about the members themselves—their trainee days, their attitude toward music, their response to other people's perceptions—*Skool Luv Affair* began BTS's exploration of the outside world with the theme of love, which requires taking an interest in other people and looking to the world beyond the self.

Skool Luv Affair also directly discusses trendy teenage fashion at the time, with "Spine Breaker" and all its social implications, but also includes "Tomorrow," which takes the personal circumstances of the members and translates them into a universal message anyone can relate to.

"Tomorrow" begins with SUGA's confession of his pre-debut uncertainties, but the lyrics "This unemployed twentysomething fears tomorrow" and "A long way to go, but why am I still stuck here?" conveyed a universal sentiment to many people in their twenties as they searched for their place in the world. By expanding their own stories to include those of their peers, BTS defined living not as "Not just being alive, but living my life," giving courage to themselves and their listeners.

It's always darkest before dawn
Later on down the road, don't you ever forget the you of now

It was a BTS signature encouragement—not leaning on baseless optimism, but not mired in negativity and despair. If "BTS Cypher Pt. 2 : Triptych" was the members' perspectives on everything that came before, including the diss from B-Free, "Tomorrow" was a glimpse into the future of BTS. The music they would bring to the scene later with

Skool Luv Affair

THE 2ND MINI ALBUM
2014. 02. 12

TRACK

01 Intro : Skool Luv Affair
02 Boy In Luv
03 Skit : Soulmate
04 Where You From
05 Just One Day

06 Tomorrow
07 BTS Cypher Pt. 2 : Triptych
08 Spine Breaker
09 JUMP
10 Outro : Propose

VIDEO

 COMEBACK TRAILER

 "Boy In Love"
MV

 ALBUM PREVIEW

 "Just One Day"
MV TEASER

 "Boy In Love"
MV TEASER

 "Just One Day"
MV

THE MOST BEAUTIFUL MOMENT IN LIFE series was already taking shape in *Skool Luv Affair*. RM looks back:

———Even when I think about it now, I think "Tomorrow" could only
    have been released because of SUGA. Because he's the one who
    wove together the beats and the themes. Actually, that was when
    our BTS Season 1[17] exhaustion was at an all-time high.

According to RM, "Tomorrow" arose from the series of obstacles
the members faced from their debut onward. The disappointing sales
of *O!RUL8,2?* and B-Free's diss had drained them, and BTS needed
something to break them out of their funk. To make matters worse,
SUGA developed acute appendicitis during production of "Tomorrow."
He recounts,

———I was preparing the album while performing in Japan when my
    appendix ruptured, so I had to come back to Korea and get surgery
    and recover. But my fever went past 40 degrees Celsius and there
    was pus buildup in my stomach. So I had to get surgery again.

Their previous album had fallen below expectations, and SUGA had
work on the next album waiting for after his recovery. An album that
had no guarantee of success. So he poured his anxieties and his determination to overcome them into "Tomorrow."

———We thought, 'I want to see the light, for once,' 'If nothing else,
    we want to have one concert at least.' Without those feelings, we
    wouldn't be who we are today.

SUGA adds,

———I wanted to make the kind of music that I used to listen to,

---

17 Although this is not an official term, BTS members like to divide up their history into eras.
   BTS Season 1 here refers to the time from their debut to the release of their 2014 album
   DARK&WILD.

something that could give people strength like "Tomorrow." I still feel the same now.

Public response to *Skool Luv Affair* restored SUGA's hopes for the future. "Boy In Luv" exposed BTS to even more people than before, successfully serving its purpose as a title song. "Tomorrow" cemented BTS's identity even further.

Now everyone's attention—BTS members and Big Hit Entertainment alike—was focused on the next album, *DARK&WILD*. As *Skool Luv Affair* had propelled them to candidacy for the top place on music show rankings, naturally their next goal was to win first place. Little by little, the future was growing brighter, and the members were renewing their determination. Around this time, Jimin was fighting to improve his singing abilities, which he had been struggling with since the debut. He remembers:

———People used to say that. That BTS's vocals were lacking. Every time I heard that, my heart broke.

BTS's vocals, which utilized R&B melodies on a hip-hop backdrop, were an outlier in the trend of K-pop idols, whose music tended to climax with high-pitched vocals. BTS's approach of riding a groove with their voices topping the beats was an unusual style in the idol industry, and the absence of the spectacular high notes that decorated other idol songs made it seem as though BTS's vocal capabilities were not up to par. But Jimin explains that he got himself back on his feet:

———I didn't just fall down each time.

Above all, their slowly growing fandom acted as their emotional support. SUGA says:

———The fans we saw for the first time. Every one of them meant so much to us.

Even after the debut, SUGA wavered internally between his initial identity as a hip-hop artist and his new identity as an idol singer. It was hard for him to cross over from his longtime love. But what eased his transition into that new world was his fans.

————It's really fascinating, that people show up to see me. And how dedicated they are. To be honest, I can't be a fan like that for someone else. I used to perform in front of like two people in Daegu, but now I had all these fans in front of me, who loved me. Think about how heart-pounding it was for a kid like me. That's when I understood everything, like 'Oh, I have the duty to do what these people want.'

This vibe helped the entire team acclimatize to idol life. Jimin recalls how he felt:

————RM and I talked a lot. We weren't really famous or anything, but we couldn't exactly spit on the streets without consequences at this point . . . And we were gradually building up a sense of responsibility to know the value of our work.

Though it wasn't always easy, it was clear that BTS was making headway, little by little. That is, until something unexpected happened.

"Bitter" Again

In interviews, j-hope tends to keep his tone consistent. Even when he discusses BTS's biggest hardships and successes, he always keeps a cool head, almost like an objective observer.

But sometimes, very rarely, j-hope's voice fills with emotion. One of those moments happened when he discussed the practice sessions leading up to the December 3, 2014, MAMA award show:

————At the time, we were really in "combat mode," and wow . . . it was like we were shooting that movie *300*, training like no tomorrow. Block B and our circumstances overlapped, too, so we thought, we couldn't let ourselves lose. Jimin and I had our teeth gritted as we practiced our solo performances. We wanted to look cool enough to kill, so we prepared with all our hearts.

Block B, the group that was slated to perform on a joint stage with BTS at MAMA, had been frequently compared with BTS at the time. Like BTS, Block B's music was also grounded in hip-hop, with members including rappers like leader ZICO. And like BTS, Block B's music was wild and direct.

The grueling practice sessions leading up to the MAMA performance, however, were not solely because of the friendly competition with Block B. BTS was truly desperate. j-hope says:

————All those performances for "Danger" were really exhausting. When we had that comeback with "Danger" releasing the *DARK&WILD* album, we'd done about twenty music show pre-recordings and then went to a different program where they announced first place. We were told we had to be there, so we went up there live, completely out of it. Then, it turned out we weren't even candidates for first place, which I think was a big shock.

j-hope's shock was not purely due to their performance on the rankings. V tentatively goes into further detail about the situation:

————It's fine if other teams are named as candidates for first place. We just need to work harder. But at the broadcasting stations, we'd

[B]ut now I had these people in front
of me, who loved me. Think about
how heart-pounding it was for a kid
like me. That's when I understood
everything, like 'Oh, I have the duty
to do what these people want.'

—SUGA

always be the first to say hello and greet everyone, the seonbaes and the hubaes alike, but some people just ignored us and passed right by. Or mocked us for not even being candidates for top place.

The incident was a heavy mental blow to BTS. V continues:

——After the broadcast, we all got into the van together . . . Someone was crying, someone was getting really mad, and someone just couldn't speak. That unspeakable disappointment and that tear-jerking emotion was too much.

V describes how the incident impacted BTS:

——That's when we thought, 'Hey us, let's do really well. So that no one will ever look down on us again.' Looking back, I'm glad we at least got a hold of ourselves back then (laughs). Because we all found our resolve, we had that determination, and we all came together as one, swearing to become a really awesome group together.

Part of the reason BTS was so hurt—and resolved to succeed—was because their first full album, *DARK&WILD* (released on August 20, 2014, with the title song "Danger") was especially important at that point in their career. Unfortunately, "dark and wild" would also turn out to be a description of what awaited the members.

Jin even describes the period between their debut and *DARK&WILD* this way:

——To be honest, I don't remember that time very well. First off, I was so busy, I'd be at the dormitory then come out to practice, record, go to the broadcasting station for performances, perform at events, and then go back to the dorm, on and on. Of course, I remember the debut showcase and our debut performance, and the fan autograph sessions, but other than that . . . for my activities from "No More Dream," "N.O," "Boy In Luv," and "Danger," there isn't much I can remember.

That was the schedule in which BTS released *DARK&WILD*, an all-or-nothing move that put the future of the team on the line. Unfortunately, reality was not so kind. SUGA describes their disappointment:

———We suffered so much for it, so why . . . ?

American Hustle Life

We go back two years to the summer of 2012, when Jung Kook went to the US for one month to learn dance. This was one year before BTS's debut, when Jung Kook was still a trainee. He recalls:

———Maybe because I didn't have a strong sense of purpose when I first became a trainee, the company said I wasn't expressing my unique character. I did everything I was told to do and I had talent, but there was something that didn't show. I think I couldn't express my emotions very well because of my personality. I think, they sent me there to go and get a feel for things in person.

The overseas study trip was a success. Jung Kook was a junior high student at the time, with no clear idea of what it meant to be an artist, but the trip transformed him. Jung Kook explains,

———The fascinating thing is, I didn't do anything special there. Instead of typical lessons, we learned dance workshop-style, and since I didn't have that kind of experience, I was a little shy and hesitant. When we had time off, I went to the beach to hang out, ate jjamppong, and when I came to the dormitory by myself, I'd have cereal with milk . . . I was heavier when I came back (laughs). But when I danced after coming back to Korea, the company and the hyoungs said I was totally different. I honestly don't think I did much there, but they said my personality and my dance style had all changed. I think my skills improved a ton then.

Following their performances of *Skool Luv Affair*, BTS took part in the Mnet real variety program *American Hustle Life*,[18] shot on location in Los Angeles in 2014. This was a natural extension of Jung Kook's 2012 study trip, intended to help the members grow in the home of hip-hop and add to the momentum they'd built with their latest album.

However, the members would not be "studying" hip-hop as if studying for a math test. Just as Jung Kook had improved both his abilities and his attitude toward his work during his first trip, the immersion in music and dance in the foreign country would be what transformed the newly debuted BTS members. Jimin looks back on some of his fondest memories from the *American Hustle Life* shoot:

————The things we experienced then were more fun than I'd expected because . . . it wasn't shown on the broadcast, but we tried shooting a music video there, and I honestly thought I'd become a real hip-hop warrior (laughs). I tried dance-battling, too. When I met Warren G, I got this homework to try writing a melody and lyrics, and he was the first person to give me an assignment like that. So, we were on the shoot, but RM and I would go outside, and in the garden, the two of us would discuss, "What do you want to write about?" "What melody do you want to use?" and it was a lot of fun. I got choreography-design homework, too.

18 An eight-episode show broadcast from July 24 to September 11, 2014.

Around this time BTS was looking at making a reality show of its own. The public loved *Skool Luv Affair*, and building up fan momentum during the airing of *American Hustle Life* would, Big Hit Entertainment predicted, lead to an explosion in popularity once the new album was released.

At the time, real-time fan meetings with idols on V Live[19]* were not yet a reality, meaning that one of the most effective ways for an idol group to gain recognition was to appear on a variety show featuring only the members. Big Hit Entertainment determined that the production of such a show would be one of the most important media initiatives for BTS, alongside their YouTube channel.

For instant promotional effect, appearing on established TV variety shows would have been the best choice. Bang Si-Hyuk himself featured on *Star Audition: The Great Birth*, and Jo Kwon from 2AM's appearance on the MBC variety show *We Got Married* had also proven that point.

But variety shows that feature a single artist or idol group exclusively serve a different purpose: these formats appeal strongly to fans of idol content, especially to fans of the specific artists the shows feature. They are the third-most awaited content for fans, beaten only by new album promotions and live concerts.

And as BTS showed consistent growth since its debut, such a show

---

19 A video platform serviced on Naver from 2015 to 2022 that allowed idols and other stars to communicate with fans in real time. Following the closure of this service, some of the paid content was migrated to the fandom platform Weverse, run by HYBE's child company Weverse Company.

would allow new fans drawn from album releases to quickly and easily learn more about the members. This effect would later be showcased in *Run BTS!*,[20] serviced on V Live. *Rookie King: Channel Bangtan* on the SBS MTV channel, which was shot soon after BTS's debut, is still viewed by fans curious to learn more about the team's early days.[21]

American Hustle Life was filled with uncontrollable variables. It was completely unlike any other Korean reality show, as it was shot in America and featured not only BTS but also legends from the hip-hop scene. The production period also overlapped with preparations for the *DARK&WILD* album.

For K-pop idols—especially recently debuted ones—there is only a short time between album releases, which meant the overlap between the shoot schedule and album production was already expected by those involved. However, a surprising new variable turned the *American Hustle Life* shoot into an unforgettable experience for BTS, in more ways than one.

You're in Danger

———Writing the title song was really exhausting. The melody just wouldn't come, so I got together in the US with Bang Si-Hyuk and everyone . . . it was almost a state of emergency.

As RM recalls, the creative process of the *DARK&WILD* title song "Danger" was a difficult one. This was a marked contrast to the previous album's title song "Boy In Luv," which was so clearly a title song from

20 The first episode was released on August 1, 2015. The show can be watched on channels such as the YouTube BANGTANTV channel and Weverse.
21 A real variety program broadcast from September 3 to October 22, 2013, with eight episodes in total.

the outset, and its working title was set as final as soon as the track was finalized. "Danger," on the other hand, required adjustment after adjustment until the final version was completed.

The reason for this sudden difficulty was the "leveling up" problem faced by all idol groups. To use BTS as an example, "No More Dream" was a hit song in its own right, which allowed them to find a foothold in the male idol market. But if they wanted to rise to the level of established groups like EXO and Infinite, they had to release multiple hits that shined even brighter than "No More Dream." This is an important principle for idol groups in particular, as their popularity is rooted largely in their fandoms. In order to retain and grow the momentum created by one hit song, an idol group must continue to produce stunning hits that visibly grow the scale of the fandom.

Improved sales numbers and stream counts are not enough. Leveling up requires explosive public response on a scale beyond what came before, a fandom response that goes wild at the newly released content. Present-day BTS achieved this with the series of hits "I NEED U," "RUN," "Burning Up (FIRE)," "Blood Sweat & Tears," "Spring Day," "DNA," "FAKE LOVE," and "IDOL," which were followed by more hits that consistently and visibly grew the scale of their fandom.

The problem was that releasing more than two back-to-back hits was a staggering achievement. If a new song was too similar to the previous hit, the public would think BTS was too predictable. It might lead to commercial success, but not the kind of passionate fandom response the previous release received. On the other hand, a completely new style might alienate the established fanbase because it was too different from what they liked. This was a dilemma faced by all artists fighting to produce their next hit.

BTS could carry on in the style of "Boy In Luv" and secure stable popularity, but that approach would never lead to later works like "I NEED U." Indeed, the songs they had promoted on music shows up to this point—"No More Dream," "N.O," "Attack on Bangtan," and "Boy In Luv"—had a consistent tone, but all had completely different vibes.

Now that they'd drawn the public's attention with "Boy In Luv," BTS needed to showcase themselves to even more people with an explosive title song for *DARK&WILD*. The title itself pointed at their character, teasing the dark and wild side of the group. And since BTS was already known for spectacular performances, their new title song also needed to live up to and exceed that expectation.

These factors all came together into one massive maelstrom during the shoot of *American Hustle Life*, packing their already-crowded schedules to the limit. V looks back on their day-to-day:

——We were shooting that show and working on the album at the same time, so we recorded the song in America and practiced the "Danger" choreography there too. When the shoot ended at eight in the evening, we'd immediately go into choreography practice until dawn, get a bit of sleep in between, and go back to the shoot in the morning. If someone said we were taking a ten-minute break in the middle, we all laid down where we were standing and fell asleep instantly.

The superhuman schedule led to some unbelievable incidents. V continues:

——We practiced all night and came back to the accommodations at sunrise, covered in sweat, but we were so heated that steam was rising from us. So someone said, "Whoa, look at him! He's literally smoking!"

RM succinctly describes their LA experience:

———It was a time when I asked, 'What's in me? What could be in me?' and pushed myself to the limit.

The Worst Timing

Unlike "Boy In Luv," BTS's new song "Danger"· did not become a first-place music show candidate. According to the Gaon Chart, *DARK&WILD*'s net shipments were at 100,906 units, putting it at 14th place. It was only a 14,902-unit increase from *Skool Luv Affair* half a year earlier, and was as good as no growth at all.

The album that had pushed them to their physical limits and given them the highest hopes of all ended up on the wrong side of the "sweet, bitter, sweet, bitter" cycle. The members were despondent. This was not unrelated to the aforementioned belittling during a music show shoot, which was a powerful emotional blow. It was also the reason SUGA sighed, "We suffered so much for it, so why . . . ?"

SUGA's disappointment would eventually propel him to pour his very soul into music through the album series *THE MOST BEAUTI-FUL MOMENT IN LIFE*. But at the point of *DARK&WILD*'s release, no one knew if BTS even had a future. SUGA recalls:

———For "Danger," we were changing the choreography until just before we shot the MV. We'd rehearse the dance, and if we had a bit of time, we'd sleep for about ten minutes and then go back to shooting the MV. And I began to feel resentful, like, 'I thought there was a God, but at this point, don't we deserve a little something from God?' Like at least a "Hey guys, you guys have worked really hard," that kind of acknowledgment.

V is even more frank about BTS's predicament at the time:

———Put simply, we were "a team that was only still alive thanks to ARMY." A group that was only alive because the fans were listening. A group that only released its album thanks to them.

BTS was once again in trouble. But the disappointment of *DARK&WILD* was not the end of their tribulations. If the history of BTS could be placed into the dramatic frame of "introduction, rising action, climax, and conclusion," *DARK&WILD* was only the introduction. And 2014 still had more curveballs to throw.

American Hustle Life began airing on July 24, 2014, and *DARK&WILD* was released on August 20, 2014. However, the summer of 2014 is remembered for another momentous occasion in the K-pop industry: Mnet's hip-hop survival program *Show Me the Money 3*, which began airing on July 3 that year.

It would be an understatement to say that the *Show Me the Money* series, specifically the season that aired in 2014, transformed the Korean hip-hop scene forever. This season of the show established an annual tradition of rap battles between the best rappers on the scene, appealing to both hip-hop fans and variety show viewers. Ironically, one of the people who established this tradition was an idol-in-training: Bobby, who would go on to become a member of the male idol group iKON. Having already featured on *WIN: Who Is Next*, Bobby had already developed a following, but he was still a trainee because his team had lost

DARK&WILD

THE 1ST FULL-LENGTH ALBUM
2014. 08. 20

TRACK

01 Intro : What am I to you
02 Danger
03 War of Hormone
04 Hip Hop Phile
05 Let Me Know
06 Rain
07 BTS Cypher PT.3 : KILLER
   (Feat. Supreme Boi)
08 Interlude : What are you doing
   now

09 Could you turn off your cell
   phone
10 Embarrassed
11 24/7 = Heaven
12 Look here
13 So 4 more
14 Outro : Do you think it makes
   sense?

VIDEO

 COMEBACK TRAILER

 "Danger"
MV

 "Danger"
MV TEASER 1

 "War of Hormone"
MV

 "Danger"
MV TEASER 2

the competition on that show. His management company, YG Entertainment, chose to have him appear on *Show Me the Money 3* alongside fellow future iKON member B.I. The duo made waves throughout the show's run, and Bobby was crowned the winner.

This outcome had a tremendous impact on both the idol and hip-hop scenes. The victory of an idol rapper on *Show Me the Money 3*, a show featuring a significant number of accomplished rappers, was a sort of turning point that opened the way for idols to be recognized for their skills by both the hip-hop scene and mainstream audiences. The following year, *Show Me the Money 4* featured WINNER member Mino, among other idol rappers who showcased their impressive abilities.

The new paradigm of idol rappers competing against established rappers from the hip-hop scene became a sensation and led to even more interactions between artists from the two scenes. A case in point was Epik High's song "Born Hater," released soon after the end *of Show Me the Money 3*, which featured Bobby, B.I, Mino, and some of the biggest names in Korean hip-hop like Beenzino and Verbal Jint.

Show Me the Money 3 added yet another obstacle to BTS's struggle for recognition. Following the diss from B-Free, BTS—in particular, RM and SUGA, who were rappers from the hip-hop scene—felt pressured to prove themselves. It was at that point that *Show Me the Money 3* showed other idols taking the lead in securing recognition from the hip-hop scene. And in the process, Bobby released the song "YGGR#Hip Hop" on the show, where he dissed all idol rappers with the exception of the few he personally respected. In his later song "GUARD UP AND BOUNCE" and the song "Come Here" in which he featured, he specifically dissed a number of idol rappers, including BTS. RM's stage name at the time, Rap Monster, was directly targeted.

To be clear, Bobby's diss was completely different in character from B-Free's insult. B-Free had mocked BTS out of the blue mid-conversation, but Bobby's rap diss adhered to hip-hop culture, where artists pick fights through rap and diss one another in a sort of dare to prove themselves.

Seen in this context, Bobby's diss was a challenge to idol rappers other than the ones he already respected. His lyrics to "Come Here" explicitly dared his peers to battle. RM, too, took the diss as a friendly challenge rather than an insult, and remarked that he respected Bobby. Unfortunately, the diss could not have come at a worse moment. BTS was going through a mountain of struggles all at once, and the diss was just one more in a pile of difficulties. Making matters worse was the fact that "Come Here" was released on December 2, 2014, precisely one day before the MAMA stage: the stage where BTS was already slated to give the performance of a lifetime.

200%

In the hours between the release of "Come Here" and BTS's performance at the MAMA, the BTS members and everyone at Big Hit Entertainment were only just barely holding themselves together. RM was already in Hong Kong, where the MAMA performance would take place, when he heard the news about "Come Here." He did not have much time to think of a response.

———I kept agonizing about whether or not to mention Bobby onstage. I couldn't sleep at the hotel, just thinking, 'Do I? Do I not? Do I? Do I not?' My mind was a mess.

If RM didn't respond to Bobby at the MAMA, which would be his first performance after the diss, any later responses would lack all impact. But RM had less than a day to compose new lyrics responding to the diss in the midst of the rap he'd prepared for the collaborative performance with ZICO from Block B.

Meanwhile, Big Hit Entertainment staff exchanged constant communications between Korea and Hong Kong, considering all the issues that might arise from RM's response to Bobby and potential response measures to such issues. It was only right for RM to respond to rap with rap. He had been dissed three times so far, and responding with silence was out of the question, especially considering his fans.

At the same time, BTS could not afford to mess up on the MAMA stage. After everything they had been through in recent months, they had to put on the perfect performance. RM would have to respond to the diss properly, but at the same time, BTS as a whole had to make certain the audience focused on the team's performance.

On the day of the 2014 MAMA, Mnet introduced the BTS/Block B collaborative performance as the "Next Generation of K-pop." But in reality, the performance was more of a war to become the next generation of K-pop: the teams would take turns showing off their rap and dance, then perform their songs in a battle format.

RM looks back on his feelings about the performance:

———We were in the position of trying to crawl up somehow. In those days, every day was full of really upsetting, underhanded, and frustrating situations, and then in my case, that thing happened with Bobby. I was already really eager and desperate, so I was somehow dragging myself forward, and I thought I was really on the verge of a big burst, when it felt like someone came with a pin and popped a balloon.

Jimin recalls his emotions prior to the MAMA stage:

———We had to win, no matter what. I didn't want to fall behind in any way.

All these circumstances came together with the members' venomous determination and desperation, propelling their MAMA preparation to new heights. RM describes the team vibe exactly as it was:

———Not just me, everyone thought the same thing. If a hyoung got mad, I got mad, if a dongsaeng got mad, I got mad. We were moving as one at the time, so we were just on exactly the same wavelength.

According to Jimin, RM often said the following to the members before the performance:

———There's this thing RM used to say to us. "Don't get all excited. We're not anything yet, we're nothing." He said that every time we were about to go up onstage.

Before even pulling off the MAMA stage, BTS accomplished many things as they practiced. One big accomplishment was the perfection of the choreography for "Danger."

At the time, "Danger" boasted the most difficult dance choreography of anything BTS had released. It involved a host of moves where details had to be matched to perfection, and although the dance appears to maintain a consistent tempo, discreet speed changes between individual moves required the members to constantly adjust their pace.

The biggest draw of the choreography was when the members froze in unison throughout the dance, which meant that everyone had to be fully tense throughout the performance, adjusting arms and legs in turn to change speed, and also remain in perfect sync with one another. Jimin explains:

———Compared to everything up to "Boy In Luv," "Danger" had a ton more details and the movements were faster. When I did moves that my body had never used before, that my body had never done, it just needed a completely different kind of strength, which was the hardest part.

Jimin adds:

———And the thought of, 'We're still not much . . .' All of it converged, so that's why it was so tough.

However, the difficult choreography of "Danger" would work to their advantage at the MAMA. The sustained intensity of BTS's moves left a powerful impact on the stage, when all eyes were locked on them. There was a concern that broadcast cameras might not be able to capture all the details of their choreography, but the issue was solved by adding a large number of back dancers to the stage to mimic the performance. The visual image of the BTS members in white and the back dancers in black was a sort of starting point for the group's later large-scale performances shown in songs like "Burning Up (FIRE)."

V remembers the MAMA "Danger" performance:

———At the MAMA, we brought out 200% of this song.

Like V says, the MAMA stage was the first opportunity BTS had to showcase "Danger" and their strengths to a mainstream audience. The intensity and the explosive, rock-inspired ending was a perfect fit for the large venue, and the stage, being massive in comparison to

Korean music show stages, allowed BTS to pull off a large-scale performance that utilized the effect of back dancers. The MAMA performance showed BTS how to maximize the effect of "Danger" and sowed the seeds for the group's unique performance style to come.

The "Danger" performance was impressive on its own, but even more importantly, the BTS show as a whole that night, from j-hope and Jimin's appearance to the climactic performance of "Danger," had a consistent, dramatic flow.

When asked what about the performance he pored over the most, j-hope replies,

———In my case, it was really the dance. I wanted to really push things to the edge when it came to the parts I could do.

During the opening solo battles, j-hope made a powerful impression by raising himself slightly into the air and landing on the ground with all his weight on one knee.

———That was the "knee slam of my soul!" I revived that feeling from my debut and smashed my knee on the floor with all my strength. So as soon as the performance ended, I grabbed that knee and said, "Ow, that hurts . . ." Versus, or competition, was the whole concept, so I had this really strong feeling that we mustn't lose no matter what.

Jimin's following performance, where he tore his shirt open mid-performance, was the result of sheer willpower and determination. He recalls:

———Anyway, we had to face Block B, so we kept ending up talking about how to make it a little more impactful. Then I think someone said, "Gotta tear some clothes here!" (laughs). Because the other side (Block B) were great dancers too, so we were thinking about how to one-up them.

I thought I was really on the verge
of a big burst, when it felt like
someone came with a pin and
popped a balloon.

—RM

Jimin also remembers a small touch he added to give him an edge over the competition:

———When we were doing the collab stage, Block B looked really strong on the visual front. So I'm petite to begin with, but I didn't want to look small, so when we were walking, I purposely walked with big strides (laughs).

RM's rap that day also added to the publicity surrounding the performance. The day Bobby released "Come Here," that is, the day before the MAMA performance, RM posted a tweet of himself listening to "Do What I Do" by Verbal Jint, and highlighting a specific section of the lyrics as a preview of what was to come.˙ Then during the MAMA performance, he gave a direct response[22] to Bobby's provocation, which instantly blew up online.

BTS threw themselves onto the stage, pulled in audiences with brilliant new ideas, and refused to hide the reality of their lives. Although j-hope, Jimin, and RM's solo performances leading up to "Danger" were wildly different from one another, each was brimming with dynamic energy that threatened to break past the boundaries of idol music and the idol industry.

If the world of idols is a fantasy genre, the BTS performance brought in the rough, raw, and wild essence of the more dramatic hip-hop genre, without compromising their identity as idols. Everything

---

22 At this event, RM showcased the mixtape song "RM (for 2014 MAMA)."

˙

came together for the climactic final performance of "Danger," which was also a preview of what the group had in store for the world.

One Day in December 2014

Even before the MAMA stage, BTS had already recovered somewhat from the disappointing reception to "Danger." Just as they had recovered from "N.O" in *O!RUL8,2?* with "Attack on Bangtan," they followed up "Danger" with "War of Hormone," which received a positive public response.

"War of Hormone" was a sort of emergency measure by Bang Si-Hyuk, being grounded in a different philosophy from previous BTS songs. Judging that "Danger" had ironically put the team in danger, Bang thoroughly produced the performance, MV, and costume concepts for "War of Hormone" to fit the most mainstream and popular idol trends of the time.

The MV stood out in that it was shot to appear like a long single take, but in all other respects, it was as close as Bang could get to what he understood to be "the kind of idol performance mainstream fans wanted." In the MV and choreography, BTS members charm audiences with boundless cheer and optimism, alongside a hint of tough-guy swagger, to match the title's reference to hormones. And, as SUGA explains, this approach was a success:

———After "Danger," the company said, "We can't just end it like this," and our schedules suddenly got filled while we were resting. We shot concept photos and an MV for "War of Hormone," and the response was great. It was the impetus for us to bounce back.

At the same time, "War of Hormone" was a sort of wall that BTS had to overcome. Thus far, their hits—"Attack on Bangtan," "Boy In Luv," and "War of Hormone"—retained BTS's trademark wildness while showing off a lighthearted side. But Bang Si-Hyuk and BTS were well aware that maintaining the same style going forward would not allow them to level up. Not only that, the style of "Boy In Luv" alone would not fully capture the messages and realities that had filled their albums and music thus far.

This was what *DARK&WILD* was meant to address. This album is not as frequently discussed today, caught between the first three albums often called the "School Trilogy" and the paradigm-shifting *THE MOST BEAUTIFUL MOMENT IN LIFE* series, but *DARK&WILD* nonetheless played a crucial part in propelling BTS into the post–*THE MOST BEAUTIFUL MOMENT IN LIFE* era.

DARK&WILD also set itself apart from the "School Trilogy" by veering away from R&B elements rooted in hip-hop, shifting to a more intricate soundscape and establishing a new style of self-expression for the group. This change asserts itself with the very first track, "Intro : What am I to you,"* which, unlike previous intro songs, fills previously sparse gaps in the aural experience with complex sounds, magnifying the scale of the sound and dramatically pushing the composition forward.

"Hip Hop Phile"** is the biggest departure from previous songs, allowing the members to express the impact hip-hop had on their lives and growth, and confess their love for the genre. It follows the trend of other BTS songs in that it emphasizes the hip-hop aspect of their music, but the scaled-up soundscape gradually builds up to a powerful climax that leaves a lasting impression on the listener.

At the same time, the vocalists held their emotions in check to avoid sounding too dramatic. This was yet another departure from the mainstream K-pop idol style, and allowed the members to express more intricate, complicated emotion with the masterful use of R&B and soul music: the crystallization of what would become the "BTS vocal style."

The album was a rediscovery of BTS's dark and wild side, which had each been showcased separately in previous albums: the wildness in "No More Dream," and the darkness in "N.O." "Boy In Luv" was on the wild side and was upbeat and cheerful. The tracks in *DARK&WILD*, on the other hand, maintain a consistent dark tone that simultaneously builds a larger scale and a powerful emotional foundation that fills each song with passion. Dense with intricate details, each track starts off dark and builds up to a pounding finish that unleashes the wild side of the members while retaining the dark and heavy energy of the song.

DARK&WILD cemented a style unique to BTS, and the MAMA performance was the group's first opportunity to show the wider world their full potential, dark and wild and dramatic at once. The "Danger" performance gave them the time to tell a story onstage, where BTS were free to show off their disparate but unified style of teamwork.

And the public began to respond. RM was soon cast in the tvN variety show *Problematic Men*, where he brought even more public attention to BTS. This casting was especially significant because it was owed almost entirely to the explosive response to the MAMA performance.

————I had at any rate responded to Bobby at the MAMA. Because of that, it ended up a little controversy on its own and I was cast in *Problematic Men*. The director of the program at the time saw my name in the real-time search rankings on Naver and looked me up, wondering, 'Who is this person with the weird name?' and thought, 'Seems like he's studied up quite a bit,' and sought me out . . . It happened with the B-Free incident too, but I felt like whenever something bad happened, something good happened too.

The MAMA performance did not instantly rocket BTS to the top of the popularity rankings, but it was a capstone on everything the team had fought for thus far. Audiences who watched the MAMA performance or read about BTS after RM's response at the award show, began to consume BTS music and MVs.

And so, the year 2014 drew to a close, and j-hope celebrated four years in Seoul. Around this time, one of the Big Hit Entertainment staff members who had been monitoring public response to BTS made a sudden report to then Big Hit vice president Choi Yoo-jung.

"Something's happening. Uh . . . they're getting more and more fans."

CHAPTER 3

THE MOST BEAUTIFUL MOMENT IN LIFE PT.1

THE MOST BEAUTIFUL MOMENT IN LIFE PT.2

THE MOST BEAUTIFUL MOMENT IN LIFE : YOUNG FOREVER

LOVE, HATE,
ARMY

THE MOST BEAUTIFUL MOMENT IN LIFE PT.1 | THE 3RD MINI ALBUM

THE MOST BEAUTIFUL MOMENT IN LIFE PT.2 | THE 4TH MINI ALBUM

THE MOST BEAUTIFUL MOMENT IN LIFE : YOUNG FOREVER | THE 1ST SPECIAL ALBUM

| | | | | | | LOVE, HATE, ARMY | | | | | ||

Born Singer

On July 12, 2013, BTS released "Born Singer," their first mixtape song since debuting, on their official blog. It was exactly one month since their debut, and three days since their fandom had adopted the name ARMY[23] on July 9. SUGA explains what was behind the lyrics of "Born Singer":

———I remember in the week after we debuted, Bang Si-Hyuk said, "We should make a record of how we feel right now," "We should make it into a song." He said that, as time went by, we wouldn't remember these emotions. So when we were at the broadcasting station, I wrote down the lyrics on a notepad.

At the time of the song's release—a new interpretation of J. Cole's original, "Born Sinner"—it had been uncommon for idols to produce tracks that were not part of an album, or to release them via anything other than the ordinary streaming platforms. At the time, there were some ARMY who didn't know where or how they could listen to the song, and so asked other ARMY for help. By directly producing, releasing, discovering, and listening to the song in this way, BTS and ARMY were making history.

This history is ongoing. Anyone listening to BTS's "Born Singer" for the first time now can experience the meeting of past and present. BTS—now iconic figures within the global music industry—defined

---

23 Selected by a fan vote, it is an acronym of Adorable Representative M.C. for Youth.

themselves with the phrase "I'm a born singer" early on, and we witness them laying bare their present in "perhaps an early confession."

SUGA discussed BTS's concerns about identity, talking about "the line between pre- and post-debut, between idol and rapper," while RM admitted of his mental state when they debuted, "Frankly, I was scared, said I'm all that, but proving myself." And then, j-hope's rap goes:

> *The blood and sweat we shed, I can feel it drenching me*
> *My tears well up after our performance*

BTS lived inside these sentences, not only before "Born Singer" came out, but in the moment it was released and even after that. A small accomplishment was soon followed by despair, and as much as BTS ran full force toward success, their goals would remain far off in the distance. Their daily routine—practicing, throwing themselves onstage, coming back down again, and working on their songs—repeated itself, but what would allow them to believe they'd proven themselves remained beyond their grasp. Whenever they came down from the stage, it wasn't glory but tears that piled up.

It'd been hoped they would do well when they debuted in 2013. In 2014, they believed they could rise to the top. But what about in 2015?

SUGA says:

——When you do this work, you feel a big disconnect. Separate from my idol career, I was nothing at that age. I would have been nothing if I hadn't ended up doing music. So, to be honest, there was no other answer. 'Guess there's nothing I can do other than this.'

The members of BTS left their hometowns, the hip-hop scene, and the ordinary student life behind them and ran headfirst into this world. However, almost three years since their debut, the thing that would prove they'd made the right decision was still beyond their grasp.

In the same way, in a vlog* recorded on December 19, 2014, j-hope wondered, "Did I have a good 2014?" He reflects:

——2014 was pretty hard, both physically and mentally. This was because it was the first time since we'd debuted that I'd started to have doubts . . . This was also the period when I was having a lot of doubts about myself, as well as the path I was taking, and I was thinking 'Is this right?'

As time went by, the members were preoccupied more and more by uncertainty. Even when their sales went up a little after the release of a new album, or when their name was being mentioned more within the idol fandom following the MAMA Awards, it wasn't encouraging. In fact, these successes made things all the more difficult for the members.

RM says of his mindset back then:

——It was like . . . things would work out, we had visible results, but it felt as if nothing was within our grasp? To be blunt, I think this had a big impact on us. That part was really difficult.

SUGA unsurprisingly recalls a sense of haziness:

——I knew our fans were increasing, but it wasn't like we could see them all. Because there was a limit as to the number of fans we could see at the TV stations or autograph sessions.

It was thanks to ARMY he met at a concert that SUGA wasn't completely eaten away by anxiety while working on *DARK&WILD*. BTS's first concert on their own in October 2014, BTS 2014 LIVE TRILOGY: EPISODE II. THE RED BULLET,[24•] became an opportunity for them to feel anew what the fans were giving them. SUGA says:

———The first performance really sticks in my memory. It was my first ever concert, and I thought, 'Wow, so many people have come to see us,' 'I'm truly a happy person.'

The uncertainty continued. Of course, they weren't without reassurance. And they didn't have many options, anyway. So, as BTS were preparing to work on their third mini album, *THE MOST BEAUTIFUL MOMENT IN LIFE PT.1*, SUGA decided:

———'If this doesn't work out, I won't do music anymore.'

Cottage Industry Production

Throughout the production of *THE MOST BEAUTIFUL MOMENT IN LIFE PT.1* mini album, SUGA essentially locked himself up in the studio. Aside from when there was something on their schedule, he hardly ever came out of the five-meter-square studio attached to the underground training room. It was also around then that SUGA began drinking.

---

24 The Seoul performance was across two days (October 18–19, 2014), but presale tickets sold out immediately upon release, so an extra date was added on October 17.

————Until then, I was such a lightweight that I didn't even drink. But it was because we couldn't go out anymore . . . The time preparing for the album really was like hell.

The other band members and staff listened to the songs SUGA was creating in real time. RM recalls of that period:

————Back then, we all worked together in this studio at the back of the second floor of the Cheonggu Building. The floors weren't ten meters long and we'd squeeze by each other. We would listen to the melodies SUGA wrote as soon as he'd written them. That was a time when in one room we were going, "Huh, this isn't bad," and Bang Si-Hyuk would come over from another room and say, "Pdogg, what do you think? Not bad, right?" Our dorm at that time was right around the corner. If the company told us to come to work, we would go right away.

This process of working on *THE MOST BEAUTIFUL MOMENT IN LIFE PT.1* recalled by RM can be summarized, to use his own words, as "cottage industry production." Regardless of role or position, everyone in the group and the company involved in the album's production worked together as one, and the end product was achieved through constant conversation. When they were happy with the song they'd made, they immediately called the others in from the other rooms to have a listen or share the track via Messenger. If the response wasn't very good, someone would edit the song right away or make a new one. Almost all the song production process would happen in real time, and the quality of the end product swiftly improved accordingly.

RM explains how he felt at the time:

————It felt like I wanted to get angry at the whole world. I don't know how to explain it other than like this, 'easily flying away, vanishing, coming together, crumbling again, being captured once more . . .' These feelings repeating themselves.

There's a real irony to all of these stories because it was *THE MOST BEAUTIFUL MOMENT IN LIFE* series that put BTS and Big Hit Entertainment on the fast track to success. It was also the start of a drastic shift in which the Korean popular music industry's influence would expand worldwide, and even idol groups who, like BTS, had debuted in smaller companies had hopes of reaching the top. Not to mention that following *THE MOST BEAUTIFUL MOMENT IN LIFE* series, more and more idol groups began to release albums as a series under a single concept just as BTS had done, and the importance of "story-planning"—the so-called "Universe"—was also becoming clear.

However, this album—a key milestone in the history of the Korean popular music industry, and especially that of idols—was also the end product of the members pouring out their most private emotions. It was also a result of how those involved in production clung together both physically and emotionally, rather than following any clearly defined system.

It was inevitable that "youth" would become both the albums' subject matter as well as their concept. "Intro : The most beautiful moment in life"' from mini album *THE MOST BEAUTIFUL MOMENT IN LIFE PT.1* begins:

> *The rim seems farther away today*
> *Sighs pile up on the court*
> *A boy afraid of reality*

In these lyrics, which SUGA rewrote dozens of times until he perfected them, he talks about coming up against the wall of reality through his favorite sport, basketball. And in "Moving On,"* which effectively acts as the final song before "Outro : Love is Not Over," he shares a very personal story.

> *From the first days in my mother's womb*
> *I used to count the days to my very first move*
> *Vague memories, the cost of my move was*
> *A medical device attached to my mother's heart and a huge scar*

———The song "Moving On" is like an aching finger for me.

His voice calm, SUGA continues the story:

———You'll see from the lyrics, but it was when I was two years old, or was it three . . . ? What I still remember is, I'd been sleeping and when I woke up, I was leaning on my mom, and I could hear a sound like a clock coming from her heart. I asked her why it was making that sound. She'd had surgery after having me. My mom had got really sick because I was born. It made me feel somehow guilty. Ever since I was little, I would think, 'Was it right that I was born?' I need to do everything I can for her, no matter what it is. Maybe that was why I was hungry for success. That was why I called my birth "Moving On."

The beginning of a huge success story, the *THE MOST BEAUTIFUL*

THE MOST BEAUTIFUL MOMENT IN LIFE PT.1

THE 3RD MINI ALBUM
2015. 4. 29

TRACK

01 Intro : The most beautiful
    moment in life
02 I NEED U
03 Hold Me Tight
04 SKIT : Expectation!
05 Dope

06 Boyz with Fun
07 Converse High
08 Moving On
09 Outro : Love is Not Over

VIDEO

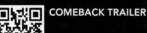 COMEBACK TRAILER

 "I NEED U"
MV

 ALBUM PREVIEW

 "I NEED U"
MV (Original ver.)

 "I NEED U"
MV TEASER

 "Dope"
MV

MOMENT IN LIFE series came out of the most private confession. Each of the youths came together and made a record of a period in a single community's life—the "most beautiful moment in life"—before drawing it to a close. Like in "Moving On," BTS moved accommodations for the very first time since their debut while preparing for *THE MOST BEAUTIFUL MOMENT IN LIFE PT. 1*. Jung Kook reflects:

———In my part of this song, there are the lyrics, "Leaving the empty room with the last of my things / When I turn back for a second," right? In reality, I do remember looking around my room in the accommodations once before leaving. I felt that we'd grown, and on the one hand I was looking forward to what exciting things would happen in our new place.

As in the lyrics of "Moving On," in the accommodations they worried about "[a]n uncertain future," and among the members there were "[a] few times we quarreled," but they went through the process of "[s]maller the house, stronger the bond." Leaving that place and moving into their new accommodations proved that something was changing, or at least allowed them to believe this was the case.

In moving accommodations, Jung Kook felt that the group's situation could change:

———First of all, there were more rooms. One, two, three rooms, and a bathroom. I bought a computer for the very first time, and I had my own workspace. I didn't have a separate room for my clothes, and so I set up rails in the living room and hung them there, and in between I placed a desk for me to use. And that was why later my studio name became "Golden Closet." The accommodations were roomier, and so it definitely felt comfortable. It kind of felt like I had more room to breathe. Way back, all seven of us slept in one room, right? Then we started to divide out the rooms.

Jin was also able to feel more at ease in the new accommodations:

——I shared a room with SUGA, Jung Kook was in a room with RM, and V, Jimin, and j-hope shared the biggest room between them. Our day-to-day life changed a lot. Before that, it was really crowded, but from then on, there was the fun of going to each other's rooms.

In this way, the series was expressed through a storytelling method based on keywords like "youth" and "the most beautiful moment in life," with the personal experiences and emotions of the members providing the foundation.

In this respect, BTS and Big Hit Entertainment, without even realizing it themselves, were in the process of tearing down boundaries. They were an idol group telling a story through an album in the style of hip-hop, an album that would come to linger long on people's lips.

Rules Broken, Then Changed

With *THE MOST BEAUTIFUL MOMENT IN LIFE PT.1*, Bang Si-Hyuk threw much of what was considered common sense (or even "rules") within idol content production at the time out the window.

Generally, idol groups would have a dance track as their album's title song, and there would of course be choreography performed by the members in the music video. However, the music video for *THE MOST BEAUTIFUL MOMENT IN LIFE PT.1*'s title song "I NEED U" has no scenes that contain dancing. What's more, the characters in the video roam around not elaborate sets, urban centers, or foreign countries, but what looks like city outskirts.

The reason for this is connected to the video's contents. There are two versions of the music video for "I NEED U": the official version* (the final edited version submitted to the broadcasting company), and the original version** released only on YouTube. The original version runs around two minutes longer than the official version, and those two minutes depict violence, emotional trauma, and so on—almost unheard of in the music videos of idol groups at the time.

Within the Korean idol industry, experimenting like this was no different from intentionally trying to ruin yourself. In Korea, idols are seen as offering up a fantasy. In their music videos, whether the concept involves smiling brightly or rebelling against the world, in most cases this is all part of the same objective: looking cool. Dividing concepts into "fresh" or "dark," depending on the vibe of the visuals and the song itself, is also part of this practice. Aspects of reality are intentionally cut away a bit at a time—only then can the fans accept the idols' content as a safe fantasy. BTS, however, brought something more realistic into the world of idols. This wasn't just a problem of the intensity of expression. The characters in "I NEED U" find themselves in dismal, oppressive circumstances, in which nothing has been resolved, and the members vent the emotions they feel toward their situation, in which everything is becoming worse and worse. Until "youth" was accepted as a single idol-music concept like it is now, it was hard to pinpoint exactly. This was, in all respects, almost alien to the fans who had gotten accustomed to the existing products of the idol industry.

"I NEED U" is only the first song of *THE MOST BEAUTIFUL MOMENT IN LIFE* series, and in order to fully understand the ongoing storyline, fans needed to watch a variety of related footage, including the music video for "RUN," the title song for the upcoming mini album *THE MOST BEAUTIFUL MOMENT IN LIFE PT.2.*

However, this was the only path available to Bang Si-Hyuk. Just like the characters in their music videos, the members of BTS were lingering on the outskirts, unable to make it into the heart of the world they were living in, trapped between their uncertain position and a longing for success: an unresolved, suffocating situation. It was these emotions that made *THE MOST BEAUTIFUL MOMENT IN LIFE* series possible. This was also why "I NEED U" could come out as a song on its own.

An ordinary producer could have chosen "Dope," which demonstrated BTS's intense choreography, as *THE MOST BEAUTIFUL MOMENT IN LIFE PT.1*'s title song. In fact, until "I NEED U," BTS's title songs had all had an intense atmosphere. Their performance at the MAMA Awards at the end of 2014 further solidified this image. Despite this, Bang Si-Hyuk chose to represent the album with "I NEED U," a song so relaxed it feels almost fragile, one that opens on a low tempo beat.

The song's choreography˙ even begins with all seven lying on the ground, and none of the remaining members get up until SUGA's rap in the first verse is over. Likewise, it is not immediately clear what the song is trying to convey. Instead, from the very beginning of the song, a melancholy and complex emotion is conveyed through the lyrics.

> *Fall Fall Fall scatters*
> *Fall Fall Fall falls*

"I NEED U" captures the members' mindset at the time, which RM described as "easily flying away, vanishing, coming together, crumbling again, being captured once more . . . These feelings repeating."

However, "I NEED U" was more than just an adventurous and risky experiment. When it came to this particular song, Bang Si-Hyuk had conviction. He'd decided that BTS needed to go beyond the boundaries of what they'd done so far. BTS's unique style, encapsulated within their previous album *DARK&WILD*, seemed to be floating in exactly the same space, repeating the same cycle.

"I NEED U" added a deep sorrow like falling petals to BTS's dark and gritty core. The title song, with its complex emotions, wasn't an ordinary choice within the idol industry. Bang Si-Hyuk was sure, however, that as a song on its own, it would elicit a universally positive response from people. In "I NEED U," a calm and delicate sound is layered against SUGA's incensed rapping, and then, when the sound suddenly speeds up, he sings in a low and sorrowful voice, "Sorry (I hate u) / Love you (I hate you) / I forgive you (Shit)." With intensity and sadness appearing constantly alongside one another, listeners feel sad while also becoming more and more elated. Then, in the chorus, these emotions fuse together and explode. The way in which the drawn-out chorus suddenly switches to a powerful beat demonstrates the song's cathartic element alongside its explosive dance routine.

The BTS members were the first to show a positive response to the song. "I NEED U" wouldn't be called hip-hop, or EDM, or dance music of the kind that previous idol groups had produced. The members, however, intuitively accepted this song born out of the boundaries between genre and genre, emotion and emotion. Jimin reflects on when he first heard "I NEED U":

————This song comes on, then we hear the album's concept and the remaining tracks, but you could tell from the atmosphere that everyone was sure. That the song was good, and that the concept was also good.

Jung Kook even felt that "it was too good for words." He adds:

————I was totally sure it would "work." It was so good. So much so that everything that'd happened until then crumbled away, and I forgot everything about "You're in danger"[25] (laughs).

Jung Kook also expresses the hope that "I NEED U" gave BTS at the time:

————It was like, this was the beginning. Our beginning.

A Moment That Comes Once in a Lifetime

They'd broken industry rules, and for the end product to be considered a success, BTS needed yet another new approach. With "I NEED U," Jin changed the way he sang.

————Until that point, I often used to oversing, but when I did this song, for the first time, I breathed as I sang. During recording, I

---

25 Part of the lyrics from *DARK&WILD*'s title song "Danger."

sang the whole song all in one go like that, and a few parts of it went into the actual song. At the time it felt awkward, but it was the right thing to do.

The dancing also needed extensive changes. j-hope explains:

——Before, we just needed to throw all our energy into the dance like 'Argh!,' but for "I NEED U," the way we expressed the emotions was really important. The choreography would only work if we expressed the sentimentality well, and so it was basically like "half dance, half facial expression acting."

To express the emotions, j-hope would imagine these kinds of things:

——Hmm . . . It was like, when I danced, I got into the character of a boy hanging off the edge of a cliff. I felt really anxious. Like there was a lot at stake.

The emotions that j-hope speaks of directly carry over into *THE MOST BEAUTIFUL MOMENT IN LIFE PT.1*'s concept photos, as well as the film set for the "I NEED U" music video. He reiterates:

——It was pretty unique. At the time, we took many shots of this and that, but like . . . I think I felt like I wasn't living as a celebrity, but as a person enjoying their youth. It was the same when I was going around filming with the other members, and maybe during the filming I was thinking about anxiety and about a period of feeling lost . . . but it didn't much feel like a process you went through as a celebrity preparing for an album.

It was like,
this was the beginning.
Our beginning.

—Jung Kook

RM felt something similar, too:

———If I look back on it now, maybe something more could have been brought out of us. I'd thought there wouldn't be anything like that after "Danger," but that wasn't the case. And the presence of the song called "I NEED U" was undeniably large. I think it started from a feeling of 'Oh, this might just work?' and us wanting to try and create our "most beautiful moment in life" was hidden within our emotions, too.

Jimin explains the effect the members' emotions had on the filming of "I NEED U":

———I think I fully immersed myself in the concept itself of "the most beautiful moment in life." Doing it together with the other members was so good, and I kept thinking how this was such a beautiful moment, that I really could call it the best in my life. By immersing myself in the music video's role like that, I was often told that this suited the emotions of the role well.

The members identified a substantial part of themselves within the music video roles, and this allowed them, though they had almost no experience acting, to immerse themselves deeply in the characters. V still holds the role he acted in *THE MOST BEAUTIFUL MOMENT IN LIFE* series in a corner of his heart. He says:

———I believed he was a person who'd had no choice but to become "evil." If there's such a thing as good and evil, he was a person whose situation meant he suddenly switched from good to evil. And so, when I look at the character, I just feel sad for him.

In this way, before the later commercial success of *THE MOST BEAUTIFUL MOMENT IN LIFE* series, the members had grown internally through its production process.

Jimin reflects on filming the music video for "I NEED U":

———For me, it was just, I'd always had this dream since way back, and that was why I was doing this work. But it was so good. Talking, singing, practicing the dance routine, filming while saying "We're the youth!" . . . We were basically doing the filming as one big group as well, and I was so happy we were going around together like that. Doing the one thing I liked to do, no less. And so I got the impression that, if I looked back on my life later on, I wouldn't be able to explain it without this part I did together with these people.

This experience working on *THE MOST BEAUTIFUL MOMENT IN LIFE* series became an opportunity for Jimin to grow as an artist.

———Comparing before and after *THE MOST BEAUTIFUL MOMENT IN LIFE*, when it came to the image I presented on the stage, it was like, I'd found my balance? I think I'd gradually found what I was good at.

Jin became even closer with the other members. He says:

———During that time, my bond with the members got stronger. They were really like family. And we filmed the music videos like a movie, right? After watching it, it really felt like that for us members. Before, we just thought we were idols, but since then, when I think of the members, it feels kind of like we're playing the lead roles in a movie.

A unified spirit began to emerge among the members. Jimin explains the atmosphere within the group prior to the release of *THE MOST BEAUTIFUL MOMENT IN LIFE PT.1* album very simply as:

———I think our mindset of 'We can do it' had grown much stronger.

Expectation

As the title suggests, the song "SKIT : Expectation!"* from *THE MOST BEAUTIFUL MOMENT IN LIFE PT.1* captures the members' feelings of expectation about the upcoming album release. To be precise, rather than expectation, it was closer to a hope that this expectation would be realized. The words the members kept repeating—that they needed to be "number one"—sound almost like a spell to wash away their anxiety. j-hope reflects:

——Work was important to me, I had a dream and wanted to be successful, and so I had quite a lot of anxiety over whether we'd do well. I think I wondered, 'Will this work make me really happy?' I was always hovering around that point.

As j-hope says, the members wanted to break away from the cycle of "sweet, bitter, sweet, bitter." They weren't asking for much. To have a number one on a chart music TV program. To come out on top, not on the yearly album charts or at a music awards ceremony, but simply on one of those programs that aired multiple times a week.

Getting a number one on a chart music TV program is a rite of passage for every idol group in Korea. Each chart music TV program runs weekly. Every terrestrial channel has its own, and put together this basically means that, other than Monday, there's one on every day. Each program also calculates rankings differently. For some, good digital music figures lead to a high chance of hitting number one, and for others, first place can come from having good physical sales.

Only after being ranked number one in one of these programs can you talk about popularity or success. If an idol group doesn't achieve a number one within a set period of time, it is likely to disappear from the programs altogether. Aside from those belonging to large management companies, idols that don't make number one in just one of these chart music TV programs that air all week long find that their companies are reluctant to keep waiting and investing in production costs.

BTS were now between albums *DARK&WILD* and *THE MOST BEAUTIFUL MOMENT IN LIFE PT.1*, and a chart music TV program number one trophy was within reach. At the time of their previous album, *Skool Luv Affair*, they had been contenders for number one with "Boy In Luv," and by the MAMA Awards at the end of 2014, their fandom had begun to increase rapidly in size. However, the numbers for *DARK&WILD* didn't live up to expectations, and their new album still hadn't come out. Neither BTS nor Big Hit Entertainment had any way of getting a true feel for their popularity.

When discussing with the company about the group's direction at the time of *DARK&WILD*, V apparently said:

———There are groups above us when it comes to popularity, and groups below us, too, but I don't think there are any groups like us. BTS are in a position unique to BTS.

Going on from this, V pointed out a condition for BTS to grow further:

———"What's called a "Legend Stage," giving an awesome performance."

A few months later, this Legend Stage took place at the 2014 MAMA Awards. Even so, they still hadn't got their hands on the number one trophy. Among all the groups who hadn't yet hit number one on a chart music TV program, they were the closest. Yet they still hadn't made it. "SKIT : Expectation!" captures all the expectations and anxieties of the members.

j-hope explains how he felt back then:

——We also wanted to reach that spot, we wanted to make number one . . . We thought a lot about wanting to achieve something.

A Shout of Joy at One in the Morning

At midnight on April 29, 2015, *THE MOST BEAUTIFUL MOMENT IN LIFE PT.1* was released across all music streaming platforms. At the time, due to the effect of real-time chart tallying by the hour, most idol groups released their songs at midnight, and the fandom would listen to the songs over and over to increase the song's entry position on the charts.[26]

An hour later, at one in the morning, the director of Big Hit Entertainment at the time, Lenzo Yoon, shouted out in surprise when he saw the results. The title song "I NEED U" had entered at number two on the Melon live chart, which at the time had the greatest market share among all the music streaming platforms in Korea.

The members were similarly shocked. j-hope recalls the moment he saw the Melon live chart:

——I think we must have all looked at the chart together mid-practice. It was so exciting. We'd never entered the music charts [at such a high position] before—it was the first time I felt that 'so many people are listening to our songs,' and it was thrilling. I also thought, 'This is what we made music for.'

---

26 This type of tallying method has since been abolished from Korean music streaming platforms, and tracks are now generally released at 6:00 P.M.

Shortly after debuting, one of SUGA's wishes had been to reach "number one on the Melon live music charts." For him, this was the marker of success. He says:

———Back then, I believed that was everything. I thought it was the very edge of this world. I think I saw it as like, 'reaching number one on Melon means you've made it as a singer.' I looked at the chart almost every day. It wasn't as if I was watching stock charts, but I calculated this and that and carried out analyses, too.

Though "I NEED U" couldn't make SUGA's wish a reality, at the time, number two on the Melon charts felt similarly—if not even more—difficult to achieve than number one on a music TV program.

Compared to singers who were widely known and popular among the masses, for idol groups, whose activities centered around their fandom, it was difficult to get good results on the streaming platforms used by the wider public, especially Melon, which had the most users. Live charts, which determined their rankings based on the number of listeners per hour, were of course favorable to artists with a strong fandom, but ranking high on the charts wasn't easy back then and isn't easy now. Even "Danger," the title song of BTS's previous album, *DARK&WILD*, didn't reach a notable position on the live charts. The significance of BTS hitting number two on the live charts was simple. Their fans had started to increase so much in number that even the staff at Big Hit Entertainment could hardly believe it.

Every one of their results went up. Based on the Gaon Chart criteria, 203,664 copies of *THE MOST BEAUTIFUL MOMENT IN LIFE PT.1* were sold, more than double the sales of *DARK&WILD* back in

2014. Then, BTS finally hit the top spot on a chart music TV program. On May 5, 2015, they got their first ever number one on cable music channel SBS MTV's *The Show* with "I NEED U," and three days later, on May 8, they reached number one on KBS's *Music Bank*, their first on a terrestrial broadcast channel.

Jimin explains how he felt at the time:

———There was a strong sense of being rewarded. That we'd done something together as a group—I was overwhelmed by that feeling, I think. I didn't really care how hard I'd prepared, or how hard I'd worked. I was so grateful we'd achieved something from all of us members working together.

The other members felt similarly. To them, a number one meant that BTS, both as a group and as individuals, had finally been recognized, and this felt like happiness. j-hope explains:

———It felt like our presence was being recognized. We started from music, and we were making it known that one album, my name, our group—all these things were "alive" . . .

j-hope elaborates on the happiness that comes with popularity:

———Making it known through my work that "This is the person I am," it tasted so sweet. I acknowledged for the first time that I was loved a lot.

The Effect of Victory on Youth

As BTS began to grasp success, the world outside them began to change. This can also be seen in videos related to their TV music program appearances, uploaded to YouTube under the subcategory "BANGTAN BOMB."[27.]

The footage captured from their debut in 2013 up until *THE MOST BEAUTIFUL MOMENT IN LIFE PT.1* generally showed the members playing pranks on one another in the green room, getting ready for their stage performances, and so on. Videos taken after their follow-up album, *THE MOST BEAUTIFUL MOMENT IN LIFE PT.2,* often showed BTS getting ready to appear as "special MCs" on music TV programs alongside the album release.

This gives an idea of what *THE MOST BEAUTIFUL MOMENT IN LIFE PT.1* meant to BTS. A special MC was a particular person chosen from among the various artists active at the time to host the program as a one-off. Being chosen as a special MC basically meant that the person "had arrived." The video content also captured the members' reactions to reaching number one on the chart music TV program.

Jimin explains the inner changes that the members, including himself, went through at the time:

———I think it was from that point onward . . . we started to properly become aware of these people called "fans." We hadn't properly defined the fans before that. We were like, "What do we call them?" The members would just be saying, "Let's do our best,"

27 "BANGTAN BOMB," a subcategory on BTS's official YouTube channel, BANGTANTV. The videos contained not only their onstage performances, but also candid footage of the members backstage, in the green room, and in other shooting locations.

"Let's do a good job." But once we'd made number one, I kept remembering our first broadcast the day we debuted. That day, around ten fans came, right? Those people—without those people cheering us on, there would have been no demand for us to exist, and we felt a sense of urgency that we needed to be truly thankful to these people called fans.

Success made BTS conscious of everything they'd gone through to get this far, as well as what they wanted their goal to be from that point on. j-hope recalls the atmosphere among the members following *THE MOST BEAUTIFUL MOMENT IN LIFE PT.1*:

———I think the members all had ambition. We'd made one dream come true, but we weren't satisfied, and wanted to present an even more impressive image of ourselves. All of us were thinking, 'I want to go even higher.' Maybe that was why our group had gotten this far already . . . I think that if even one of us had thought differently, it would have been difficult to do.

Success had allowed the members to expand their goals, and it was just by great coincidence that they had been working on "Dope"' as the follow-up to "I NEED U."

"I NEED U" and "Dope" were, so to speak, two milestones that encapsulate the BTS of that time. "I NEED U" almost seemed to portray the hardships and despair BTS had experienced prior to *DARK&WILD*, whereas "Dope" captured how, despite everything, they'd somehow made it this far.

Ah stink! Stink! Stink! Smell of sweat in our dance studio
See! Loud! Loud! Loud! My dance answers

The song's title "Dope," or "jjeoleo" in Korean, generally means "on a roll," "awesome," similar to the word "swag," but in the lyrics, BTS use the other meaning of "jjeoleo": "to stink with sweat." While other idol groups who'd had a sudden boom in popularity would boast, "We're dope," BTS came forward declaring, "We practice until we stink with sweat."

With "I NEED U," BTS were rapidly on the rise, and their follow-up "Dope" became a song that captured the underdog spirit of pushing their way to the top. The opening of "I NEED U" has a lyrical atmosphere, after which a deep sorrow gradually builds up; "Dope," however, comes straight in with its highlight and storms through right until the end. And while "I NEED U" maximizes its melancholy emotion through the chorus and a long and complex melody, "Dope" maximizes its exhilarating atmosphere through the two characters of "jjeol-eo" and the beat.

Welcome, is it your first time to meet BTS?

RM's lyrics at the very beginning of "Dope" became a declaration full of meaning. These lyrics weren't included as a prediction of *THE MOST BEAUTIFUL MOMENT IN LIFE PT.1*'s huge success. Instead, "Dope" was a song that explained the group's identity to those who had discovered BTS for the first time through *THE MOST BEAUTIFUL MOMENT IN LIFE PT.1*.

In this sense, "I NEED U" and "Dope" capture the core of BTS at the time. Fighting as an underdog: enduring everything imaginable, but

— I think it was from that point onward . . .
we started to properly become aware
of these people called "fans."

—Jimin

never losing the will to go on. The group's spirit was revealed through "I NEED U" and then, with "Dope," grew out of control. This was not limited to the realm of chart figures: everyone in the idol industry felt it.

Korean idol groups hold mini fan meetings in front of the broadcasting station after a music TV program has finished filming. Here, they meet fans who've been waiting at the set since the early hours. You can judge the scale and enthusiasm of a group's fandom based on the mini fan meetings: these are the fans who have come to see the group in person. Sadly, if the group is unpopular, the number of fans can be less than the number of group members themselves.

That day,[28] BTS went to the mini fan meeting still in their "Dope" stage costumes, and the outside of the broadcasting station was so full of ARMY that they had to stop letting people in for safety reasons. BTS's fans were no longer the "single line" Jimin had spoken of.

The Self-Produced Content Era

Just like with all industries, the idol industry has its own know-how regarding certain "standard" roles. Though they are not explicitly stated to be idol industry standards, once this production know-how has been established within several key companies, it soon becomes a standard the whole industry must follow in order to succeed.

For example, for Korean idol groups, it went without saying that dance music would be chosen as the title song, which would be accompanied by elaborate choreography based around the concept of "kal-

---

28 July 5, 2015, the day of the SBS broadcast *Inkigayo*.

gunmu." SM Entertainment's role had been absolute in setting these standards. Through their unique dance routines, SM Entertainment's idol groups were redefining music, and the music industry's consumers did not remain simply as listeners, but became fiercely devoted fans. In addition to this, with BIGBANG and 2NE1, YG Entertainment had fused the international hip-hop and pop trends of the time with the structure of K-pop melodies. They also utilized street and high fashion—something rarely attempted by idols before then—and through this, their influence went beyond the fandom, to the masses and the fashion industry itself.

After *THE MOST BEAUTIFUL MOMENT IN LIFE PT.1*, Big Hit Entertainment presented a new standard other than those offered by SM Entertainment and YG Entertainment. On top of their series concept for albums, and the album planning method that allowed for multiple interpretations within a single story, they also made use of beats that raise a song's energy, like the part in "Dope," "I have worked all night, everyday / When you are hanging around in da club yeah," for example. These methods were later applied by several other groups.

It also seems that, by focusing on online platforms rather than the ordinary TV channels, they were hailing a new generation. BTS had been using YouTube in a similar way to YouTubers nowadays since before their debut. Here, through the live streaming platform V Live, BTS perfected their unique ecosystem of activities.

In August 2015, three months after the release of *THE MOST BEAUTIFUL MOMENT IN LIFE PT.1*, V Live, which offered a variety of Korean idol content directly to fans, had been running a beta version on Naver. On V Live, artists could communicate instantly with fans through online live broadcasting, which they could initiate spontaneously or prearrange for a specified time, and reply to fans' comments there and then. This was the start of the "self-produced content" era.

With the emergence of V Live, the generation in which idols would shroud themselves in mystery offstage, restricting their content and releasing it little by little to fans, had come to an end. At the time of BTS's debut, the idol industry was already a red ocean among red oceans. With the advent of V Live, self-produced content made by the idols and their representatives themselves, so-called "teasers," became much more important. Continuously handing out teasers in this way meant that even when the idols weren't working on an album, fans couldn't look anywhere else.

For BTS, who had been making a variety of content available through their blog and YouTube channel since before their debut, the era of self-produced content was like an "ancient future." Their experience communicating recent news with fans through vlogs on YouTube made a natural transition to the V Live streaming function, and the variety of self-produced content acted as continuous teasers to the fans who followed BTS on their V Live channel.

Run BTS!, the variety show started by BTS and Big Hit Entertainment on V Live, was the final piece of their new ecosystem of activities. For idol groups, not only did special appearances on variety programs allow fans to enjoy domains beyond music, but they were also important in highlighting each member's unique personality. Both before and after 2000, the first generation of boy groups in Korea formed the basis of their popularity through variety show specials. However, until *Run BTS!*, the production of idol variety shows remained exclusively within the domain of the broadcasting companies. Idol groups affiliated with large management companies would also regularly make their names known through variety show specials as soon as they debuted. But broadcasting companies also had to consider their ratings, and it was standard to cast popular idols.

Through *Run BTS!*, Big Hit Entertainment carried idol variety programs over into the realm of self-produced content. Making their own variety program was a huge gamble for a smaller-sized company. In the end, however, it wouldn't be an exaggeration to say that *Run BTS!* was more successful than not only *Rookie King: Channel Bangtan* and *American Hustle Life*, but all idol variety shows of the time.

Unlike broadcasting companies' variety show idol specials, *Run BTS!* could continue running without there needing to be an end, and since it was created by BTS's management company, the producers also had a good grasp on the members' physical conditions. Now, after watching chart music TV programs in which BTS featured, ARMY could then watch live streams on V Live where the members discussed their reflections, and could also check out related behind-the-scenes footage and photographs on YouTube and Twitter. In between all of this, they could watch variety programs like *Run BTS!*. If you were someone who had become ARMY through *THE MOST BEAUTIFUL MOMENT IN LIFE PT.1*, you could easily stay up all night watching the teasers accumulated over the past two years.

However, the era of self-produced content didn't stop at transforming how idols worked. As idols shared what went on behind the scenes and beyond the stage, as well as talking directly with fans, the definition of an idol itself began to change. While in the past it had been taken for granted that an idol would only show fans their good side, in the self-produced content era, idols began to reveal aspects of their situations as well as what was really on their minds. They spoke of being upset at the general public and the press, and even occasionally aired criticism. Now, in the 2020s, idols speak much more openly about the difficulties and problems they're experiencing, and occasionally, if they're going through a difficult time physically or psychologically, they give up the idol career entirely. And so, Korea's idols began to take on their own identities, different from the idols of Japan and America.

These activities made BTS all the busier. Even while preparing for *THE MOST BEAUTIFUL MOMENT IN LIFE PT.2* album, they still had to remain active on V Live and social media. How did the members respond to this increase in work? V explains it clearly:

———I just followed the group's decisions. I didn't see my own personal decisions as important at all. If I'm against something, but everyone else isn't, I'll think that the members are right. If the members go, "I want to do this," or "We have to do this," then I of course go along with it.

Asked how that was possible, V responds:

———"Because we're BTS," I think.

He goes on:

———I've bet my life on this group, I can't just decide something based on my own individual opinion. That's why I do it, and all of us have the attitude, 'Let's do it,' for all those different activities. And my attitude is to go along with it.

j-hope reflects on how he felt back then:

———I think it was a feeling like, 'Surely we can't lose now?' In thinking, 'We can do even better,' we did more. Once we did something, we did even more, we didn't do less.

In among all this, from May 20, 2015, the BTS YouTube channel began its own "mukbang" with Jin, "EAT JIN."· This move reveals to us not only BTS's determination to give anything a try, but the impact of the changing generation. Jin, who had been sharing his cooking via the BTS official blog since before the group's debut, after *THE MOST BEAUTI-FUL MOMENT IN LIFE PT.2*, began filming himself eating, too.

———At the time, there wasn't really any way to communicate with the fans, and as I liked eating, I thought I should upload that at least, and began filming. I wanted ARMY to be able to see my face, and that's how it started.

When Jin first started filming this content, he was worried about inconveniencing the other members, and so he shot the show in the smallest space he could, as quietly as possible. However, the content immediately got a good response, and Jin moved from YouTube to the BTS V Live channel and started live streaming. Jin recalls:

———When I was doing V Live the scale grew bigger. In the beginning, I was by myself, and all I needed to do was put the phone in front of me, eat, and film, but for V Live we do it together with people from the company. I hated being a burden to others and so personally, I was concerned, but the crew said it was no big deal at all, and not to worry. It was a live stream too, and I think at first, I wasn't very good. At the time there was also this preconception that I needed to have full makeup on because it counted as a broadcast.

However, in contrast to Jin's fears, "EAT JIN" became BTS's leading self-produced content. Even now, Jin maintains the image of a skilled cook, and this has become one of his signatures. Right from when he was an unknown trainee, to the superstar he is today, he has presented a consistent personality by sharing videos of himself cooking and eating. As it has for BTS, the self-generated content era has made the emotional relationship between idols and their fandom closer and more enduring.

BTS's relationship with ARMY, formed thanks to the Internet, became their unintended path to salvation. This relationship they had built with ARMY became their biggest support through the series of events that followed *THE MOST BEAUTIFUL MOMENT IN LIFE PT.1.*

The Other Side of *THE MOST BEAUTIFUL MOMENT IN LIFE*

In interviews, SUGA would always talk in a small, calm voice. Even when discussing unimaginably tough times, he spoke about them like they were nothing. There was one occasion, however, when SUGA briefly raised his voice.

It was in a video uploaded to BTS's official YouTube channel on March 19, 2015. The focus was on SUGA, who'd had his birthday, and the video captures the members preparing gifts to pass on to their fans. Preparing Polaroids of himself and handwritten letters for fans who'd been selected by a draw, SUGA debates what to write to each of those chosen, and the members wrap the presents with love and care.

When asked why they put in so much care, SUGA replied adamantly, in a loud voice:

———I believe they're the reason for my existence, these people.

He continues:

———Speaking like that, others might say, "Hey, come on now," but that's how I feel. If you remove the fans from my life as an idol, I'm a really pathetic person. I'm just nothing. I always feel so guilty toward the fans . . . Responsibility, I think I have to take responsibility. I think that's one of the driving forces that moves me. If it wasn't for that, I don't think I could have done this work. I need to take responsibility, perform, and satisfy those people. That was a big part.

SUGA's reason for saying as much is as follows:

———Back then, the world I saw was like, in one word, hell. I wasn't hoping for much, we were a group in our early twenties and there were even teenagers among us . . . What did they dislike so much to do that to us? Why did they hate us?

RM once admitted later in "ARMY Corner Store" that 2015 to 2017 was a difficult period for BTS. Though running the real path to success, they were also the ongoing targets of large-scale cyberbullying.

The reason for this we'll never know for sure, but there's also no need to know. Perhaps the hateful comments that first started to appear on articles announcing their debut had been a prediction of what was to come. BTS were subjected to abusive language for being from an unknown company and criticized at public events for being idols pursuing hip-hop. The first large-scale cyberbullying attack on BTS was because they had "sold too many records."

When the songs from *THE MOST BEAUTIFUL MOMENT IN LIFE PT.1* landed much higher on the digital music charts than those from *DARK&WILD* had, it was perfectly reasonable to predict that physical album sales for *THE MOST BEAUTIFUL MOMENT IN LIFE PT.1* would also increase dramatically. The fact that groups like BTS, who were centered around their fandom, were making a name for themselves in the digital music rankings (the general public overwhelmingly listened to digital music, while far fewer people bought physical records) meant that their fanbase had also increased rapidly in size.

However, the response to their results was neither surprise nor cheers, but fake news produced under the justification of "suspicion." *THE MOST BEAUTIFUL MOMENT IN LIFE PT.1* had sold so much more than *DARK&WILD*, and people claimed this was due to fans hoarding multiple copies. The fact that record sales had suddenly increased by several thousand copies was presented as grounds for suspicion.

In Korea, the volume of records purchased directly by consumers is announced via the Hanteo Chart.[29] The Hanteo Chart reflects total real-time sales, but Hanteo are notified by record stores of advance order and sales figures from autograph sessions to commemorate album releases, which generally take place on weekends, and these figures are lumped

---

29 Hanteo receive and present sales figures from the on-and offline sellers registered with them.

together. This means that sales numbers on the Hanteo Chart suddenly go up, and fans say that "[sales] exploded."

At the time, this fact was not as well-known as it is now. However, you only needed to send a query to Hanteo Chart to find out. One ARMY did in fact send a query to Hanteo Chart, and the reply stated that there had indeed been no hoarding. An employee of Big Hit Entertainment was also in tears on the phone protesting that it wasn't true to the ARMY who'd called up to query.

Though compared to *DARK&WILD*'s first-week record sales of around 16,700, *THE MOST BEAUTIFUL MOMENT IN LIFE PT.1* sold almost triple as much, at around 55,500 copies, giving a difference of only around 38,000. Three times as much seems like a lot, but an increase of 38,000 copies is neither a huge surge nor difficult to believe.

The cyberbullies, however, couldn't see any of this. They didn't believe that BTS's popularity could have suddenly gone up. Why they didn't believe it, we can't know. However, this suspicion, as if completely natural, progressed into hatred and attacks directed at BTS. The members' words and actions were taken completely out of context and distorted into fake news, which continued to spread across the Internet community and social media.

BTS were viewed as the "villains" of the idol industry, and attacks on the group continued. When the album *WINGS* was released in October 2016, for example, the hashtag #BREAKWINGS spread all over social media abroad. Though it didn't have all that much influence, it does demonstrate that by around this time, the public attacks on BTS had reached the international stage. Use of abusive language, for the simple fact of not liking how the members looked, became something that was "okay to do," almost like a trend, and people taking the members' past words or actions completely out of context and saying "Die" would be retweeted and shared like it was nothing.

Following the cyberbullying directed at BTS, cyberbullying of idols within the fandom stuck around almost like an institution. Sensationally worded documents were uploaded to social media and the online community, and people who agreed with the claims propagated them; without the opportunity to confirm their veracity, they became truth and spread. In response, the fandoms of the idols in question came forward and used various methods to explain and minimize the damage.

This is why the term "checks" is commonly used within the idol fandom community in Korea. When a particular idol begins to become popular or experiences a comeback, anti-fans perform checks, meaning they use various reasons to criticize the idol or foster an atmosphere in which it's okay to do so. If there really is no way of performing these checks, they resort to bringing back up things that were already laid to bed years ago, doing what is called "BUMP" (Bring Up My Post), and trying to muster up negative press. These actions create a situation in which idols are essentially unable to step a foot out of place, and the tiniest mistake makes it okay for people to criticize them however they please.

The cyberbullying of BTS foreshadowed the changes brought to the Korean idol industry by the advent of social media, as well as the personality of the idol fandom. Cyberbulling that took place either out of random hatred for an idol or for the purpose of carrying out checks, began to occur far more frequently among the consumers of idol music than in the past.

Idols and Fans

This "war" surrounding BTS had an important impact not only on BTS themselves, but also on ARMY as a fandom. In 2015, alongside the release of *THE MOST BEAUTIFUL MOMENT IN LIFE PT.1*, ARMY was growing considerably in size. You couldn't call the fandom small, but it was also difficult to say that it was large or strongly cohesive. As one might expect for a group that had just started to rise in popularity, their fandom consisted mostly of teenagers. In other words, they were lacking in the numbers and experience needed to fight and win a war.

One of the desired effects of bullying idols was that fans would leave the fandom. It was not easy for teenagers, heavily influenced by peer pressure, to cope when the online community, or even their friends, criticized their favorite idols.

Ironically, though, it was what BTS went through from 2015 to 2017 that turned the relationship between BTS and ARMY into something very special. Whenever BTS came up with a particular goal, ARMY would leap headfirst toward it or offer up an even bigger vision. ARMY went from putting their all into helping BTS survive in the industry, to making them into international superstars, and today many of ARMY are contributing to society in various ways. To BTS, ARMY were not only fans, but powerful supporters, and that made them a huge brand. It is not entirely clear where ARMY's unique characteristics or their powerful bond with BTS came from. Perhaps it all began with the fans wanting their presence in the world to be acknowledged, just like BTS did. Having been attacked in every way imaginable, in order to prove that they'd been right all along, the fandom had to start by growing their influence within the idol industry. Another reason was perhaps that, with the cyberbullying ongoing, the members and fans were gradually strengthening their relationship via Twitter, YouTube, V Live, and so on.

Regardless of the cause, in the end, this new relationship with ARMY came to play a decisive role in the steps BTS took. j-hope's remarks confirm what exactly this was:

———When I heard "I keep living my life thanks to you," I thought, 'Oh, I guess I'm giving someone strength.' I also get strength from them, too. It's pretty interesting, each side giving each other strength. And so it's like, I'm more reluctant to get tired and have a hard time. I thought that, 'even if just for these people, I can't give up now.'

They'd been through everything imaginable to achieve their success, but it had been discounted just one week after their album release, and the criticism drowned out the shouts for joy as they worked. RM expresses, in a roundabout way, how he felt at the time:

———Around that time, we took the MBTI. For some reason, I didn't want it to come out as saying I had an extroverted personality, I think. I think I wanted to come across as someone introverted.

It's still difficult today for celebrities to take a stand on the cyberbullying they are subjected to. Even making a statement could unnecessarily proliferate a problem into the wider domain, a problem that had thus far been raised only within certain circles, and in the end could impact their image negatively.

BTS didn't directly respond to the cyberbullying, either. Their only choice was to keep on working. Despite the relentless outpouring of every kind of fake news and personal attack, BTS continued their work. The lyrics from "Born Singer," released shortly after their debut, "The blood and sweat we shed, I can feel it drenching me / My tears well up after our performance," came to take on an even more extraordinary meaning. For all their hard work and sweat, they had expected to rise just as high, but the only place they could feel at ease was with the fans onstage.

This was where their story with the fans, which would unfold through their albums, first began.

RUN

The production of *THE MOST BEAUTIFUL MOMENT IN LIFE PT.2* album had to take place in among all the excitement and support, as well as all the negativity directed toward the group. RM reflects:

———2015 in itself was a trial for me. Whether we were writing a song or shooting a music video, I felt like 'Aw, dammit!,' and 'Argh!' I didn't realize back then, but recently I rewatched the videos related to "RUN," and all the members, me included, feel like lead roles. We're just running randomly with that 'Argh!' feeling, but I realized how natural it was . . . Even though we were running only because when we were filming, they told us to run.

Just as RM remembers, whether consciously or unconsciously, the members' feelings at the time are captured within *THE MOST BEAUTIFUL MOMENT IN LIFE PT.2.*

THE MOST BEAUTIFUL MOMENT IN LIFE PT.2

THE 4TH MINI ALBUM
2015. 11. 30

TRACK

01 INTRO : Never Mind
02 RUN
03 Butterfly
04 Whalien 52
05 Ma City
06 Silver Spoon

07 SKIT : One night in a strange city
08 Autumn Leaves
09 OUTRO : House Of Cards

VIDEO

 COMEBACK TRAILER : Never Mind

 "RUN" MV TEASER

 ALBUM PREVIEW

 "RUN" MV

I still can't believe it
This all feels like a dream
Don't try to disappear

. . .

Will you stop time
After this moment passes by
What if this becomes something that never happened, or I lose you
I'm afraid, afraid, afraid

As in the lyrics of "Butterfly"· from the album, everything seemed like a dream, and the members feared that none of what they'd done had ever really happened. SUGA reflects:

———Our song "INTRO : Never Mind"·· has the lyrics, "If you think you're gonna crash, accelerate even more," right? I injured my shoulder on my motorbike, but I still rode it sometimes even after that. Even so, I thought, 'What if I'd accelerated a bit more in the moment of the accident?,' and that's what those [lyrics] are about. I don't ride my motorbike anymore and it's been shoved in storage, though.

These lyrics of *THE MOST BEAUTIFUL MOMENT IN LIFE PT.2*'s opening song tell SUGA's story, but they also refer to the situation BTS were in at the time. In "Intro : The most beautiful moment in life" from the previous album, *THE MOST BEAUTIFUL MOMENT IN LIFE PT.1*, SUGA is alone on the basketball court, and in "INTRO : Never Mind," he is standing in a concert arena, cheers resounding. BTS struggled through the release of four albums, and with *THE MOST BEAUTIFUL MOMENT IN LIFE PT.1*, they were well on the road to success. However, as much as love for them had increased, they were also the target of intense hostility from some, and anti-fans and ARMY were constantly embroiled in offensives and defensives, almost like a war. For BTS to break their way through this reality, they needed to take the stance of "If you think you're gonna crash, accelerate even more."

> *No matter How far I reach for you it is just an empty dream*
> *No matter how crazy I run I remain on the same place*
>
> . . .
>
> *Let's Run Run Run again. It's ok to fall down*
> *Let's Run Run Run again. It's ok to be injured*

In the title song "RUN"· from *THE MOST BEAUTIFUL MOMENT IN LIFE PT.2*, while they are afraid in the moment that "it is just an empty dream," they shout out "Let's Run Run Run again." "RUN" therefore encapsulates their sense of resolve at the time. In the next song, "Butterfly," they are afraid "That you might fly away or fall apart with just a touch," but they still need to push on ahead. Right until the final song, "OUTRO : House Of Cards," BTS express this sense of precariousness—that the slightest touch could cause everything to collapse. "RUN," meanwhile, portrays the BTS who keep on running ahead despite everything.

THE MOST BEAUTIFUL MOMENT IN LIFE PT.2, and particularly its title song "RUN," were thus born out of an even more trying process than previous albums DARK&WILD and THE MOST BEAUTIFUL MOMENT IN LIFE PT.1. It was decided early on what track would be used for "RUN." The track was so good that Bang Si-Hyuk and the other producers at Big Hit Entertainment went, "That's the one!" All they needed to do was put a rap and melody over the track.

That was also the problem. THE MOST BEAUTIFUL MOMENT IN LIFE PT.2 was originally supposed to come out in September. However, the album was in fact released on the last day of fall, on November 30, 2015.

Sophomore Jinx

The crux of the chorus of "RUN" consists of two brief repeating melodies: "Let's Run Run Run again. I can't stop running" and "Only thing I can do is run." This might sound simple to the listener compared to the complex chorus of THE MOST BEAUTIFUL MOMENT IN LIFE PT.1's title song "I NEED U." However, for topliner[30] Bang Si-Hyuk, who wrote the chorus for "RUN," this melody was both incredibly important and a tricky winning move. It's fair to say that this brief melody was the deciding factor in whether BTS would remain where they were with THE MOST BEAUTIFUL MOMENT IN LIFE PT.1, or head toward a bigger future.

As such, THE MOST BEAUTIFUL MOMENT IN LIFE PT.1 was

---

30 A creative who makes the central melody and key lyrics.

essentially BTS's sophomore album. Artists whose debut albums have been well received are commonly unable to get a similar response to their follow-up. Ideally, factors that had been successful in the previous work would be incorporated alongside a new style. If this were so easy, however, then Bang Si-Hyuk, who'd already reeled off countless hits before working with BTS, wouldn't have spent more than two months agonizing over this brief melody.

Perhaps another song similar to "I NEED U" would have gotten a reasonable response. However, as a title song, "I NEED U" stood out in BTS's discography at the time, and by repeating that same style, it would be difficult to capture their signature dynamic energy. On the other hand, a style like *THE MOST BEAUTIFUL MOMENT IN LIFE PT.1*'s "Dope" lacks the deep, dark, and sorrowful emotion of "I NEED U." Either way, BTS were at risk of limiting their potential, and they could easily have ended up stuck where they were with *THE MOST BEAUTIFUL MOMENT IN LIFE PT.1*.

This wasn't just about the album's results. For BTS, who had shouted out, "If you think you're gonna crash, accelerate even more," their situation was a complex combination of hardship and expectation, sadness and hope. Within the melody of "RUN," they needed to capture this complex emotion, as well as the will to keep pressing on.

A chorus able to satisfy all these elements would need to be more than just a "good" melody. The "RUN" we listen to now has plenty of brilliant melodies aside from the chorus. However, in 2015, they couldn't find that melody perfect for the BTS who had just finished work on *THE MOST BEAUTIFUL MOMENT IN LIFE PT.1*. They'd keep writing new melodies and scrap them, and there were even suggestions to go for a different title song entirely.

One melody made it through all these hurdles, and this is what forms the chorus for "RUN." As in the lyrics, "Let's Run Run Run again," the melody focuses solely on the sense of running, without the need for a fast tempo or a great exertion of energy. And then again with the line "Only thing I can do is run," the melody elevates the emotion a little more, further contributing to that picture of running until breathless. This portrayed the image of BTS: they had to keep on running, no matter what the situation, no matter what anyone said.

And so, the title song "RUN" was complete. In *THE MOST BEAU-TIFUL MOMENT IN LIFE PT.2*'s first half, while "INTRO : Never Mind" deals with BTS's attitude in changing circumstances, "RUN" deals with how this attitude would be put into practice, and "Butterfly" is about BTS's internal anxiety and sadness, which existed both in the real world and within their music videos. The album goes deeper and deeper into the members' inner world, and with "Whalien 52," BTS begin to speak more directly of how they felt following *THE MOST BEAUTIFUL MOMENT IN LIFE PT.1.*

> *In the middle of this vast ocean*
> *A whale speaks in a low and lonesome voice*
> *No matter how much it shouts, it won't reach anyone*
> *Feeling so lonely, it quietly shuts its mouth*
>
> . . .
>
> *Words easily thrown out to me builds a wall in between*

Even my loneliness looks fake in your eyes

. . .

The world will never know
How sad I am
My pain is like water and oil, it can never mix

In "Whalien 52," the members are "[a] whale . . . in the middle of this vast ocean," and feel so isolated from people that they say "even my loneliness looks fake in your eyes." The world has no idea "[h]ow sad I am," and their pain is like "water and oil, it can never mix."

The group had experienced a certain amount of success. However, their relationship with ARMY aside, they felt in some ways even more isolated than before. It was only after BTS went deep within themselves and came up with a definition of who they were that they could sing facing the outside world, like in "Ma City" and "Silver Spoon."

RM explains how he felt while making *THE MOST BEAUTIFUL MOMENT IN LIFE PT.2*:

———Lots of things were happening, which overlapped with things like our standing at the time, and I think I was trying to hide. Inside my shell.

Even after the release of *THE MOST BEAUTIFUL MOMENT IN LIFE PT.2*, BTS were at the center of all sorts of issues, and during that period, RM found a way to reflect on himself:

———I went around by myself a lot. And for a long time, I would go to Ttukseom. I felt calm whenever I went there, and the reason I felt calm was because at night, people went there in groups, but I was alone. No one talked to me, and around me people ate their chicken, talked about school, about dating . . . I would sit off to one side and drink beer by myself and feel like I was being comforted. 'A place like this exists in the world. There's a place where I can feel at ease.' The group was doing well, and at the same time, music and what I'd made as an individual were being disregarded, and I felt an extreme emotion, that in some ways everything I had done up until then had been worthless. Looking back on it now, I wonder how I managed to stand it.

Growth

The concerns RM and the other BTS members experienced were in fact what brought *THE MOST BEAUTIFUL MOMENT IN LIFE* series together. If what they went through making *THE MOST BEAUTIFUL MOMENT IN LIFE PT.1* were the growing pains of youths trying to prove themselves, then in *THE MOST BEAUTIFUL MOMENT IN LIFE PT.2*, they were facing the world head-on as it watched them. Amid this success and hardship, the members could have new thoughts and experiences of themselves.

While working on *THE MOST BEAUTIFUL MOMENT IN LIFE PT.2*'s "Ma City,"' j-hope began to open his eyes to the relationship between himself and society. In "Ma City," he depicts his hometown, Gwangju, and wrote these lyrics:

Everybody dial 062-518

"62" is Gwangju's area code, and "518" refers to the May 18 Gwangju Democratization Movement of 1980. While there are still those online who denigrate the May 18 Gwangju Democratization Movement and promote regionalism, j-hope has pride in his hometown. Through studying up on the history of where he was born, he could reflect on himself:

———I didn't know much about regionalism. To begin with, I didn't have any feelings of regionalism myself . . . However, when I came to Seoul, I realized such a thing existed, and felt it for the first time. 'What's this? What is this feeling? Why do I have to hear these things about the place I was born, why do I have to feel like this?' And so, I looked up the history. Honestly, I'm still lacking when it comes to that kind of knowledge, but at that time I found out a lot. While studying, I thought about how I could express this in my work. But it was so interesting. It was like, I suddenly felt for the first time, 'Wow, so this is how telling my story and putting my emotions into music feels.'

Introspection became an opportunity for j-hope to grow as an artist:

———During that time, the question of 'Who was I? What kind of person was I?' occupied more than half of my brain. Because the choreography for "I NEED U" was so different to the styles I'd done in the past, I often wondered what kind of dance I was doing before. So, I ended up starting "Hope on the street." Dancing in the training studio in front of the mirror became a time for me to reflect on myself once more.

I would sit off to one side and drink
beer by myself and feel like I was
being comforted.
   'A place like this exists in the
world.
   'There's a place where I can feel
at ease.'

—RM

"Hope on the street" consisted of an irregular YouTube feature, as well as occasional live streaming on V Live, and showed j-hope as he practiced dancing. It was an opportunity for him to communicate with fans through dance. Self-directed concerns turned into a new understanding of his work, and yet another experiment became possible. j-hope says:

————For me, since *DARK&WILD* it was like . . . I could hear my voice in the album. And so, I think I had a really strong desire to improve quickly, to establish my place.

For Jimin, too, the concerns and efforts surrounding the events that unfolded after *DARK&WILD* began to bear fruit after *THE MOST BEAUTIFUL MOMENT IN LIFE* series. He reflects:

————I learned what parts of me people liked, and how they liked it when I expressed something in a certain way and in a certain body shape, and so I also ended up focusing on maintaining those things. I do that when I sing, and sometimes I find even the movement of my very fingers slowing down, then speeding up . . . I think I changed a lot in this respect. And I had to make a lot of effort trying to calm myself.

By building a relationship between himself and others, and between himself and the world, V was able to refine the ways in which he expressed himself. When acting in music videos and performing onstage as part of *THE MOST BEAUTIFUL MOMENT IN LIFE* series, he channeled Colin Firth:

————At that time, Colin Firth was my role model. I liked his vibe so much, and I wanted to give off that vibe myself.

V's approach to his work came out of how he felt about his relationship with the other members:

————For me, just one look and I can immediately see that they're becoming more amazing as time goes on. If I have no comparison point, my timing ends up slower than the other members. For example, I need something specific, like if there's a singer I really like, thinking, 'I want to be like that singer,' or 'I want to perform onstage like that one day,' and only then will I be on fire. If I don't have that, then I really do get a bit slow. That's why the other members get targeted by my ambition.

V adds one more thing about the members:

————I often cried because I felt guilty that, 'I don't want to become a burden to BTS.' I was worried that, because of me, cracks would form in the heavy and stable wall called BTS. I didn't want to fall behind these perfect people.

Oldest Jin and youngest Jung Kook were experiencing small yet important changes to their daily life. Jin, who valued work-life balance, had begun to gradually adjust his daily routine after moving accommodations for the first time since their debut in spring 2015:

————Until then, I didn't really have the time to go out. Even when I was a college student, my friends would ask why I wasn't involved in university life and told me to take part. I wanted to, myself (laughs). And so little by little, I started going out more, signed up to a boxing hagwon and got lessons in the afternoon, then in the middle of the night I'd go and work out . . .

Jung Kook talks about his new interests:

————I started to get a taste for shopping. Until then, I just dressed how I liked. 'I'll dress in my own style,' I'd thought. Then maybe after a while I got a bit fed up, too, and I also got caught while out shopping by the other members (laughs).

This was also a process of finding ways to express himself. Jung Kook adds:

———Until then, I would just do as I was told, all I'd think was that I needed to do well no matter what, and I didn't have my own values. Then, I started to think about what I should do and how I should do it, how I'm supposed to take things, how I came across on the stage while singing. Guess you could call it a "skill tree," like in video games? It's similar to that. Once you accomplish one thing, that divides into two branches, and divides again into more branches, and develops from there. It felt kind of like clearing one level at a time.

Jung Kook's skill tree led him to dive right into making music:

———I didn't have even the slightest fear about learning. This was because the hyoungs had done music before, whereas from the start, I couldn't dance, sing, or play instruments well.

And then, SUGA. He looks back on the music he made during that period:

———Stories about my hopes and dreams always appeared in my songs. "Tomorrow," which I'd written earlier, was the same. My songs are half about my hopes and dreams. Who will tell these stories if music doesn't? And that music, looking at it now, it's like those are words speaking to me. A few years later, listening to the songs I made back then, I feel comforted. They're like a letter written to my future self.

Going on from this, he considers the many people listening to BTS's music:

———At the time, I wasn't really sure why people listened to our music. I couldn't know whether it was because the songs were well made, or because the people listening understood the meaning contained in our songs and related to them. But I think I understand now.

That Name, BTS

THE MOST BEAUTIFUL MOMENT IN LIFE PT.2 album made number five in the 2015 Gaon Chart album rankings, having sold 274,135 copies. At number six was *THE MOST BEAUTIFUL MOMENT IN LIFE PT.1*, and numbers one to four were all EXO albums. This was the first time in the decade that an idol group not from the so-called "big three" companies had occupied two spots in the top ten. What's more, these were the results just one month post-release, and in 2016 *THE MOST BEAUTIFUL MOMENT IN LIFE PT.2* sold an additional 105,784 copies, making number 21 in the album charts that year.

However, the value of *THE MOST BEAUTIFUL MOMENT IN LIFE* series cannot be explained simply in BTS's rising position in the album charts. Throughout their work on the *THE MOST BEAUTIFUL MOMENT IN LIFE* series, the members talked about what they'd experienced and were still experiencing, and were growing little by little as a result. Each somewhere between boy- and adulthood, the members—from high school student Jung Kook to Jin in his early twenties—worried, wandered, and experienced a mix of joy and sorrow, before finally coming face-to-face with the outside world.

In this respect, it was during *THE MOST BEAUTIFUL MOMENT*

IN LIFE series that BTS and ARMY—and in broader terms, the youth of Korea—were "syncing." Though their lives are very different from that of their fans and young people their age, idols also need to survive in society, and experience an unwanted period of turmoil, too. The BTS generation doesn't constitute as much of the population as that of their parents. Furthermore, after the IMF crisis, the gap between the rich and poor in Korea had become even more pronounced, and people would find themselves pushed out amid a fierce competitiveness, in which the phrase "every person for themselves" could be commonly heard. The large entertainment companies and popular idol groups of the previous generation had already cemented their position—BTS needed to make a place for themselves within this environment, too.

For this generation, though exhausting and suffocating, you can't give the world a piece of your mind if you want to survive in society. Thus, in this generation, though you can rebel, it's hard to resist. BTS took the picture of this generation of young people and brought it into the world of idol groups: here, they defined their own generation through the means of hip-hop.

> *They call me baepsae*
> *We've got it tough, our generation*
>
> *. . .*
>
> *Switch up the rules, change change*
> *Hwangsae want want to maintain*
> *Oh no, you don't BANG BANG*
> *This ain't normal*
> *This ain't normal*

These lyrics from "Silver Spoon,"* featured on *THE MOST BEAU-TIFUL MOMENT IN LIFE PT.2*, refer both to BTS's own generation and to the world as they saw it. *THE MOST BEAUTIFUL MOMENT IN LIFE* series was also BTS's response to that world, the BTS who appeared to be the Korean idol industry's "baepsae" or "imposter." Even if others saw them as "baepsae," they sprinted on and on and tried to jump the walls standing before them. In *THE MOST BEAUTIFUL MOMENT IN LIFE* series, BTS kept their promise about their name. They speak about the world's prejudice and the difficulties experienced by young people in their teens and twenties as if fending off raining gunfire. That name, which had been anonymous individuals' target of ridicule when BTS first started out: three years post-debut, BTS were able to prove what it meant.

When asked whether *THE MOST BEAUTIFUL MOMENT IN LIFE* series had provided an opportunity to collect his thoughts and feelings, RM responds:

———Rather than that . . . It was more of a feeling like, 'Oh, I can breathe.' This was because we'd gotten a number one (laughs). And even at music awards and things like that, how should I put it? It felt like we'd finally been "invited." Before that, when we went to those kinds of places, it felt lonely. We'd been invited, but it didn't feel like that in reality. This was because our crew were way over there, and the seven of us were seated together, and I thought, 'There's really no one on our side.'

In fact, *THE MOST BEAUTIFUL MOMENT IN LIFE* series only made up the first out of the three difficult years (for both BTS and ARMY) from 2015 to 2017 that RM refers to. More trials and unexpected events lay in wait for them. However, after *THE MOST BEAUTIFUL MOMENT IN LIFE* series, the world finally sent BTS an invitation, and the group could understand their relationship with that world and grow.

It was also around this time that RM and the other members started to organize their thoughts about the so-called misogyny controversy raised against them. Once BTS had achieved success, they were criticized, on the grounds that some of their lyrics were misogynistic. RM, who'd been exposed to hip-hop from a young age, had come to understand its misogynistic elements as characteristic of the genre. When the controversy was first brought up, he, SUGA, and the other members had to learn about the concept of misogyny and what it constituted.

———I can talk about it. Looking back on it now, I think it was something I needed to go through.

Having responded to whether he could talk about what happened at the time, he continues:

———About this kind of concept and awareness, I have come to think that as someone living in the 2020s, it's something you come up against at least once. And because I was criticized early on, I could recognize the problem sooner.

On top of the considerable cyberbullying they'd suffered, they also had to consider what changes they needed to make with regard to the misogyny issue. RM adds:

———This was because I'd received clear comments and criticism about the raps I'd written as well as my views. The Gangnam Station murder[31] happened around that time, and so from a woman's perspective I think there was no choice but to speak out even more. Someone I know said, if you call a situation of equality "0," and the world's injustice is at as much as "+10," then those experiencing injustice have no choice but to emphasize not "0," but "−10" in order to achieve equality. Those words really hit home for me.

RM also speaks about the positive impact this had on BTS.

——If it wasn't for that process, we wouldn't have made it this far.

Later, in July 2016, Big Hit Entertainment and BTS publicly announced their position on the misogyny controversy, stating, "We learned that music creation is not free from societal prejudice and fallacies," and "Furthermore, we became aware that it may also not be desirable to define the value of women and their role in society from a male perspective." Gender sensitivity training is now obligatory for all HYBE artists before they can debut.

In this way, through *THE MOST BEAUTIFUL MOMENT IN LIFE* series, BTS—both as individuals and as a group, and, by extension, ARMY—were passing through "one period of youth." These events would come to feel like nothing in comparison to what lay in wait for their future selves, but they had traveled a long, long journey since their debut. Having released the two *THE MOST BEAUTIFUL MOMENT IN LIFE* albums, they had finally arrived at a station where they could stop and rest for a while.

Before they headed to the next station, there was one thing left for BTS to do.

Let's burn it all[32]

---

31 Refers to an incident where a man murdered a woman he didn't know in a toilet near Seoul's Gangnam Station on May 17, 2016.
32 Part of the lyrics from BTS's next album, *THE MOST BEAUTIFUL MOMENT IN LIFE : YOUNG FOREVER*'s title song "Burning Up (FIRE)."

FIRE!

Following on from mini albums *THE MOST BEAUTIFUL MOMENT IN LIFE PT.1* and *THE MOST BEAUTIFUL MOMENT IN LIFE PT.2*, special album *THE MOST BEAUTIFUL MOMENT IN LIFE : YOUNG FOREVER*, released on May 2, 2016, was the final chapter that brought the various meanings of *THE MOST BEAUTIFUL MOMENT IN LIFE* to their perfect conclusion. Not only was it necessary to draw this period in BTS's life, which had unfolded within the previous two albums, to a close, but in terms of the real-world music industry, they needed to reflect their explosive growth and mark a peak with this album. Rather than scrutinize the various situations the group had found themselves in, like they had in "I NEED U" and "RUN," this was a period in which BTS could display their unstoppable energy through their songs and choreography. They could finally show off those "frenetic" dance routines that appeared in songs from "Attack on Bangtan" to "Dope," but this time in a title song.

At the time, luckily—and also necessarily—Big Hit Entertainment was ready to present all these things. The focus of the choreography for title track "Burning Up (FIRE)"· is a large-scale routine in the second half of the song, performed together with backup dancers. The dancers suddenly appear while the members are dancing, and they give an explosive performance that really is as if, like the lyrics go, they are "burning it all." In this moment, BTS allowed people to really feel their unique and unstoppable energy.

A dance routine like this requires a considerable investment of people power, time, and capital. It required hiring dozens of dancers for a set period who could keep in step with BTS, as well as a large space in which to practice. Though this would change according to the nature of the stage itself, in the practice video* for this large-scale dance routine, V swivels the camera that had been following him to the opposite side of the stage, and moves along with it before joining the remaining members and dancers already there. This was how large the training room needed to be.

Big Hit Entertainment had actually secured the funds to do all of this. For Bang Si-Hyuk, *THE MOST BEAUTIFUL MOMENT IN LIFE : YOUNG FOREVER* was the beginning: he could finally embody his vision. Thanks to the success of BTS, the company grew financially, and Bang Si-Hyuk could implement what he'd imagined in a way closer to his ideal. In this respect, "Burning Up (FIRE)" was none other than a declaration. Just like the BTS members, Big Hit Entertainment didn't sit back and relax and were determined to "push their way forward."

And so, with *THE MOST BEAUTIFUL MOMENT IN LIFE : YOUNG FOREVER* album, *THE MOST BEAUTIFUL MOMENT IN LIFE* series, created from the energy of BTS and Big Hit Entertainment, was complete, and the group was advancing toward the future. It wasn't your ordinary "repackage" album, but an epilogue that brought one period to a close. Songs from *THE MOST BEAUTIFUL MOMENT IN LIFE PT.1* and *THE MOST BEAUTIFUL MOMENT IN LIFE PT.2* were arranged in a new way, and included were new songs

"Burning Up (FIRE)," "Save ME," and "EPILOGUE : Young Forever" that would clearly convey the special album's story and message.

Following on from the "School Trilogy," the more carefully planned series structure of the two *THE MOST BEAUTIFUL MOMENT IN LIFE* albums was perfected with *THE MOST BEAUTIFUL MOMENT IN LIFE : YOUNG FOREVER*. This was possible because BTS were successful enough to release a special album, and because they were successful enough for the company to put in considerable financial investment.

The promotion for the release of *THE MOST BEAUTIFUL MOMENT IN LIFE : YOUNG FOREVER* is a particular example of what could be achieved when Bang Si-Hyuk's ambition met capital. Big Hit Entertainment released the music video for "Burning Up (FIRE)" in between the videos for "EPILOGUE : Young Forever"· and "Save ME."··

> *Forever we are young*
> *Even if you fall and get hurt*
> *I keep running towards my dream*

If "Burning Up (FIRE)" demonstrated the group's explosive energy, then "EPILOGUE : Young Forever" was an ode to the youth: to both themselves, who'd made it through *THE MOST BEAUTIFUL MOMENT IN LIFE* series, and also to ARMY, who'd been with them the whole way.

While "Save ME" on the one hand continued the stories of the characters from *THE MOST BEAUTIFUL MOMENT IN LIFE* series, it was also a message from BTS to the world.

THE MOST BEAUTIFUL MOMENT IN LIFE : YOUNG FOREVER

THE 1ST SPECIAL ALBUM
2016. 5. 2

TRACK

CD1

01 INTRO : The most beautiful
   moment in life
02 I NEED U
03 Hold Me Tight
04 Autumn Leaves
05 Butterfly prologue mix
06 RUN
07 Ma city
08 Silver Spoon
09 Dope
10 Burning Up (FIRE)
11 Save ME
12 EPILOGUE : Young Forever

CD2

01 Converse High
02 Moving On
03 Whalien 52
04 Butterfly
05 House Of Cards (full length
   edition)
06 Love is not over (full length
   edition)
07 I NEED U urban mix
08 I NEED U remix
09 RUN ballad mix
10 RUN (alternative mix)
11 Butterfly (alternative mix)

VIDEO

"EPILOGUE :
Young Forever"
MV

"Burning Up (FIRE)"
MV TEASER

"Burning Up (FIRE)"
MV

"Save ME"
MV

Thank you for allowing me to be who I am.
Allowing me to fly.
For giving me wings

And so they made three new songs, filmed music videos for them, practiced the dance routines for "Burning Up (FIRE)" and "Save ME," as well as the upcoming concerts . . . Everything was going along without a hitch. RM reflects:

——"Burning Up (FIRE)" was the period in which we really were "on fire."

RM explains in simple terms the differences between the two previous *THE MOST BEAUTIFUL MOMENT IN LIFE* albums and *THE MOST BEAUTIFUL MOMENT IN LIFE : YOUNG FOREVER*. He goes on:

——Just, it felt like being back where we were meant to be. Like how I started out in hip-hop after listening to Eminem's "Without Me." All seven of us members are silly. And we have so much talent. Onstage I could pass out I'm so excited, the song was so exciting. And the recording was so much fun. It's a feeling like 'Oh, I can live now.' Until then, I was going, "I'm seriously going to die, die, argh!" and like that, I stopped, and it felt like a party was going on here.

This experience was a new turning point for them. For Jin, "Burning Up (FIRE)" was an opportunity to considerably shift his attitude toward work:

——"Burning Up (FIRE)" is my favorite song of all time. Before that, I was living without self-confidence, but just like I did in the choreography for "Burning Up (FIRE)," I blew kisses when I met ARMY, and because I was doing it in real life rather than onstage, they really liked it. So I tried to find actions they would like, ended up finding lots, and I was able to really recover my self-confidence a lot through that. Then that became my character, and I ended up pulling gestures a bit brazenly and more often (laughs).

This attitude of Jin's developed into his own unique role, which he would perform not only onstage, but when they met ARMY, at official appearances, wherever. Later, when BTS officially expanded into America, his conviviality and good manners would create a lively atmosphere no matter where he was.

Don't try too hard
It's okay to be a loser

Looking at the history of BTS so far, these lyrics from "Burning Up (FIRE)" were yet another declaration. In the song's opening, they have no choice but to say, "I'm just nobody," but they also tell themselves, "It's okay not to try hard." Like that, they let things go a little, and onstage they fly into a frenzy. Then when it came to the Korean idol industry they work for, BTS really did "burn it all." And then finally, the Olympic Gymnastics Arena, too.[33]

Yet Another Start

When BTS debuted, RM's conditions for success were simple:
———For me, things like the industry situation and indicators go in one ear and out the other. If it feels like things are going well,

---

33 In July 2018 its name was officially changed to KSPO Dome following the remodeling of Seoul Olympic Park's main gymnasium. It can seat around fifteen thousand.

that's all I need. At the time, if we were "number one on Melon" that was enough. Also, saying, "My friends know our group's songs," for us that was everything.

Performing in the Olympic Gymnastics Arena was yet another marker of success that artists could feel for themselves. Until the Gocheok Sky Dome opened its doors at the end of 2015, the Olympic Gymnastics Arena had been the largest indoor arena in Korea. Even now, being able to perform at the Olympic Gymnastics Arena is proof of an artist's success, and is therefore not easy. In simple terms, the time between BTS's debut and their first performance in the Olympic Gymnastics Arena was longer than the time between their Olympic Gymnastics Arena performance and their first worldwide stadium tour, during which they filled the 100,000-capacity Jamsil Olympic Stadium.

BTS's concert 2016 BTS LIVE THE MOST BEAUTIFUL MOMENT IN LIFE ON STAGE : EPILOGUE'—which took place in May 2016 at the Olympic Gymnastics Arena alongside the release of *THE MOST BEAUTIFUL MOMENT IN LIFE : YOUNG FOREVER* album—was in this respect like *THE MOST BEAUTIFUL MOMENT IN LIFE* series' "epilogue of epilogues." Finally, the greatest achievement they could have imagined up until that point had become a reality. The resounding "EPILOGUE : Young Forever," sung together with ARMY, filled the arena, and the members couldn't hold back their tears onstage.

SUGA still remembers those emotions:

———The day we performed was Parents' Day. And so I looked around the arena, saw my parents, and bowed deeply. I burst into tears. I was basically wailing.

However, this elaborate epilogue gave them some new homework to do. Once everything they'd dreamed of had come true, RM realized that he was facing a new goal he hadn't even thought of before:

———When we heard our album was selling a lot, I started to think more in terms of "grand prizes" than numbers like hundreds of thousands of records.

At the time, for the members, an annual grand prize was beyond the bounds of their imagination. It was heading toward becoming a reality, however, and even greater things lay in wait for them.

V explains his feelings about BTS's success from that point onward:

———My goal had just been to debut, but then we debuted, and when someone asked me what my goal was, I would say it was to get a number one. After that, we really did get a number one, and when someone asked about my goals, I said, "My goal is to get three number ones." Once we'd achieved that, I said I wanted to get the grand prize at an awards ceremony. And then we got the grand prize (laughs). When we got lots of awards like that . . . it got ridiculous. Because we'd said only the things we thought we could never achieve, and then we achieved all of them.

V gently shakes his head and says:

———I think it's strange (laughs).

CHAPTER 4

WINGS

YOU NEVER WALK ALONE

INSIDE
OUT

WINGS | THE 2ND FULL-LENGTH ALBUM

BUS STOP

59th-61st

YOU NEVER WALK ALONE | THE 2ND SPECIAL ALBUM

||| | | | | INSIDE OUT | | | | |||

Friends

The "Dumpling Incident" between V and Jimin is one of the most famous BTS anecdotes, known to practically every member of the fandom. V and Jimin even referenced the incident in their duet "Friends" from the February 2020 full-length album *MAP OF THE SOUL : 7* with the lyrics "The dumpling incident's a comedy."

In actuality, "incident" is almost too serious a word. As V and Jimin explained to fans many times, they had a disagreement about when to eat mandu dumplings—V wanting to eat during choreography practice and Jimin after practice—and had a brief argument that ultimately only deepened their friendship. In the greater context of BTS, however, this fun but minor incident was more than just a funny memory: it was a reflection of their circumstances circa 2016.

V had wanted to eat during practice because he had been shooting the period drama *Hwarang: The Poet Warrior Youth* all day and hadn't had a chance to eat. His role on the show was just one of the many new opportunities offered to BTS in 2016 thanks to the runaway success of *THE MOST BEAUTIFUL MOMENT IN LIFE* series. Premiering on December 19, 2016, *Hwarang* had the Monday–Tuesday evening primetime slot on KBS, the national broadcaster of South Korea, and also featured then-rising star Park Seo-joon. It was clear to V, BTS, and everyone else that appearing on the show would bring BTS even further into the mainstream.

The problem was scheduling. Unlike with many other Korean TV series, production on *Hwarang* wrapped completely before the premiere, with the shoot starting in March 2016 and ending in early September the same year. This overlapped almost precisely with BTS's preparations for their second full-length album, *WINGS*. It was not unusual for members of idol groups to have overlapping independent and team commitments, but between 2015 and 2016, BTS had reached a new milestone in popularity—and not just in Korea.

To give an idea of their meteoric rise, the release of the album *THE MOST BEAUTIFUL MOMENT IN LIFE PT.2* in November 2015 coincided with THE MOST BEAUTIFUL MOMENT IN LIFE ON STAGE tour, which took the team to three cities in Korea and Japan. Then THE MOST BEAUTIFUL MOMENT IN LIFE ON STAGE : EPILOGUE tour, which followed the release of *THE MOST BEAUTIFUL MOMENT IN LIFE : YOUNG FOREVER* album, took the team to seven locations across Asia from May to mid-August 2016, with only about a week between concerts to move on to the next location. Compared to the previous year, their schedule was jammed.

V recalls this period:

———I was doing both the tour and the *Hwarang* shoot, so whenever we briefly flew back to Korea, I had to rush straight to the set. It was supposed to be a bit of a break for us back home, but I had to go shoot the drama. When the others asked, "Hey, you all right?" I'd say, "I gotta do this" and head to the shoot, and when the people on set asked, "You can really do this while you're on tour?" I'd say, "I'm fine" and go on camera . . . and then I'd go back to the tour.

Doing double duty on the tour and the *Hwarang* shoot was excruciating for V. He was pushed to his physical limits, but even more challenging was the fact that he had to juggle two completely different kinds of work. Onstage as an idol, he was free to express himself, riding the support of the audience to show off a completely new side to himself each time. However, shooting a TV show required him to perform multiple near-identical takes of the same sequence with his costars, one after another. V explains:

———With acting, reproducing the same performance is really import-
    ant. I have to do the exact same performance as the one I just shot,
    and I thought, 'What do I do? This is bad.' When I moved too
    precisely, it would look artificial. When it comes to performance,
    I'm the type who's always experimenting, 'How can I make this
    new?' so that part about screen acting was really difficult.

Another psychological weight was V's sense of responsibility as a representative of BTS.

———At one point, I had a bad shot. The hyoungs I was acting with
    taught me a lot, but I couldn't pull it off. I thought I completely
    ruined one scene where I had to show emotion. And I was worried
    that because of that, I might hear, "Bangtan's acting sucks." This was
    the first time a BTS member was acting on-screen and if I messed
    it up, people might look down on us. So I told myself, 'I'll do my
    best,' but when I messed up that shot, no one said anything bad,
    but I already felt that way in my own head. I was really depressed.

No star ever gets used to countless anti-fans analyzing every second of their life to find things to criticize. And as described earlier, BTS's surge in popularity coincided with a rise in cyberbullying. V, however, did not let his agony show.

———I'm sure the other members were really frustrated. They told me
    to talk to them if things were rough, but I didn't tell them any-
    thing. It's the way I am, I'm not good at talking about those
    things. I can't work up the courage.

This was the background behind the "Dumpling Incident." V adds,

———I was in the midst of juggling the *Hwarang* shoot and the tour, and that day, I finished the drama shoot and had to come right back to prep for the album . . . but I was so hungry. I hadn't had a chance to eat. So I asked the manager to order some dumplings, and I was eating during choreography practice. But Jimin didn't know my situation, so he said we should eat after practice, and we had a squabble. The hyoungs told us to talk it out among ourselves, so we came outside and talked, but we only talked about our own perspectives, so we just kept repeating the same things over and over again.

The spat ended several days later over drinks. V reminisces:

———Jimin told me, "There's nothing I can do for you right now, but I want you to take heart. I know that something is giving you a really hard time, and when that happens, I'd like you to talk more about it. I really want to give you strength." That deepened our friendship,

V defines his relationship with Jimin this way:

———Originally, me and him fought so much . . . but because we fought so much, later, he turned out to be someone I can't live without (laughs). It feels really empty when someone you used to argue with isn't there.

The powerful friendships V developed with his colleagues were his source of strength as he worked on both the TV drama and the upcoming release of *WINGS*.

———Back then, what kept me going was, honestly the fact that people on both sides were amazing. I survived the tour because I loved the members, all of them on a personal level, and I survived *Hwarang* because I loved the people I worked with. They taught me every last detail and took care of me. Before we went into production on *Hwarang*, I was worried because I'd never acted before, but because I didn't know a thing about acting, they went out of their way to teach me even more of the finer details and were really nice to me.

V thanks the people around him. He adds:

———When I was endlessly depressed, the BTS members and the hyoungs I was on the drama with were my strength. We drank together, and we talked a lot. I was struggling so much, so they came to me and told me they wanted to give me strength. So I managed to get my thoughts in order and kind of get out of that headspace.

New Wave

V's difficulties foreshadowed the lead-up to the release of *WINGS*. BTS had finally realized their dreams of success, taking a step into a completely new world. In their new environment, the members were faced with deeper, more complicated issues than ever before.

The full-length album *WINGS* was released on October 10, 2016. The members had gone teary-eyed at the fifteen thousand packed seats in the Olympic Gymnastics Arena that May; less than a year later, the two-day 2017 BTS LIVE TRILOGY EPISODE III: THE WINGS TOUR˙ at Gocheok Sky Dome sold the venue's full capacity of twenty-five thousand tickets, including standing room. Later in 2017, BTS would have a three-day concert in the same location.

Meanwhile, the official BTS Twitter and YouTube channels recorded a marked increase in comments in English and other non-Asian languages. The number of ARMY swelled across the world, and cyberbullying of BTS intensified proportionately.

This was all completely unprecedented—not only to BTS, but to the Korean idol industry. In December 2015, *THE MOST BEAUTIFUL MOMENT IN LIFE PT.2* ranked 171 on America's Billboard 200. The following album, *THE MOST BEAUTIFUL MOMENT IN LIFE : YOUNG FOREVER* ranked 107 in May the following year. In a vacuum, these were not high rankings. But the fact that the consecutive albums made it on the Billboard 200 immediately upon release, with the latter taking a markedly higher ranking, was of great significance for BTS.

What was responsible for this sudden surge in popularity? People began to post English-language comments on a range of YouTube channels, requesting BTS content, and not just on the K-pop MV reaction channels that had begun to grow at the time. BTS were becoming a sensation, and any content that dealt with them would spread rapidly on social media. Even before mainstream media attention, even before the Billboard 200 ranking, something unprecedented was happening.

Just as V had to juggle album production, tour prep, and the *Hwarang* shoot, the sudden success threw BTS as a whole into a completely new environment. With success, they found a chance to change their lives, and in their new world, the members had to either accept or reject the changes while also rethinking themselves.

The text at the very end of "Burning Up (FIRE)," the title song of *THE MOST BEAUTIFUL MOMENT IN LIFE : YOUNG FOREVER*, would foreshadow both *WINGS* and the things to come.

BOY MEETS WHAT

Concept Album

———To be honest, I was scared at first.

"Intro : Boy Meets Evil," the first track in *WINGS* (which was made into a comeback trailer) was a source of pressure for j-hope, and not just because RM and SUGA were the only ones who had done previous intro tracks. j-hope says:

———When I got the choreography outline, I thought, 'I could do this,' but when I actually practiced it, that wasn't the case. I wondered if I could pull it off. At the time, I really lived in the practice studio. I shot and monitored the comeback trailer more than a hundred times, and for things I couldn't do, I personally went to an expert to learn. I hurt my wrist, too. I almost lost my mind.

The "What" of "Boy Meets What" was "Evil," which for BTS was the confusion and agony of encountering something completely new, like j-hope's sudden assignment to the intro track. The comeback trailer for "Intro : Boy Meets Evil" begins with RM reciting a quote from *Demian*, and unlike the comeback trailers for *THE MOST BEAUTI-*

FUL MOMENT IN LIFE series, was a live-action trailer featuring a BTS member in person.

In the MV, j-hope is dressed not in hip-hop clothes or street fashion, but the stark combination of a white button-down shirt with black skinny jeans, as he combines elements of contemporary dance with his trademark style. The difficulty of blending a totally new style into his movement was just part of his metamorphosis. j-hope explains with a smile:

———That really was the "evil" I had to contend with (laughs). The pressure to do well was so big, and I put everything into the choreography for this song. So there were parts I could do, parts I wasn't good enough for, and parts I couldn't do at all. Somehow, I had to address them one by one.

> *Bloodstains caused by the harshness of reality*
> *Couldn't imagine*
> *That the greed would become a call to hell*
>
> . . .
>
> *Too bad but it's too sweet*
> *It's too sweet it's too sweet*

"Intro : Boy Meets Evil" was a departure from other songs in more ways than one. From before their debut to *THE MOST BEAUTIFUL MO-MENT IN LIFE* series, BTS had directly expressed their personal realities in their lyrics. But within the span of the year leading up to *WINGS*, they successfully set foot into the world of abstract literature and symbolism.

V describes his acting in the MV of the title song "Blood Sweat & Tears":

———In the previous MVs for "I NEED U" and "RUN," I had to maintain a consistent characterization. But "Blood Sweat & Tears" is different. It's a totally different character. So I wanted to put on a performance where when people saw "him," they couldn't tell if he was good or evil. Going really evil would make it too obvious, but this person seems evil but there's a brief, peculiar smile . . . I think that would have given people the sense of "giving a hint."

The shift from the directness of THE MOST BEAUTIFUL MOMENT IN LIFE series to the new approach to performance in the "Blood Sweat & Tears" MV applied not only to that one song, but the entire WINGS album. The new tracks were filled with ambiguous expressions with no clear meaning, and the Demian quote in the comeback trailer and the artworks in the "Blood Sweat & Tears" MV almost seemed to be hints pointing to a secret message. The artworks featured in "Blood Sweat & Tears" coaxed audiences into slowly developing their personal interpretations of the MV, much like works in an art gallery.

From a business standpoint, these changes were a bold move. The call to analysis and personal interpretation, some thought, might pose too high of a barrier to new BTS listeners. No one had expected the sweat shed during practice for "Dope" to come back with a vengeance in "Blood Sweat & Tears," this time in a completely new light.

However, WINGS was a necessary step for BTS at the time. They had entered a new stage in their career, and no one could give them all the answers. WINGS reflected BTS's path forward as they grew personally, pursued their careers, and grew into adulthood; a concept album packed with the members' coming-of-age stories, with all the pain and temptation that came with them. j-hope recalls:

WINGS

THE 2ND FULL-LENGTH ALBUM
2016. 10. 10

TRACK

01 Intro : Boy Meets Evil
02 Blood Sweat & Tears
03 Begin
04 Lie
05 Stigma
06 First Love
07 Reflection
08 MAMA
09 Awake

10 Lost
11 BTS Cypher 4
12 Am I Wrong
13 21st Century Girl
14 2! 3!
15 Interlude : Wings

VIDEO

 Short Film 1
"Begin"

 Short Film 6
"MAMA"

 Short Film 2
"Lie"

 Short Film 7
"Awake"

 Short Film 3
"Stigma"

 COMEBACK TRAILER :
Boy Meets Evil

 Short Film 4
"First Love"

 "Blood Sweat & Tears"
MV TEASER

 Short Film 5
"Reflection"

 "Blood Sweat & Tears"
MV

————When I think about it, I don't know how we all managed to acclimatize to it. In every way, the concept was so different from the album before. There was a bit of awkwardness, and I had to think about how I would express this in a way that fit my style. But ironically, that was why I enjoyed my work even more. I didn't give myself time to rest. It's like . . . with each album, new things came up that I had to address, to overcome. 'Wow. There's so much I didn't know. So much I have to learn.' 'And I'll have to keep doing it in the future.'

These realizations were just some among the precious fruits borne of *WINGS*. While the world showered BTS with attention, the members themselves were using their new album, with all its unusual experimental opportunities, as a lens to examine themselves.

Seven Dramas, One Medley

The seven solo tracks in *WINGS* were the beating heart of the album, with each one a critical step in the journey of each member. Jung Kook, who turned nineteen during production of *WINGS*, looked back on his first meeting with the other BTS members with the solo track "Begin."[•]

> *A 15-year-old me with nothing*
> *The world was so big and I was so small*

Jung Kook looks back on this time:

──The "me" back then was really young. There was so much I didn't know, so if I felt a specific emotion, I would wonder, 'Is it all right to feel this way?'

I can't imagine anymore
The scentless and hollow me, me
I pray

Love you my brother, thanks to all you guys
Now I have feelings, I truly became me

The lyrics went on to show how Jung Kook had been transformed by the other members. He adds:

──Of course, I had emotions even when I was young. But I didn't really know what they were, and as I grew, I started to learn more . . . so I think I was able to unleash my emotions, literally.

"Begin" started with Jung Kook's feelings toward the other members and Bang Si-Hyuk over the years. During production, Jung Kook looked back on their relationship and realized how he had come to grow. He continues:

──Being around the hyoungs, I started learning bit by bit. Like . . . being onstage, what it means to hold something dear, that kind of thing. I think I grew a lot, in a lot of ways. The members didn't teach me specific things, but I can see the other members in the way I talk and act. I watched them do music, their little gestures and the way they did their interviews, and I realized and learned things. SUGA's thoughts, RM's words, Jimin's actions,

[W]ith each album, new things came
up that I had to address, to overcome.
'Wow. There's so much I didn't know.
So much I have to learn.' 'And I'll have
to keep doing it in the future.'

—j-hope

V's unique style, Jin's cheerfulness, j-hope's optimism . . . Things like that all came into me one by one.

From the perspective of a concept album, "Begin" held yet more significance in the context of *WINGS*. Where "Intro : Boy Meets Evil" was the gateway into the album and "Blood Sweat & Tears" communicated the album's overarching tone and vibe, "Begin" signaled the solo pieces to come, where each member offered his own take on the themes of *WINGS*. It was only after each member had grappled and come to terms with the new stage of his career that the album continued to the unit tracks "Lost" (by the vocalists) and "BTS Cypher 4" (by the rappers), which were followed by "Am I Wrong," which brought all the members together again.

WINGS as a whole was a journey where BTS shifted between team, individual, and unit under a singular concept, as well as a contiguous medley featuring seven narrative dramas by each of the seven members. As "Begin" led into "Blood Sweat & Tears," which led into the seven solo tracks, the stories of the members and the music they made formed a cohesive flow that bolstered the messages of all the tracks.

"Begin" was followed by Jimin's solo track "Lie,"· whose soundscape retained the darkness of the three preceding tracks, upholding a consistent tone for the album. Jimin, however, faced a completely different challenge from what j-hope had gone through in "Intro : Boy Meets Evil."

Wake me up from this hell
I can't break free from this pain
Save me from this punishment

The despairing, anguished lyrics of "Lie" marked the first time Jimin expressed his deep-seated emotions in words. He explains:

———I had meetings with Bang Si-Hyuk about what direction to take the content, and I wound up telling him things I'd kept in my heart. Then Bang Si-Hyuk plucked out the keyword "lie" for me, like things I felt when I was young, a kid who acted like he knew everything . . . and we went on talking until the lyrics came.

It was no easy task for Jimin to draw on his inner turmoil for his very first solo track. He recalls:

———When this song first came out, to be honest . . . I didn't want to do it. Because it deals with such deep emotion. At the time, I'd been thinking of more pop-style and mainstream music, so I'd given Pdogg a song where my voice shines through clearly. That song is way too different from "Lie" (laughs).

But Jimin also explains that that was the reason he was able to perfect "Lie."

———But that's exactly why "Lie" was able to come into the world. I could only sing that song because I was that awkward kid from back in the day who didn't fully understand those emotions.

"Lie" presented challenges on multiple fronts. Not only did Jimin have to bring feelings he'd left unspoken into the forefront, he also had to publicly present his own music and lyrics for the first time, and discover a completely new method of self-expression. He reminisces:

———Production took a really long time. The recording alone took more than two weeks. I'd record the whole thing, scrap it all and start again, change the key . . . and that went on, and it took a long, long time.

In spite of the difficulties, however, embracing "Lie" allowed Jimin to discover new potential within himself.

——We talked out the lyrics together, and I didn't like them at first, but then . . . that doesn't mean I came to like them, necessarily, but as I practiced singing the song and learned the choreography, I felt something funny. I fell for its charm, and I enjoyed performing it.

The performance of "Lie,"* revealed after the announcement of *WINGS*, showcased a completely new side of Jimin. Heavily incorporating elements of contemporary dance from his time in high school, Jimin's movements reflected the content of the lyrics and came together to express a cohesive tone, relying even more on performing convincing facial expressions. Only two years earlier, Jimin had given a fiery performance and torn his shirt open on the 2014 MAMA stage. Through "Lie," he was now using dance to express the emotions of a person being crushed by the darkness in his heart.

The vocal style Jimin developed in the process of expressing these complicated emotions soon came to influence the rest of BTS. By pushing his thin, fragile voice into the spotlight and adding a layer of darkness, Jimin created a unique new voice with an off-kilter charm—which he used to powerful effect in the first part of "Blood Sweat & Tears," instantly setting the tone of the track. He explains:

————Recording "Lie" was so hard that I remember I had to learn "Blood Sweat & Tears" in between recording sessions for "Lie," before I actually recorded "Blood Sweat & Tears."

Jimin then summarizes what he learned in the process:

————But when time passed, I didn't enjoy singing with only that kind of voice. I even briefly agonized, 'Is this all I'll get to showcase?'

The challenges that had daunted him at first slowly made him more and more ambitious, determined to meet them head-on.

V faced a different set of obstacles from fellow BTS members. Just releasing a solo track was a challenge for him, as he was already pulling double-duty with *Hwarang* and the new album. The pressure of a solo track was immense, as V recalls:

————The responsibility was much heavier than I expected. If I came to dislike this song, I thought it would show onstage. So I worked really hard to love "Stigma." During production, I listened even more closely to the track and prepared myself. Because I had this strong feeling that I wasn't good enough, I had to work even harder. Especially so I could make the track shine when I performed it live onstage.

V's efforts to love "Stigma"· paid off. The track featured the kind of jazz vocals he had loved since childhood, allowing him to showcase a deeper, heavier voice than he usually used in ensemble tracks. This approach helped to unify the album under an overarching theme,

[A]s I practiced singing the song
and learned the choreography, I felt
something funny. I fell for its charm,
and I enjoyed performing it.

—Jimin

and the song's looser melody led organically into the following track ("First Love" by SUGA). The falsetto V utilized in the chorus seared the entire track into the minds of listeners, adding yet another facet to the diversity of *WINGS* with its languid jazz influence. V explains:

———The falsetto was actually ad-libbed. The song was supposed to be complete without the falsetto, but no matter how much I listened to it, it was boring . . . The company said the last take was good too, but it didn't seem to have a color of its own, so during recording, I asked, "I thought of an ad-lib, could I try singing it?" and gave it a shot, and the responses were positive, so it made it into the final version. I was glad I managed to really make that point stand out, at least (laughs).

Through the production of "Stigma," V learned to better reflect his own voice and musical preferences in his songs, which would later develop into a unique personal style that exploded onto stage in works like "Intro : Singularity" and "Blue & Grey." Like he did with "Stigma," V would continue to set ideals for his work and let his ambition propel him forward. He adds:

———I . . . just think I'm still really greedy for the stage. "Greed" isn't a nice word, from one perspective, but for an artist, being greedy for the stage is the best thing there is. That greed is what drives me to make music.

While V learned to define himself as an artist, SUGA struggled with the opposite problem: addressing a love-hate relationship with music. He recalls,

——When I was working on "First Love,"* I was also working on my first mixtape at the same time. So actually, "First Love"and "So Far Away" (Feat. SURAN)** on my mixtape are a pair of songs that go together. But to be honest, what I thought when I was working on those was, 'Ah, I don't want to do music' (laughs). 'I don't like music after all. I dislike music.' I was doing this because music was all I knew, but I really thought I didn't want to do this.

SUGA's concerns were tied directly to the reason *WINGS* was so crucial to BTS: the search for direction following the success of *THE MOST BEAUTIFUL MOMENT IN LIFE* series. SUGA continues:

——The emotional drain was just too much. Once, my emotions would drop down all the way to the pits, and then suddenly they'd soar upward like crazy . . . I'd thought I wasn't strongly affected by pressure, but looking back, it all happened because of pressure. Anyway, I'd had big success, and I had to keep doing well. Those are the thoughts that I struggled with at the time. Because if I stumbled, I thought I would really fall.

SUGA's magnum opus, *THE MOST BEAUTIFUL MOMENT IN LIFE* series, had been a massive success. His first mixtape *Agust D*,[34]**** released two months ahead of *WINGS* in August 2016, was a chance

---

34 At the time, BTS member mixtapes were released largely on the global music streaming service SoundCloud. Some of these SoundCloud mixtapes are now available as solo albums on a number of music streaming platforms.

for him to confront the emotions that had piled up in his heart since he first embarked on his music career.

At that point, SUGA may have already achieved everything he had dreamed of as a trainee. But music, like life, was an endless journey. Through "First Love," he had the chance to reflect on what led him on the path of music in the first place: the piano he used to play as a child. Looking back on his own past, he would reminisce on music and everything that gave him strength over the years.

> *Holding onto my shattered shoulder saying,*
> *"I really can't do this anymore"*
> *Every time I tried to give up you were by my side saying,*
> *"Hey man, you can do this. No doubt"*

Though he found incredible success, his triumph was overshadowed by fear. SUGA chose to face that fear by laying bare the music that shaped him, which allowed him to put words to his feelings for music.

———That was the point when I started calling music "work." Before that, I said music was precious to me, and I thought that way, too. So how could I possibly approach it casually, you know? That was when I started consciously thinking of it as work. So I thought I really hated music. For a while, I didn't listen to a lot of it. But at the same time, I didn't want my musical spectrum to narrow down, so I'd listen to a whole bunch at once . . .

SUGA pauses at this point, and continues:

———But recently, I met some people and talked, and I realized I was talking about nothing but music (laughs). I met someone much older than me, someone who does music, and they said to me that I sound like I really love music.

One of SUGA's most intricate considerations when composing "First Love" was the placement of his track in the album. He wanted to make sure his song carried on the dark, melancholy tone of preceding tracks, but also change up the flow of the album. His solution was to start off dark with a serene keyboard melody underlying quiet, almost narration-like rap, slowly adding stringed instruments like the violin and cello for an explosive finish.

SUGA's attempt at embracing music as work was his own way of honing his craft. Through this process, he learned to express himself in even deeper, more diverse ways.

Where "First Love" showed the most dramatic flow in the album, the following track—RM's "Reflection"—was the most tranquil and reflective contribution to *WINGS*. Placed in the very middle of the fifteen-track album, RM's creative direction turned out to be a much-needed moment of contemplation for both him and BTS as a whole. RM discusses the timing of the album:

———Because of all the discourse that started in late 2015 onward, that was the point when my confusion reached a climax.

RM refers to the fact that as BTS's popularity rose, so did negative discourse and related cyberbullying. This was the reason RM, for a time, loved cloudy—and especially rainy—days.

———I just felt good when it rained. I loved how I could be around people, but because my umbrella covered my face, they couldn't see me. At the time, I think I really wanted to get the sense, 'I'm also part of this world.'

"Reflection" began with ambient sound from a crowded street, with RM's voice a lone, clear beacon in the soundscape. It gave the effect of being surrounded by people yet isolated.

———It's like I'm with them, but I'm alone, feeling, 'What is this?' We're definitely doing well, and I'm still doing something, but it's like I'm digging at the ground all alone . . . It was really paradoxical. But being with the other members made me laugh. So I could set those thoughts aside and laugh with them.

People look happier in the dark than in the daylight
They all know where they need to be
I'm the only one just walking around
But I feel more comfortable just blending in
Ttukseom swallows the night, hands me a completely different world

The lyrics to "Reflection" encapsulated RM's conflicting feelings. And in spite of the confusion between solitude and the search for belonging, he could always look to his friendship with the other members for support. By facing his emotions head-on and delving into his thoughts, RM came to understand himself and pour his identity into his music.

"Reflection" was the first of a series of contemplative pieces. His first mixtape *RM,*˙ released in March 2015, was followed by his second mixtape *mono.,*˙˙ which was filled with songs that struck a powerful contrast to the previous mixtape. RM reminisces:

———Most of the songs in *mono.* came out from 2016 to early 2017. I polished them up and released them later. So then when I released *mono.* in October 2018, I even thought, 'Do I really release this now?' But in spite of that, I thought, 'I have to face the person I was back then, I can't run away from my old self.'

Just as the other members underwent their own personal journeys, RM, too, learned more about himself through those turbulent times.

———Looking back . . . in a way, that was when I came to discover myself as a professional in my own right. For the first time, this shape of an adult with a career of his own was beginning to emerge.

And as it happens, at some point, RM began to dislike rainy days and stopped visiting Ttukseom.

When placed into the context of the series of solo tracks, from Jung Kook's "Begin" to RM's "Reflection"—that is, a series of songs that begin with a look back at one's personal journey to one's contemplation with their present-day self—j-hope's solo track "MAMA"˙˙˙˙ sounds completely different than it does when heard in a vacuum.

Time travel 2006, that year
Crazy about dancing, mom had to tighten the belt

Like the other solo tracks on *WINGS*, "MAMA" looked back on j-hope's dancing and his relationship with his mother, telling the story of his journey. But in the context of *WINGS* as a whole, "MAMA" also pointed to the roots of a person who had reached maturity. j-hope explains:

———At the time, both me and the company thought, this was what I had to talk about now. It was a time when it was really necessary.

j-hope's decision to discuss his mother was connected to BTS's circumstances at the time. He continues:

———This team called BTS was starting to get a bit of international attention, so I began searching for one of the reasons I made it this far. I endured thanks to my family, and of my family, my mom helped me so much, so I wanted to talk about her. It was something I could only express at that point in time, that only the me of that time could express.

j-hope's musings on his family and their role as his starting point, which connected to his role as a member of BTS, reflected the journey of BTS as a whole. But at the same time, "MAMA" was a turning point in *WINGS*, shifting the album from the members' fears and worries to an optimistic and cheerful tone. Going from the darkness and confusion of "Intro : Boy Meets Evil" to the upbeat reminiscence of "MAMA," j-hope created a ray of hope in the melancholic vibe of the album. In the 2017 BTS LIVE TRILOGY EPISODE III: THE WINGS TOUR, which took place after the release of *WINGS*, "MAMA" injected a dose of upbeat energy, signaling a transition to a more lighthearted vibe. j-hope explains:

———I wanted to make it feel like a musical. It's a story about my mother, and as for the performance, I wanted it to be pure and let the dance express the music. I had to show it off at live concerts, so when I made the song, there was an aspect where I took performance into a lot of consideration.

While the solo tracks allowed each BTS member to deeply explore their personal perspectives, they also played important roles as pieces of a larger whole. Jin's solo track "Awake"˙ was the track that most clearly showed what function it was intended to serve as part of a bigger picture, and as a personal message.

As a sort of epilogue to the seven solo tracks, "Awake" began with a serene orchestra prelude that brought together the flow of the varied solo tracks that came before. The lyrics, "I'm just walking and walking in this darkness," were a summation of the obstacles the members faced and overcame in their individual solo tracks during the production of *WINGS*.

At the same time, "Awake" was a personal prologue for Jin, heralding a new stage in his life. As with the other members, production on the album overlapped with his personal struggles.

——The song "Awake" fit my circumstances at the time perfectly. To be honest, I was a little depressed at the time. It was a time when I wondered, 'Can I really do this work well?' All the other worries I had before vanished, so I was agonizing over new things at that point.

I don't believe in it
I'm just trying to hold on

The only thing
I can do is this

Jin confesses:

———I had to do a little better, but I didn't have the ability, but I still
wanted to do something . . . That's what it was like at the time.
Looking at the other members made me envious. They could
write melodies, and they could also write lyrics.

Jin's worries were partly due to his circumstances. He hadn't yet
made his own music, and suddenly getting into composition was no
easy task.

———Until that point, I hadn't actually seen the other members compose music. It's embarrassing for one another, you know. When
you want to record with a beat playing, you have to be loud,
too . . . The other members often say that they can't produce
anything if they try to work in the open.

"Awake" represents the radically different circumstances BTS faced
after *THE MOST BEAUTIFUL MOMENT IN LIFE* series, and the
equally different anxieties they faced. As they attained a measure of
commercial success, Jin's concerns shifted to his own creative role in the
team. As if on cue, circumstances soon improved:

———That was when I composed music for the first time. There was an
empty room, too, so I ended up giving it a shot.

Jin began by putting a melody to a beat.

———I don't know how other people work, but I was told to start by
listening to a beat and then singing the melody I wanted, so I
followed that advice.

It was this process that gave rise to "Awake." Jin looks back:

———The entire second floor of the Cheonggu Building was repurposed as composition studios, and I sat blankly in my room with the beat I received playing in the background and humming along . . . That day, we had plans to eat out, and this melody that emerged ten minutes before we left made me feel, 'Huh? This doesn't sound bad.' So I recorded it on my phone and played it back later for RM and a composer hyoung, and they told me it was all right.

Though Jin was filled with trepidation at first, the positive response gave him confidence. He recalls:

———The composer hyoung did bring in a different chorus melody, but this was my first solo track and I'd built up confidence, so I persuaded a lot of people, starting with Pdogg, and ended up going with my melody. I convinced them by saying, "I'd feel amazing if I could sing the melody I made," and "If it's not a seriously horrible melody, I really want to use it."

Once the melody for "Awake" was set in stone, Jin went about experimenting. It was this uncertain process that led up to the lyrics, his heartfelt reflections on this time.

———I was writing the lyrics based on what came from my discussions about the theme of my solo track with Bang Si-Hyuk, then I asked RM for help. I showed him what I'd been writing and said, "I want lyrics that feel like this, that don't try and dance around the point."

Through his work on the solo track, Jin eventually reached a point where he genuinely felt "Awake." His eyes were opened.

———I kept practicing for one or two hours a day on my own in the practice studio so I could sing "Awake." Then I sang it while we were on tour, and the song improved a lot.

Finally, in the 2017 BTS LIVE TRILOGY EPISODE III: THE WINGS TOUR, Jin sang his solo piece live for adoring fans and was overcome with a completely new emotion.

———On the first day of the concert, it felt amazing when I sang "Awake." It was my first time singing my own melody, and it was my first solo song. Like, it was like I went up onstage and I'd prepared it all myself. That was when I understood how the other members felt. How good it feels when you sing your own creation in front of an audience.

Jin's experiences, too, reflected the journey of BTS as a whole throughout the production of *WINGS*. Each member faced his own struggles, and in the process, learned more about himself. This passage from *Demian* encapsulates this period in their career:

> *The bird fights its way out of the egg.*
> *The egg is the world.*
> *Who would be born must first destroy a world.*

Another Level

Bang Si-Hyuk was fond of the phrase "another level," which he used to describe BTS to friends before the team's debut, to describe amazing BTS performances, and to describe the future direction of the team.

Though it was not clear how he foresaw that this new idol group

It was my first time singing my own
melody, and it was my first solo song.
Like, it was like I went up onstage
and I'd prepared it all myself. That
was when I understood how the other
members felt. How good it feels
when you sing your own creation in
front of an audience.

—Jin

from a tiny management company would rise to another level, such explosive success probably went beyond what Bang had initially expected, as BTS's incredible showing in the years following their debut could only have been predicted by a bona fide prophet. But what was clear was that Bang expected *WINGS* to indeed take BTS to another level, because nothing else could explain what he did in the lead-up to the album's release.

As the BTS members began preparation for *WINGS*, Big Hit Entertainment also got to work on the *WINGS Concept Book*, a publication that would chronicle the making-of process for the album. Published in June 2017, this book contained heartfelt, genuine reflections on the members' emotions as they prepared for the album, as well as a record of the entire production process, from the initial planning stages to the Seoul performance of the 2017 BTS LIVE TRILOGY EPISODE III: THE WINGS TOUR. The book even contained photographs of all the outfits worn by the members.

This was a risky venture by K-pop industry standards, especially because the album *WINGS* had not even been released when work on the book began. It would be much more cost-effective for an entertainment company to simply block off a few days from the artists' schedule to shoot an ordinary photo book. There was no good reason for a company to plan and publish a large, thick book (complete with slipcase) that covered half a year's worth of a K-pop idol group's schedule from album production to tour.

The same went for the YouTube documentary series *Burn the Stage,* planned alongside the *WINGS Concept Book* and uploaded on YouTube the following year.[35] Big Hit Entertainment followed BTS's international tour closely, capturing every aspect of their work on camera. The documentary made no attempt to hide the members collapsing in exhaustion or being embroiled in disagreements with one another about their performance. This was yet another departure from K-pop idol industry norms, where member chemistry—meaning closeness between members in this context—was considered a crucial element of success by both fans and management companies. Why invest so much time and money into showing artists going through difficulties and conflicts with one another?

As it turned out, there was a method to Big Hit's supposed madness. The release of the *WINGS* album was followed by the publication of the *WINGS Concept Book*, which coincided with the production on the documentary series and feature. It was at this point that the name BTS came to take on an additional meaning on top of "Bulletproof Boy Scouts": "Beyond The Scene." This new brand identity for both BTS and ARMY was unveiled on July 5, 2017, making the team's name easier to remem-

---

35 *Burn the Stage* was released in March 2018 as a series of eight documentary episodes on YouTube, which were later compiled into the feature *Burn the Stage: The Movie* (including previously unreleased footage), which premiered simultaneously in more than seventy countries in November of the same year. The *Burn the Stage* series was followed by similar documentary and feature series that covered BTS's tours and other major musical activities, including *Bring the Soul* (2019), *Break the Silence* (2020), and *BTS Monuments: Beyond the Star* (2023).

ber for both Korean and international fans, and expanding the scope the team could cover.

This was the future Big Hit Entertainment had in mind for BTS: an international sensation that anyone on the planet would recognize. Artists whose work was worth the effort to chronicle into large, thick books sold in slipcases.

BTS skyrocketed in popularity globally following *THE MOST BEAUTIFUL MOMENT IN LIFE* series. But passionate fan engagement and responses on Twitter and YouTube would not necessarily lead to tangible success. Korean idols had already carved out an international niche, which continued to expand on YouTube. But these successes were largely limited to the Asian market, with K-pop forays into other locales largely failing to garner mainstream attention.

Big Hit Entertainment, however, moved as if aware that the Bulletproof Boy Scouts would soon be called upon at international music awards, under the name BTS.

"Blood Sweat & Tears"* was clear evidence of the company's foresight, containing elements that appealed to both established BTS fans and completely new audiences. As with "Dope" in *THE MOST BEAUTIFUL MOMENT IN LIFE PT. 1*, "Blood Sweat & Tears" opened with the highlight of the song to grab the listener's attention from the outset, and made use of the international trend of the moombahton beat.

The vocals, however, struck a marked contrast—the members maintained the delicacy of Jimin's opening solo throughout the track, their voices highlighted by tasteful mixing and reverb that lent a darker tone to the song. The beat seemed to coax excitement, but the performers onstage seemed to quaver in temptation. "Blood Sweat & Tears" offered something for every listener, from longtime ARMY enraptured by BTS's trademark darkness and dynamism, to South American listeners who had never heard of BTS.

When he realized that all these factors were encapsulated by the word "temptation," Bang Si-Hyuk thought of everything that made up "Blood Sweat & Tears." Just as BTS found success and stepped into a new world, a young person stepping into the world of adulthood was faced with countless new choices, many of which were temptations that would pull them away from their goals. The depiction of the confusion between pain and pleasure and casting it as temptation was the final piece of the puzzle that perfected "Blood Sweat & Tears."

Where "Dope" showcased the members in a constant state of motion, pulling off dramatic moves with no time to breathe, "Blood Sweat & Tears" had them almost completely rooted in place, focusing their entire performance on their faces, running their hands over their own bodies, and making gestures almost reminiscent of choking. The reason behind this style of performance might not have been clear to those who hadn't been exposed to the other songs in the album or the ongoing narrative of BTS's albums, but the vibe of the performance would be crystal clear even to new audiences. This performance was about sex appeal.

Bringing together a host of complex elements, "Blood Sweat & Tears" was an intuitive blend of a multitude of messages. There was no doubt that sex appeal was the predominant flavor of the performance, but in a blatant reversal of K-pop industry trends, the members were not the tempters but the tempted. And when fans wanted to delve into these hidden meanings one by one, researching the lyrics and the symbolism behind the MV, they no longer needed to look for "방탄소년단," "Bangtan Boys," or "Bulletproof Boy Scouts" in search engines. It was now as simple as typing "BTS."

Korean fans were not the only ones typing "BTS" into their search bars now. *WINGS* recorded 751,301 net shipments in 2016, topping the Gaon Chart that year by tripling the performance of *THE MOST BEAUTIFUL MOMENT IN LIFE PT.2*, which had itself performed markedly better than its predecessor. *WINGS* was also ranked twenty-sixth on the Billboard 200—the unprecedented top performance among Korean artists—and was the only album by Korean artists to remain on the chart for two weeks running.

But even these unbelievable showings did not completely explain the things that happened following the release of *WINGS*. The 2017 BTS LIVE TRILOGY EPISODE III: THE WINGS TOUR, which kicked off about four months later, took BTS to twelve stops around the globe and was a bona fide world tour. While the previous tour, 2016 BTS LIVE THE MOST BEAUTIFUL MOMENT IN LIFE ON STAGE : EPILOGUE was exclusive to Asia, the 2017 tour also involved concerts in Chile, Brazil, Australia, and a whopping three cities in the United States.

Counting from the first days of the two tours, this explosive change had occurred in a matter of six months. BTS had performed previously in these countries with the 2015 BTS LIVE TRILOGY EPISODE II: THE RED BULLET, but the venues then had been relatively tiny at only several thousand seats. The 2017 venues were massive in comparison, with BTS performing at an arena-class venue in America, a country where they had no official promotional presence. By the time the team landed in America for the tour, they were a phenomenon. *Billboard* magazine covered the Newark show, stating the following:

> *With their loyal Army cheering them on from start to finish, the seven-member boy band kickstarted the U.S. leg of the worldwide 2017 BTS Live Trilogy Episode III: The Wings Tour with a nearly three-hour long show that incorporated the group's most boisterous hits and the introspective songs of its record-breaking* Wings *album.*

Everything pointed toward the dawn of a new era. Even with *WINGS*, BTS had neither produced English-language songs nor heavily promoted themselves to the Americas, and did not have the backing of influential international media channels to carry their names across language barriers, as with popular artists from the US and UK.

In spite of this, more and more people came to recognize BTS, searching for the group on Twitter and YouTube. In January 2017, two months before the Chile stop of the tour, Chilean public service broadcaster TVN covered local ARMY lining up overnight to purchase tickets to the show. ARMY in every country seemed to take after their Korean counterparts, going wild for BTS and growing exponentially in number.

All We Want Is Love

Ironically, the surge in popularity did not particularly affect BTS; or to be more accurate, they did not let the change affect them. According to j-hope, BTS already knew about the international following they attracted after *WINGS*. He reminisces:

————The results we got back were, well, a little different. These responses from overseas media were a little . . . like something out of another world.

But no matter how the world changed, their own world remained unshaken. Jung Kook explains:

————Well . . . for me, I was still doing the same thing I always do. And I had to keep improving, and I was working hard to keep releasing albums one by one, so to be honest, our popularity didn't really feel real to me. But then our results kept getting better and better, and we could see the data and how our old records were getting broken one after another, so I started feeling like I was in a daze, it was fascinating. So I just felt like, 'I guess I'm doing all right.' I didn't want to focus on the numbers, just keep doing what we always did.

V, too, is of a similar mind:

————I was really late to realize how popular we'd gotten. I was just happy having a good time with the other members.

According to Jimin, this attitude stemmed from a BTS-style vibe they developed together.

————Call me conceited, but I didn't spend a lot of time being aware of just how popular we were. I once got a question about our popularity, and I replied, "At this point, it would be rude to our fans to say that we don't really know how popular we are."³⁶ But before that, we never did our work with the mindset of, 'Hey, we got more popular!' Our world was limited to just our team and the audience. And it still is. So we could see how our venues were getting bigger and bigger, but we didn't get a real sense of our popularity increasing.

Ironically, their skyrocketing popularity had a sobering effect on SUGA. He explains:

──We try not to look at responses to our work. It was even more so back then. I think I had this really big concern, like, 'What if I get conceited and start slacking off?'

Considering everything they had fought through until the release of *WINGS*, SUGA's attitude was inevitable. The lyrics from the unit and group songs following the set of solo tracks on *WINGS* spoke for themselves:

> *It's so hard, I don't know if this is the right path*
> *I'm so confused, never leave me alone*
> —"Lost"•

> *What I'm saying here, bae*
> *Gibberish to some people, bae*

36 Press conference celebrating the release of the *LOVE YOURSELF* 承 *'Her'* album on September 18, 2017.

Change your dissing pattern, bae
—"BTS Cypher 4"*

All over and around HELL YEAH
Online and offline HELL YEAH
—"Am I Wrong"**

———Some people jeered us when we went onstage. So we had this idea
that there were still quite a lot of people who were hostile to us.

SUGA's statement applied to a number of stages, including the 2016
MAMA—one of Korea's biggest music awards. Two weeks earlier on
November 19, BTS had been awarded one of the three grand prizes at
the MMA (Melon Music Awards), the Album of the Year award: the
team's first ever grand prize win.*** At the MAMA, they would win the
Artist of the Year award. But even as they took center stage as the clear
winners of the year, they remained targets of hate. Some social media
users organized cyberbullying attacks on days when BTS had a concert
or was receiving an award.

Jimin reveals how he felt at the MAMA performance:

———We gave our performance with a lot of pride in being able to
show off our efforts. I think we had a lot of people watching, so
we were like, "Check this out!"

Indeed, BTS needed to put on a performance that captured audiences
at the MAMA. Two years earlier, at their first MAMA performance, they

had been exhausted, desperate, angry, and determined to counter the frigid stares of anyone who wasn't ARMY. But there was no need for that anymore. No one could look down on them now. They had gone from sharing performance time with Block B to getting eleven minutes all to themselves.

This also meant, however, that they had to prove their mettle: that they deserved the title of Artist of the Year, attained with the support of ARMY around the world. They had to silence those who continued to put them down, with a performance that went beyond just "good." They had to pull off something spectacular.

BTS made that goal a reality. Their performance* was attention-grabbing from the word go, and no one could tear their eyes away. Jung Kook was hanging in the air. Before audiences could process their shock, they were treated to a powerful dance solo by j-hope—who faded into darkness and was followed by Jimin, dancing alone with eyes covered in red cloth. Then j-hope emerged again, dancing in parallel on the other half of the stage. When the song ended, all seven members walked into the spotlight together for "Blood Sweat & Tears." In the performance** following the song, V fell to the floor and pulled up his shirt to expose his back, revealing a pair of gaping wounds from a pair of missing wings.

By reenacting otherworldly scenes from the "Blood Sweat & Tears" MV onstage, BTS stole the show at the MAMA, enthralling the audience. But "Blood Sweat & Tears" was only the centerpiece of an eleven-

•

••

minute block packed with powerful and alluring sights and sounds. j-hope and Jimin's opening performances in "Intro : Boy Meets Evil" started off as a pair of solo movements that dovetailed into one dramatic dance, and the tension of the performance carried on unbroken into "Blood Sweat & Tears" before exploding in a burst of energy with a host of back dancers in "FIRE." Jimin reminisces:

———In one sense, the dance from that stage was exactly the type that fit my strengths. In both direction and in the vibe of the song. So I got this strong feeling that I was really making an effort to genuinely express this song. And expressing this song was an incredible feeling for me as a performer, too.

Jimin's sense of accomplishment applied to all BTS members. The eyes of the world were on them as their haunting visuals, impeccable narrative composition, and captivating performance made MAMA history. They had shown ARMY and non-ARMY alike that they had what it took to take charge at a massive event like the MAMA.

V has this to say about their first ever grand prize in 2016:

———It was like, it felt like a miracle. To be honest, just being nominated was awesome. But when we got the award, the feeling I personally got was, 'I knew Bangtan would win. No matter what anyone says, Bangtan is going to win.'

And BTS did indeed secure victory at the MAMA that year: not just by taking the grand prize, but by proving themselves worthy of the prize.

———Walking this path, I always thought, 'One day we're going to get an award.' I put myself into this group called BTS, and I had faith that this team would win. Like, if I was with these people, I was going to succeed.

V's unwavering trust in the other members was what allowed BTS to fight through the wave of hate.

——Like with the other members, Big Hit was my first company, and I debuted through this first company. I'd never even heard about what other teams and companies were like. So when I looked at the other members, it's just like . . . I became fearless. For example, they're the kind of people I could brag about at school, saying, "This is my hyoung." From the beginning, these people were celebrities in my eyes.

Together, they were invincible. It was a sense of solidarity that tied together not only the seven members of BTS, but BTS with ARMY. In this context, *WINGS* was the musical expression of their growing bonds. The solo tracks allowed each member to confess his deepest fears, the unit and group songs from "Lost" to "21st Century Girl" were the team's united messages to the world, and "2! 3!"* was their message to ARMY.

As an official message to ARMY, "2! 3!" began with the lyrics "Let's only walk flower paths / Such words I cannot say." Though they were all alone and disconnected at first, BTS would sing together to the world about their pain, and meet the people who lent an ear to their music. But even though they know everything the fans did for their sake, BTS couldn't promise that everything would always be fine. In spite of this, the track ended on an optimistic note with the lyrics, "Erase all the sad memories, / take each other's hand and smile."

It was like, it felt like a miracle. To
be honest, just being nominated
was awesome. But when we got the
award, the feeling I personally got
was, 'I knew Bangtan would win. No
matter what anyone says, Bangtan is
going to win.'

—V

WINGS was an encapsulation of BTS's journey thus far as they stepped onto the stage and formed a community through ARMY. As the lyrics to "2! 3!" showed, they were no longer fighting alone: they were moving forward together.

> *For better days*
> *Because we are together*

This marked the moment BTS and ARMY became inextricably intertwined. They went beyond the traditional connection between artist and fandom, becoming a tight-knit unit defying precedent and definition.

It was for these reasons that the two-year journey from *THE MOST BEAUTIFUL MOMENT IN LIFE* series to *WINGS* boiled down to one keyword: love. When BTS won their very first grand prize, the prevailing emotion that overcame j-hope was not accomplishment or triumph. He explains:

————That was when our feeling of being loved reached a peak. That award made us feel like, 'We went through a lot,' and 'We really worked hard.'

Jung Kook, who like the rest of BTS also shed tears as they won the MAMA Artist of the Year Award, looked around at his fellow members, and at the fans in the audience.

————'Man, we went through a lot.' The things we did up to that point flashed before my eyes. That was the first thing that came to mind, because the other members were at my side, and ARMY was cheering us on from the seats, and it was all coming at us at the same time.

SUGA states that he understood exactly what the fans' love meant to him:

——Now, I look at fan responses on occasion. A lot, actually (laughs). To build up self-esteem. Because I get the feeling that I need to know that I am loved.

BTS longed for success. But when that success finally became reality, what they then began to want was, ironically, love—that is, love from ARMY.

In 2016, Jimin celebrated his birthday on a music show set for a pre-recording shoot. The ARMY on-site sang him "Happy Birthday," and Jimin came to treasure his birthday for the first time in his life.˙ When asked to elaborate, he replies:

——Before, my birthday was just something that's nice to get congrat-ulated for, no more than that. Like an excuse to see my friends again, or get some attention? (laughs). That was what I liked, otherwise I didn't place too much meaning on it. But then right in front of me, there were these people I loved, people I wanted to work hard for, but they were the ones celebrating for me. That feeling . . . it's hard to put into words.

And to Friends

After the successes of 2016 marked by the keywords "victory" and "love," BTS kicked off the new year by stepping into the spotlight yet again, this time from a completely unexpected direction: the media reported that in January 2017, BTS donated KRW 100 million to 4/16 Sewol Families for Truth and a Safer Society, an organization composed of families of the victims of the 2014 sinking of the Sewol ferry.

Because of this charitable act, people began to interpret "Spring Day" from the February 2017 special album *YOU NEVER WALK ALONE* (a spinoff of *WINGS*) as a reference to the 2014 tragedy. The lyrics begin with the words "Miss you," and the MV featured mountains of clothing, which were taken to symbolize the 304 dead and missing from the capsized ferry—an interpretation fueled further by the fact that most of the casualties had been high school students on a school trip. The investigative TV show *Unanswered Questions* on the SBS channel even featured the song on its April 2017 episode covering the third anniversary of the sinking.

BTS never gave an official explanation behind the meaning of "Spring Day," save for brief comments at a press conference at the beginning of the 2017 BTS LIVE TRILOGY EPISODE III: THE WINGS TOUR stating that they would like to leave the interpretation up to the listeners.

According to RM, "Spring Day" began as a message to friends:

———When I wrote the lyrics to that song, I remember I really tried to write to my friends. Friends like the ones who left my side, the ones I see once in a while but are so far away that even though we're under the same sky, in some ways they're someplace else.

SUGA, the other lyricist for "Spring Day," is more specific:

———I just resented my friend so much.

YOU NEVER WALK ALONE

THE 2ND SPECIAL ALBUM
2017. 2. 13

TRACK

01 Intro : Boy Meets Evil
02 Blood Sweat & Tears
03 Begin
04 Lie
05 Stigma
06 First Love
07 Reflection
08 MAMA
09 Awake
10 Lost
11 BTS Cypher 4

12 Am I Wrong
13 21st Century Girl
14 2! 3!
15 Spring Day
16 Not Today
17 Outro : Wings
18 A Supplementary Story : You
    Never Walk Alone

VIDEO

 "Spring Day"
MV TEASER

 "Spring Day"
MV

 "Not Today"
MV TEASER

 "Not Today"
MV

He adds:

———Because I couldn't meet them, even though I really wanted to see them.

Later, SUGA would quote lyrics from "Spring Day" in "Dear My Friend" (Feat. Kim Jong-wan of NELL)," part of his May 2020 mixtape *D-2*, implying that the two songs were about the same friend. According to him, the friend was "a friend [he] held very dear." But a number of things happened between them, and they drifted apart and could not meet again. At one point, when the longing got to be too much, he even reached out to acquaintances to reconnect with the friend. Unfortunately, there would be no reunion.

———When I was going through a hard time, that friend was the only one I could lean on . . . When I was a trainee, we'd talk together, "Hey you think I can really debut?" and break into sobs, and then make resolutions together like, "Let's conquer the whole world!" But now I wonder how that friend is doing . . . That's why I resented them.

SUGA had suffered a great deal before "Spring Day," but that suffering was what had gotten him so far. Unfortunately, his old friend was no longer at his side. For him, "Spring Day" was a way of coming to terms with emotions that continued to burn inside his heart after all those years. The resulting track became a source of comfort to him.

———Even back then, I didn't remember the last time I was uplifted by listening to music . . . it had been a really long time. So at the time, I didn't know. I do know now, though.

You know it all
You're my best friend
The morning will come again
No darkness no season can last forever

SUGA was far from the only one comforted by "Spring Day." The Sewol disaster had left an indelible mark on the season in Korea, and spring was no longer purely a time of warmth and restoration. April in particular remained a "cruelest month" for those left traumatized by the sinking. RM explains:

———Studying art, I learned that a lot of writers talk about springtime as a cruel season. Like T. S. Eliot's poem "The Waste Land" says, "April is the cruellest month." Being exposed to works like that, I thought, 'Why did the idea of springtime being cruel never occur to me?' But then again, spring can also be thought of as something that happens at the end of winter. And "Spring Day" is about a certain feeling of missing someone . . . That's why I think people like this song.

Indeed, "Spring Day" came to be a symbol of the season for Koreans. Even now, it remains on the Melon Top 100 playlist, and rises again in the standings in spring each year, a testament to its sustained popularity. The hopes RM planted into the song blossomed beautifully:

———I wanted to make a song that would be long-lasting in Korea.

RM's recollection of the production process gives a sense of destiny, or fate, to every aspect of "Spring Day." He recounts:

————Even now, it's an unprecedented experience, but when I wrote the melody for the first time, I just knew, 'This is it.' Experienced musicians say that some songs emerge out of the blue in only five minutes, and for me, "Spring Day" was exactly that.

The period from the donation to the Sewol victims' families to the release of *YOU NEVER WALK ALONE* was a turning point in BTS's career. "Spring Day" made no direct references to the ferry disaster, but was—and remains—a universal song of consolation and support for those hurt by similar incidents. At the same time, the donation was a show of determination from BTS to do their part as members of society.

"Not Today,"* another new track on *YOU NEVER WALK ALONE*, sent a reassuring message to "All the underdogs in the world."

> *Till the day of the victory (fight!)*
> *Never kneel down Never fall apart*

From *THE MOST BEAUTIFUL MOMENT IN LIFE* series to *WINGS* and *YOU NEVER WALK ALONE*, BTS sang of previously disconnected individuals coming together in solidarity through community. It was a journey of growth, where an adolescent learned to look beyond the self and toward the lives of others. Indeed, BTS would go on to find even more ways to contribute to the world.

Part of their actions stemmed from a desire to give back to ARMY for their love and support, to show their biggest fans that BTS were now capable of taking the lead. They were no longer simply walking together, they were now trailblazers, forging a new, more meaningful path forward. BTS would go from telling their own stories to listening to other voices, actively seeking out meaningful causes to champion and defend.

RM discusses how BTS began to perceive the world around this time:

———Whether it was for the people listening to our music or for myself, I scolded myself to 'have something to say about the world around me.' After all, I started with Nas and Eminem. In one sense, we could be said to be in an unstable and hypocritical position, but in spite of that, there will always be something to say . . .

When they fought their way out of the egg, they found a seemingly endless world filled with things to do—even after being named Artist of the Year.

CHAPTER 5

LOVE YOURSELF 承 'Her'

LOVE YOURSELF 轉 'Tear'

LOVE YOURSELF 結 'Answer'

A FLIGHT
THAT NEVER LANDS

LOVE YOURSELF 承 'Her' | THE 5TH MINI ALBUM

LOVE YOURSELF 轉 'Tear' | THE 3RD FULL-LENGTH ALBUM

LOVE YOURSELF 結 'Answer' | REPACKAGE ALBUM

||| | | | | A FLIGHT THAT NEVER LANDS | | | | |||

May 20, 2018

On May 20, 2018 (local time), BTS ascended to the stage at the Bill-board Music Awards (BBMAs), held in the MGM Grand Garden Arena in Las Vegas. They were about to perform the title song "FAKE LOVE" from the new album, *LOVE YOURSELF* 轉 *'Tear,'* released a few days before, for the very first time.

The BBMAs meant a lot to BTS—they had attended for the first time the previous year, where they were awarded Top Social Artist,* and they would finally also be performing there for the first time.** They were awarded Top Social Artist for the second year in a row, and *LOVE YOURSELF* 轉 *'Tear'* became their first Billboard 200 number one album.

However, it was during this period of tremendous glory that BTS were also experiencing their most serious crisis to date. This fact was only made known seven months after the 2018 BBMAs, at the MAMA Awards on December 14.

On this day, BTS were awarded Artist of the Year for the third year in a row, and mid–acceptance speech, j-hope said through teary eyes:

> *I . . . I think I would have cried whether we'd won or not. This year. Because we went through so much, because we received so much love from all of you, I wanted to repay you no matter*

what, really . . . thank you so much, really, I want to say in this moment when we're all here together, to the members, "Thank you so much."

Jin, who was already in tears listening to the other members' speeches, said, in a trembling voice:

Uh, really . . . this year . . . I'm reminded of its begin-ning. At the beginning of this year, we really, we had a very hard time emotionally. So . . . we discussed between us and debated whether to break up or not . . . but, we really got our acts together and ended up getting such good results . . . I think it's a real relief . . . I am so thankful to the members for getting our acts together, and I want to say how thankful I am to ARMY for always loving us.

"Breakup." This is the last word you would associate with BTS now, and it was no different at the beginning of 2018. Before *LOVE YOUR-SELF* 轉 '*Tear*,' *LOVE YOURSELF* 承 '*Her*,' released in September 2017, had been their first album to sell over a million copies, and it had also reached number seven on the Billboard 200, BTS's highest ranking so far. However, while BTS were soaring up toward the sky, those very same heroes of the story were in fact plunging to the bottom of the sea, with no end in sight. SUGA summarizes the atmosphere within the team at the time:

——We all wanted to say, "Let's quit," but none of us could bring ourselves to do it.

Bohemian Rhapsody

At the end of 2018, once BTS had made it through their breakup crisis, RM watched *Bohemian Rhapsody* (2018), which tells the story of legendary British rock group, Queen. RM says that the many things BTS had been through flashed through his mind as he watched the movie:

———In a fight with the other members, Freddie Mercury says that the repeated cycle of "album, tour, album, tour" is exhausting, right? Then Brian May makes a comment. Watching that scene, so many thoughts came to mind.

In this scene, Freddie Mercury is depicted as being cornered psychologically. He was exhausted—with Queen's enormous popularity, their schedule was accordingly hectic, the press was digging into their personal lives, and as a result, they were flooded with every kind of misunderstanding and criticism. When Freddie Mercury says he no longer wants a life that's a repeat of albums and tours, Brian May answers back:

That's what bands do. Album, tour, album, tour.

Like Queen, BTS couldn't escape "what bands do." Going back a little in time, to between the release of the album *YOU NEVER WALK ALONE* in February 2017 and *LOVE YOURSELF* 承 *'Her'* in September of the same year, BTS had performed thirty-two concerts across ten different countries and regions as part of the 2017 BTS LIVE TRILOGY EPISODE III: THE WINGS TOUR.

Then, less than one month after the release of *LOVE YOURSELF* 承 *'Her,'* BTS performed their remaining five concerts in Japan, Taiwan, and Macau. The show in Japan's Kyocera Dome Osaka was their first dome performance since debuting.

Though this will be covered later on, around two weeks later, on November 19 (local time), BTS became the first Korean artists to give a solo performance at the American Music Awards (AMAs),˙ one of the US' biggest three music awards. The awards were held at the Microsoft Theater in Los Angeles, where BTS also performed. They then made back-to-back appearances on the leading talk show of America's "Big Three" television networks, NBC, CBS, and ABC.[37]˙˙

After returning to Korea, BTS prepared for performances at various award ceremonies, including the MAMA Awards and the MMAs. They also held three concerts as part of the 2017 BTS LIVE TRILOGY EP-ISODE III: THE WINGS TOUR, that would draw to a close the voyage of their previous world tour. They rang in the new year of 2018 having made it through all the preparations and appointments for each Korean broadcaster's end of year special music programs and award ceremonies, and immediately had to get to work on their new album, *LOVE YOURSELF* 轉 *'Tear.'*

When asked how he felt at the time, Jin raises his voice slightly and explains the pressure and exhaustion they were experiencing:

---

37 BTS were guests on NBC's *The Ellen Degeneres Show*, CBS's *The Late Late Show with James Corden*, ABC's *Jimmy Kimmel Live*, among others, where they gave interviews and/or performances.

———We really had almost no days off. So, at the time, I wondered whether it was right for a person to live life as exhausted as this.

Album production and promotion, and then tours, countless awards ceremonies and performances, producing yet another album . . . Just as it had been for Queen in *Bohemian Rhapsody*, this repeated schedule was exerting more and more of a psychological toll on the BTS members. To be precise, however, BTS were experiencing a pain different from that expressed by Queen in the movie. This was because BTS were in a situation that no British rock band or Korean idol group had ever been in before.

As mentioned earlier, Korean idol groups had been gaining popularity in the western music market even before BTS. K-pop music videos were already popular on YouTube. However, being invited to the BBMAs and winning, or making the top ten on the Billboard 200 with a Korean-language album: these were achievements on a whole new level. BTS were already unmatched in popularity within the Asian market and were also experiencing soaring popularity in the West, including in the US.

While on tour, Jin would take his PC into the accommodations and play games. He says:

———With games, it doesn't feel like I'm gaming but that I'm doing it to chat. I need to spend my time doing something so that I can sleep. When we go abroad, there's so little to do.

Because of the interest in BTS, it was difficult for them to leave the accommodations. Jin continues:

———Whenever a concert was over, I'd eat a meal, and then I'd log onto the game and chat with my friends, that was basically it. This was because we had to spend most of our time in the hotel.

Once they'd returned to Korea after the tour, their new daily life began in full swing. V reflects:

———It was stressful. Before, I could quietly go wherever I wanted and just quietly do what I wanted. But from that point onward, at the same time as starting to feel, 'Oh . . . Guess we really have become more famous,' I began to think, 'Guess this kind of private life won't be easy now.'

How V was feeling wasn't because of ARMY's interest in BTS. No Korean artist had ever experienced so much success abroad, and they had therefore attracted a huge amount of interest. It wasn't only in the idol industry—BTS were becoming a topic across the entire Korean popular music industry, as well as the general public as a whole.

As SUGA explains, it was like trying to solve a problem that had no answer:

———If history books are the answer sheet to the present, then our sunbaes who did music before us are our answer sheet, right? However, with us, we had to deal with an additional something else.

Following BTS's debut, SUGA had fairly sizable goals as an artist. He reflects:

———Even back in 2016, performing once at the Olympic Gymnastics Arena, getting a grand prize, and financially, getting a house and the car I wanted—if I could have these four things, I would have achieved all my life's goals.

Most artists have similar dreams. SUGA was in fact in the small minority who actually *did* receive the grand prize at a music award ceremony in Korea, and who *did* get to perform at the Seoul Olympic Gymnastics Arena. However, from 2017 onward, SUGA's reality began to surpass everything he'd ever dreamed of:

———To give an example, it was like this. I'd suddenly become the protagonist in a martial arts novel, and there, I meet a really strong opponent. And so I go, "Oh well, whatever" and strike them, but somehow, I win with a single blow. It felt like that. "Wait, since when was I so strong? This wasn't what I'd intended."

SUGA sums up his mindset back then:

———You mean we can do even more than we're doing now . . . ?

Hesitation & Fear

The anxiety SUGA felt at the time is evident in "Skit : Hesitation & Fear" (Hidden Track), found only on the CD version of the *LOVE YOURSELF* 承 *'Her'* album. This track is a voice recording of the BTS members as they rewatch the video of the 2017 BBMAs Top Social Artist announcement while preparing for *LOVE YOURSELF* 承 *'Her.'*

Seeing their name called out once again, BTS talk about how happy they had been, and soon they open up about what this unexpected success had felt like. RM expresses his concerns, saying, "How much farther up do we have to go," "How far down do we have to go when we must," while SUGA says, "When we go down, well . . . Back then, I was worried it would be faster than our rise."

World Business (bang bang) core
Number 1 favorite for casting (clap clap) sold out

Above is part of the lyrics from *LOVE YOURSELF* 承 *'Her'*'s "MIC Drop."* The song appears immediately after "Skit : Billboard Music Awards Speech," a recording of the 2017 BBMAs Top Social Artist acceptance speech, with the background noise left in as it is. As "MIC Drop" depicts, BTS felt pride at this new level of success they were experiencing.

However, as mentioned in "Skit : Hesitation & Fear" (Hidden Track)—which you could call the epilogue to their win—with great glory, comes anxiety. As soon as they debuted, BTS were subjected to a baptism of malicious comments online and were even insulted to their faces at public appearances. Though their popularity had soared, they were quite literally being "pummeled." The praise and interest they were suddenly one day showered with made them just as confused as happy.

SUGA recalls how he felt at the time:

———Apart from those who loved and supported us, everyone else felt like an enemy. We were really worried about how much criticism we'd get if we put even a foot out of line.

SUGA's words clearly show us the "hesitation and fear" BTS were feeling at the time. After the release of *LOVE YOURSELF* 承 *'Her,'* reaching number one on the Billboard 200 was no longer an unrealistic goal. However, when they really did reach that goal, the fact that no one could predict what the future would bring inevitably filled them with fear.

At the time, as it so happens, BTS had been doing their utmost to respond to the love ARMY had given them thus far. On November 1,

LOVE YOURSELF 承
'Her'

THE 5TH MINI ALBUM
2017. 9. 18

TRACK

01 Intro : Serendipity

02 DNA

03 Best Of Me

04 Dimple

05 Pied Piper

06 Skit : Billboard Music Awards
   Speech

07 MIC Drop

08 Go Go

09 Outro : Her

10 Skit : Hesitation & Fear (Hidden
   Track)

11 Sea (Hidden Track)

VIDEO

 COMEBACK TRAILER :
Serendipity

 "DNA"
MV TEASER 1

 "DNA"
MV TEASER 2

 "DNA"
MV

 "MIC Drop"
(Steve Aoki Remix)
MV TEASER

 "MIC Drop"
(Steve Aoki Remix)
MV

2017, BTS began the "LOVE MYSELF"³⁸• social initiative in collabo-ration with UNICEF. This campaign, still ongoing, was decided upon after BTS realized that their influence was as great as the love ARMY gave them.

Their support for children and young people, especially those ex-posed to violence, also rang true with BTS's message, which, since their debut, had grown by reflecting on the reality faced by teenagers. This was the reason why they not only donated a portion of the profits from each of their albums, but actively promoted this campaign, too. Through their promotional activities, they hoped to raise awareness of the problems children and young people faced.

However, it was during their preparations for this campaign, from early 2017 onward, that BTS were invited to the BBMAs for the first time. Furthermore, all the records they had broken with *WINGS* for being "the first ever Korean artist to [fill in the blank]," they were break-ing all over again (and by huge margins) with *LOVE YOURSELF* 承 *'Her.'* BTS's popularity, which could be easily described as "out of con-trol," not only gave each one of their actions tremendous influence, but with each of these actions also came huge responsibility. Even the "LOVE MYSELF" campaign, which had started out of only the purest

38 A campaign supporting the global project "#ENDviolence," started by UNICEF in 2013, which aims to create a safe world free of violence against children and young people. The donations collected through the "LOVE MYSELF" campaign were given to help children and young people who were the victims of violence, and were also used to exhort a systematic overhaul of regional-based violence prevention.

intentions, became yet another reason that they neeeeded to take social responsibility for each of their actions and words.

SUGA says he felt a lot of pressure from the huge outpouring of interest in BTS as well as the excessive meanings assigned to them:

————It was the same then, but even now, in fact, the names attached to us are a big burden. Words like "good influence," and the responses to all the economic impact we're having . . . After all, it wasn't our intention to rise so high, and we can come tumbling down without intending to, too. It was during this time that I was most worried and bewildered.

Then, SUGA adds:

————It was like performing a perfectly synchronized dance in front of people.

On the one hand, at the beginning of the "LOVE MYSELF" campaign, Jimin also wondered what its impact on the world would be:

————I think you could call it "the power to change hearts." Actually, I once went to find RM and asked him what his thoughts were behind working on the campaign. I suddenly became really curious, which is why I went to see him. We make donations knowing it's a good thing, but I thought that the mindset behind it was more important.

The conversation Jimin shared with RM solidified his thoughts about the work he was doing:

————RM said, "If with the money I donated, or with my singing, I can make life better for just one person, not a few people but just one person, then I want to keep on doing this work." After I heard this, I think I started to see things really differently. What I'd always wanted to do was perform for people, and if for them sharing their hearts with me makes them happy and what we can do makes them feel that small emotion of, "Today was fun" and "Thanks to this, I'm in a good mood," that's something we can do.

As Jimin says, for BTS, the emotional exchange with ARMY and those listening to their music was an important driving force that allowed them to continue work on the *LOVE YOURSELF* series.

In this respect, *LOVE YOURSELF* 承 *'Her'* and the subsequent album *LOVE YOURSELF* 轉 *'Tear,'* were like the "exterior" and "interior," the "light" that leads them and the "darkness" that makes them afraid. "Pied Piper" in *LOVE YOURSELF* 承 *'Her'* depicts what the BTS fans—in other words, the people living as ARMY—might be going through, and lets the fans know that the members are aware of how they're feeling. Title song "DNA" describes BTS's meeting with ARMY as the "commandments of religion" and "providence of the universe."

j-hope reflects on how he felt around that time:

———Actually, I didn't want to let them know we were going through a difficult time emotionally. I only wanted to present a good image to them, and only good things, I didn't want to show them a shadow.

Just like j-hope wanted, with *LOVE YOURSELF* 承 *'Her,'* BTS did their best to present a fun and positive image in front of ARMY. Alongside the difficulties they were experiencing, they had also embarked on a new era of glory days, surpassing the glory days of before. ARMY were ready to enjoy *LOVE YOURSELF* 承 *'Her,'* the first album in BTS's history centered entirely around an atmosphere of brightness.

j-hope explains how, even while the group's problems were becoming more and more serious, they were able keep to working on the album:

———I don't know. Like . . . we had a slightly insufficient sense of calling? (laughs). Actually, I don't think we were people who lived life thinking about so many things. In fact, if we had thought a lot, it would have been harder, and because we were just seven really simple people, maybe that was what made it possible. The interesting thing is, at the time everyone was struggling, but everyone had a professional mindset. It's really funny. Even while struggling and going, "Dammit . . . !" we'd go, "Oh, whatever. Gotta do what we gotta do."

j-hope continues:

———Even in a situation where it would only be normal for at least one of us not to turn up, everyone turned up to every practice and every recording. There were times when we didn't look so good, but we did what we had to do.

It's difficult to put a finger on exactly how, no matter what the situation, BTS managed to do their work, while sending their intense love to ARMY and demonstrating how trustworthy they were. Maybe it was because BTS and ARMY had always gone through everything together, or perhaps it was the members' inborn nature, or because they'd naturally communicated and shared their emotions with their fans from the very beginning.

However, what's clear is that the will that allowed them to train, and to create songs and performances no matter what, brought the *LOVE YOURSELF* series into new territory.

The Joy of Love

Despite everything the BTS members were going through, the *LOVE YOURSELF* series meant something important to them.

Their popularity—which had exploded through 2015 to early

2017—turned everything BTS and Big Hit Entertainment had wanted into a reality. Simply put, Big Hit Entertainment music producer Pdogg was able to buy the same equipment used by the sound engineers in America when producing the *LOVE YOURSELF* series and install it in his own studio. With this foundation, BTS could not only set the direction they wanted for the album's overall sound, but also draw up a concrete picture for each song.

Though "DNA," the title song of *LOVE YOURSELF* 承 *'Her,'* is a dance music song accompanied by intense choreography, it describes the love between the narrator and their counterpart as a cosmic relationship. "DNA"'s sound aligns with this and maintains the intensity of the beat while also creating a sense of space through the reverb. The proportions occupied by each of the sounds are then reduced, and a variety of noises then fill that space, move, and spread out in all directions, creating a space that almost seems to express the mystery of the cosmos.

It could be said that this sound direction is what tells, through music, the stories flowing through the album as a whole, almost like the original soundtrack to a film. While *THE MOST BEAUTIFUL MOMENT IN LIFE PT.1*'s "Intro : The most beautiful moment in life" and *THE MOST BEAUTIFUL MOMENT IN LIFE PT.2*'s "INTRO : Never Mind" both take sounds directly from the spatial background— the basketball being bounced around a court, an arena full of screaming fans—in the *LOVE YOURSELF* series, BTS were able to express a more abstract concept of space through their desired sound.

The opening songs to *LOVE YOURSELF* 承 *'Her,'* "Intro : Seren-dipity"˙ and *LOVE YOURSELF* 轉 *'Tear,'* "Intro : Singularity"˙˙ present opposing images of love, and their sounds create entirely different spa-tial atmospheres.

It is Jimin who sings "Intro : Serendipity," and he expresses his love for someone as the "providence of the universe," referring to himself as "your flower": here, sounds as bright and light as the lyrics are arranged in every part of the space, and the slow beat makes it seem almost as if Jimin is dancing inside a flower bed.

"Intro : Singularity," on the other hand, is a song about the pain of love, and is centered around a low and heavy beat, creating a dark and cramped sense of space. V, who sings, emanates two opposite poles of emotion, and creates an atmosphere almost like a one-person play.

On top of their technological capabilities that allowed them to re-alize everything they wanted, BTS's popularity in the US—which had begun to grow with *THE MOST BEAUTIFUL MOMENT IN LIFE* se-ries and had continued to do so through to the 2017 BBMAs—allowed them to collaborate with a wider variety of artists. In *LOVE YOURSELF* 承 *'Her'*'s "Best Of Me," BTS collaborated with the Chainsmokers' An-drew Taggart, who'd held the number one spot on the Billboard Hot 100 for twelve weeks running with "Closer" (Feat. Halsey), while Steve Aoki, who had also remixed "MIC Drop," produced *LOVE YOURSELF* 承 *'Her'*'s "The Truth Untold" (Feat. Steve Aoki).

BTS's popularity in the US allowed them to collaborate with artists who were the trendsetters of American pop music, and BTS used this opportunity to include a wider variety of sounds through more complex methods in their albums. BTS, who had created Korean idol music with a hip-hop sound, were now able to capture the contemporary trends of the American pop music sound, too. Though a mix of sounds from various genres, "DNA" is at the same time upbeat pop—you could even call it easy listening. It was yet another landmark demonstrating that BTS had arrived somewhere new.

It was BTS's unique way of working that allowed them to finish work on *LOVE YOURSELF* 承 *'Her'* and *LOVE YOURSELF* 轉 *'Tear,'* regardless of their situation. For example, in "DNA"'s choreography,* similar to what the sound does, there is not only movement left and right across the stage, but the moment the beat drops, for example, there is a sudden withdrawal backward, creating three-dimensional movement. The choreography creates a three-dimensional feeling, not only thanks to the spaciousness of the stage, but through continuous movement in all directions. This was yet a new style of performance, different from that of "Burning Up (FIRE)," which mobilized dancers on a large scale, and also from that of "Spring Day," which fused modern dance elements with an idol group dance routine.

The choreography was, unsurprisingly, difficult, and even as the problems within BTS gradually bubbled to the surface, the group was still coming up with the best possible end product. j-hope comments on BTS's capabilities during that period:

———It was when we debuted that we practiced the most. Practicing step-by-step, we each learned what we needed to adjust and what we needed to do. By *LOVE YOURSELF*, it was possible to only practice for the length of time in which we could fully concentrate. Three or four hours? If it was a bit longer, we would practice only for five or six. We had that kind of teamwork.

The members, having made it through a wave of personal concerns following the success of *WINGS*, demonstrated their expanded capabilities in *LOVE YOURSELF* 承 *'Her'* through a variety of methods.

Carrying on from *WINGS'* "Lie," Jimin continued to show his presence as a solo artist through "Intro : Serendipity,"· Jimin says:

———First, even when deciding the key, I discussed with Slow Rabbit, who I worked on the song with, for around two days. Going, "Should we raise it a bit? Lower it?" We kept debating how we could make the song feel lighter and breezier.

As well as this, during his performances of "Intro : Serendipity" at concerts, and so on, Jimin also made use of the modern dance elements he'd learned.

RM, meanwhile, had captured an overall theme for the *LOVE YOURSELF* 承 *'Her'* album's song lyrics. He recalls:

———As a comparison, I thought of this album as that moment of first meeting someone as well as pushing the limits of fantasy. In that respect, it's a familiar subject within popular music, and tells a story of having fallen in love, so much so that you could call it sacred, and it was actually pleasant to make. It was like painting a canvas pink and drawing a picture on top of it. Actually, when we were making the album, we went to the BBMAs for the first time, too, and it was enjoyable.

Of course, just as for every one of BTS's previous albums, work on this one wasn't all smooth sailing. Humbly, Jimin was also concerned about how he would pull off the lyrics to "Intro : Serendipity." Jimin smiles and says:

———I didn't understand "I'm your calico cat" or "You're my penicillium," and so I asked RM. I asked him, imagine you had a girlfriend and she called you "mold," would you feel good? (laughs). But I learned it was discovered by chance that you could get penicillin from penicillium, and so I thought that the lyrics fell into place well. And so, I felt I could sing it with a comfortable heart.

After "Intro : Serendipity," a rather difficult problem awaited the following song, "DNA," as you might expect for a title song. As soon as they'd come up with the sound of "DNA"—in which a whistling and an acoustic guitar instill a refreshing atmosphere, alongside a trap beat and EDM elements—it was clear that they wouldn't come up with anything better. This was the bright atmosphere of BTS, who were finally singing about the joy of love, and yet they'd still kept their unique toughness alive. However, finding a melody to match this amazing arrangement proved incredibly difficult. Jimin recalls:

———"DNA"? I remember it being really funny. We were at the height of preparations for the album, and Bang Si-Hyuk wrote the melody, but it was really bad (laughs).

Jimin continues, and, for some reason, looks to be enjoying himself more than usual:

————When I heard it, I thought, 'Oh no, this isn't good.' We had to tell Bang Si-Hyuk, right? I was the first one to say straight up, "I don't like it." At the time, we were getting ready to film a music video, my hair and makeup were being checked, and the members were all together in the training room, when we heard the melody. Between us we went, "What's this? This is bad," "This is unbelievable," "We need to tell him we can't use this" (laughs). So, RM told the company, and I was scheduled for a recording and went to the company, too.

Bang Si-Hyuk, having been informed of what the members thought, went into the studio while Jimin was mid-recording.

————He looks at me and asks, "Do you not like it either?" To be honest, it was really stressful (laughs). That was when I felt it. 'Ah, our leader RM really has got it tough.'

However, it seems that Jimin's resolve didn't weaken in the slightest:

————When Bang Si-Hyuk did that, I panicked, but what was I supposed to do? I say, "Yes," and he tells me to go home for the day. That I didn't need to do the recording, and to go home.

That single word, "Yes," changed a lot of things. Bang Si-Hyuk rewrote the melody for "DNA," and this is the version we hear today. Immediately after the song's release, BTS entered the Billboard Hot 100 singles chart for the first time in their history—they were only the second Korean artists to do this—at number 85. The music video for "DNA" hit 100 million views in only around twenty-four days, record-breaking within K-pop history at the time.

Not only was this an interesting episode, but the way the members expressed their opinions of "DNA" also reveals how BTS had changed. Bang Si-Hyuk was their producer, but was at the same time their teacher, who offered up the vision for the group and had instructed them on all they knew about music and dance. The members, however, now had their own clear views on the songs Bang Si-Hyuk created. They had made it through all the troubles that come with success, and at some point, their abilities, as well as their views on work, had developed dramatically.

Starting with "Intro : Serendipity," and followed by "DNA," "Best Of Me" and "Dimple," the first four songs of *LOVE YOURSELF* 承 *'Her'* capture the butterflies and joy of love, as well as a passionate confession, something BTS had never done before in their music. These songs capture the joy of love under a single theme, and each one portrays a different moment and emotion. While "DNA" depicts the butterflies and delight, which can even feel like nerves, of a love for someone you believe to be your destiny, "Best Of Me" talks about unconditional passionate love, and "Dimple" contains every kind of praise for the one you love.

BTS were ready to express all these emotions of love. The recording process, as Jimin describes it, hints at how *LOVE YOURSELF* 承 *'Her'* became the album that really kicked off their success worldwide:

———All of the songs in the album are cheery, but they each need to be cheery in a different way, right? I felt this whenever we were recording, and I found that the lyrics helped so much. I also used my imagination a lot while singing . . . And there's no doubt that it sounds more pleasant if you smile when you sing. If you do, it really feels like you're excited when you're singing, and so we adjusted the amount we smiled when we recorded each song. "Oh, for this song, we should smile only half of the time," "For this song, we should smile a lot when we sing," like that. Each time, it was the lyrics that helped the most. RM wrote a lot of the lyrics for the album, and there are some really beautiful ones.

All the conditions were set, and the members were ready to show off the best of their abilities. This was the product of their attitude, to always turn up at the training room, no matter what emotions they were feeling in the moment.

While making *LOVE YOURSELF* 承 *'Her,'* however, the problems that had been giving them a hard time psychologically were eating away at BTS. As mentioned earlier, SUGA had been overwhelmed by the outpouring of interest in the group. From one end, the attacks were still coming, while there were yet others who were supporting them with everything they had. The people around him, including the other members and ARMY, were the only ones SUGA could trust. He says:

———I thought a lot more about people. I learned how cunning and cruel some can be. So from around then onward, I didn't look much at the responses to us online. I tried hard to regain peace of mind. Even if there was something good about BTS on the news, I deliberately didn't look at it. I didn't want to get caught up in that.

In "Outro : Her,"˙ SUGA captures exactly how he felt at the time:

Perhaps I'm your truth and lie
Perhaps I'm your love and hate
Perhaps I'm your nemesis and friend
Your heaven and hell, pride and disgrace

. . .

I always struggle to become the best for you
I hope you never know this side of me

———What I wanted to say through the *LOVE YOURSELF* 承 *'Her'* album as a whole, is summed up exactly in the lyrics I wrote for this song. One person's love can be another person's hate, and the occupation called idol can be a source of pride to one person and of humiliation to another. I'm not perfect, but I'm working hard for you. You can't know about the effort I'm making, though. I'm talking about things like this in the song, right? I don't want to reveal the underside of my emotions, I'm trying my best and I'd prefer you not to know that, beneath it all, I'm struggling like this . . . You could even say that every other thing I wrote in the album was in order to say this.

At the time of working on the *LOVE YOURSELF* series, BTS had fallen into a cruel irony. Like SUGA says, even though BTS weren't perfect, they were doing their best for the people who loved them. Perhaps they would have felt guilty if they hadn't done their best. The group—having made their debut while essentially hanging off the cliff of the idol industry—were reaching as far as the heavens, thanks to ARMY. BTS were now in a position to pay back the love they'd received.

However, this success—so incomprehensible it felt as if the whole world was playing a trick on them—made it difficult for them to fully focus on returning the love they'd been given.

The November 2017 AMAs were when the psychological pressure and confusion really amplified for SUGA. BTS were the first ever Korean artist to be invited and were the only artist from Asia to perform that year. Before they went onstage to perform "DNA" from *LOVE YOURSELF* 承 *'Her,'* SUGA had been extremely nervous:

———It was probably the most nervous I'd been before a performance
    in my life. I was white as a sheet. My hands were properly shaking.

For SUGA, who was beginning to meet a future that had no answer sheet, the AMAs were when his anxiety had fully become reality:

———The gap between the ideal and reality was the hardest. Usually,
    the ideal is so high, and in most cases, you suffer because reality
    can't keep up with it. But we were the opposite. It was like . . .
    the ideal was beating up my reality?

Getting Tickets

The AMAs became another turning point for BTS. About two months before, immediately after its release, *LOVE YOURSELF* 承 *'Her'* had hit number one on the iTunes charts across seventy-three countries and regions. Soon, Twitter and YouTube were none other than BTS's home ground, and the group was making waves across countless countries.

On the other hand, the records they'd broken—including their first attendance at the May 2017 BBMAs, and their number seven on the Billboard 200 with *LOVE YOURSELF* 承 *'Her'*—reveal that such waves were now also occurring within the world's largest music market of America. Now, with their performance of "DNA" at the AMAs, BTS were showing America what they were really made of.

RM, reflecting on the situation at the time, sums it up with a simple analogy:

———"We got tickets."

At the time of the AMAs, however, BTS had no idea what would happen at this place they'd managed to "get tickets" to. Jimin says:

———Actually, I don't know much about award ceremonies like the BB-MAs (laughs). So, when we went to the BBMAs for the first time, I asked the hyoungs what kind of award ceremony it was, and how big.

Jung Kook wasn't very familiar with the US music award ceremonies, either:

———I knew this was something really impressive, and understood that it was something to be really thankful for, that it was an honor . . . What I felt personally was really simple. When the staff briefed us beforehand about various things, I just said, "Sounds good," that was all. And at the awards ceremony, I got so much confidence from the fans cheering us on, it was so good. We just had to do a good job at what was handed to us, then leave the stage.

For Jung Kook, it was outside of the award ceremony stage that he felt the pressure:

———Interviews were hard. My English isn't good and so it was difficult to understand the conversations. RM had to do the lion's share of the talking, and I felt bad, I wanted to help out in some way, but I couldn't.

Immediately after their appearance at the AMAs, *LOVE YOURSELF* 承 *'Her'* reentered the Billboard 200 at number 198. Then, a few days after the AMAs, Steve Aoki's remix of "MIC Drop" entered the Billboard Hot 100 at number 28, before staying on the chart for ten weeks running.

As soon as they got their tickets to enter the American market, BTS began to expand their position in the US with staggering force. At the same time, the members were being flooded with work with a similar staggering force. And that was in another language, too.

Chaos and Fear

———To be honest, I had never felt as much pressure going onstage as I did at the AMAs. Though I was always nervous, of course. But I found the interviews and talk shows so difficult.

Here, j-hope is discussing his memories of when they really started to become active in America. He reflects:

———If I was good at English and could express my thoughts and attitudes properly, I would have enjoyed myself more. This problem really held me back. I think I was okay, despite this, because I believed that performing onstage, and even the nerves and anxiety, they were so precious that I had to accept all of it. There were things where I was like, "Okay, yeah, let's give it a try!" But the other things beyond the stage, what I felt about that was just different. For example, when I was asked questions like "How does it feel to have so many fans who love you?" if I were to express it in Korean, I could convey how I felt from the heart, but the language is different . . . At times like that there's an overall flow to the program and there are basic comments you have to say and trying to familiarize myself and memorize all of that, I could sense that I was in over my head.

As these situations continued, j-hope realized that something was becoming more and more difficult:

———When I don't have enough mental space, I burn out. Talk shows, the red carpet, and endless interviews . . . I felt myself burning out as a result of these things.

This wasn't only about the pressure of a busy schedule in an unfamiliar environment. Repeatedly finding himself needing to at least do something, but being unable to contribute a thing, j-hope drew in on himself:

———It was frustrating. I'm whipping myself to at least do something, but I can't. I do feel the necessity to study English, but seeing myself not able to do it properly in practice, I think, 'Wow, I seriously . . . I can't believe this is all I'm capable of,' and berate myself. If I'm lacking in something onstage, I can resolve it by practicing, but it doesn't work like that for studying English. Each time, in the hotel room I thought to myself, 'Oh, so guess this is all I amount to.'

One of the reasons why BTS could keep moving forward in any crisis, was that, in the end, victory or defeat would always be decided onstage. No matter how disadvantageous their position, and even when it felt like the whole world hated them, all they needed to do was prepare a good song and a great performance, and give it their all onstage.

However, after their performance at the AMAs, their activities in America sent them into chaos. Given all the members other than RM found it difficult to give interviews in English, it wasn't easy for them to speak their opinions frankly. It was also hard to put across their unique interview style, in which they talk among themselves, allowing their teamwork to come across naturally. And so, the interviews became an even bigger burden to RM.

j-hope pays tribute to RM's role at the time:

————If it wasn't for RM, we would have been in serious trouble (laughs). It would have been difficult for us to get so popular in the US, in my view. RM's role is huge.

For RM, the first time he had to give an interview in English in the US was like suddenly being thrown into a battlefield. He recalls:

————It was our first time at the BBMAs, and they tell us we're going to be interviewed live for a whole hour. Out of nowhere. That we're going to be interviewed by eleven US broadcasters. And in ten minutes from now. It felt like I was having a mental breakdown. All the interviewers had different accents and it was difficult to pick up what they were saying . . . Even so, I got through it.

Recalling that time, he pulls a quizzical smile and says:

————Then, after getting through it, I realized, 'Okay, we're really in big trouble. There's just no going back now.'

English wasn't the only problem. This was of course the first time a Korean idol group had become so popular in America, and the US media didn't only ask the group about BTS, but about the idol industry, and the Korean popular music industry as a whole.

When responding, RM had to trim his message to make it brief and so as not to cause misunderstanding. If the meaning didn't come across properly, questions would arise that could cause problems for both Korea and America.

————Until around the end of 2018, I found it stressful every time. I couldn't always come up with answers just like that. So, I learned

English really as a matter of "survival." I still find it difficult when technical topics come up. And for sensitive questions, I didn't think that just avoiding answering left a good impression. So, I had to respond tactfully without being provocative or causing misunderstanding, and I had to do that in English. Truly . . . there were a few really hairy moments.

Each and every moment in which RM had to speak English in front of the media was critical, and he needed the wisdom to make it through those critical moments.

Now some time has passed, RM summarizes the concerns he went through back then as follows:

——Because I always thought that, when it came to interviews, I had to be the one to go ahead and open the door, it felt like I was carrying out assignments as they came at me, and I was overwhelmed. So, I didn't have the space to think of things like, 'Uh . . . this is getting big,' 'Whereabouts are we now?,' 'Right, should we take a quick look around us?' I was going, 'I don't know what this is, but I have to do it quickly,' 'I have so much to do.' Tomorrow I needed to do interviews on the red carpet with twenty media outlets, but I couldn't think about whether it was hard or whatever. I needed to learn one more expression and do the interview well . . . It all flew by as I went, 'I'll give it a go for now!'

Then, after getting through it, I
realized, 'Okay, we're really in big
trouble. There's just no going back
now.'

—RM

On April 13, 2018, Jimin filmed a vlog. In the video, uploaded to You-Tube almost a year later on February 26, 2019, Jimin opens up about the mental anguish he was going through. He had come to consider what his "dreams and happiness" were, and a few months earlier at the beginning of 2018, all of the members, not just him, were exhausted physically and mentally. When asked about that time, Jimin admits:

――I felt like that for a while as we went from 2017 to 2018. But I
　think the other members probably weren't aware back then.

Jimin continues:

――One time, I grew dark for no reason . . . In the accommodations,
　there was a three-meter-square room, and I once went in there
　alone and didn't come back out. I don't know what I was think-
　ing in doing that, I don't know why I was being like that, but it
　was a period where I just suddenly became depressed. And then,
　I began to question myself, 'Why am I putting my life on the line
　like this?' and that calmed me down a bit. I think I was locking
　myself away in that room.

Jimin doesn't know himself exactly why he got lost in those worries. However, what's clear is that these complex emotions had been building up over a long period of time. Jimin reflects:

――Until around then, we were really busy. Every day we just worked,
　and powering through like that, I guess you could say I had

doubts. It was like . . . we'd started to feel the things we'd lost in becoming singers, celebrities. I often thought, 'Is this happiness?' and particularly, feeling people's gazes, not just those of ARMY, the thoughts grew bigger.

"G.C.F. in Tokyo (Jung Kook & Jimin),"[39]* released on YouTube on November 8, 2017, is a record left by Jung Kook and Jimin from the period that was hardest for them mentally:

———In the accommodations, us two went to bed the latest. We liked hanging out when we were awake. Jung Kook and I had lots of similarities in things like that. So, we were like, "Should we go on a trip?" "How about Japan?" and we actually went.

When the two first revealed the plans for their trip, Bang Si-Hyuk and the other BTS members were initially concerned. BTS were already international stars. The others couldn't help but be worried for their safety. In the end, the two were helped by a Big Hit Entertainment employee in Japan, and taking the necessary safety provisions, they left for their trip. Jung Kook looks back on that time:

———When we arrived in Japan, an employee from the company was at the airport. They'd already got a taxi, and as soon as we arrived at the airport, we zoomed out with our luggage and got in the taxi as if we were fleeing and left. There were fans there.

---

39 An acronym of "Golden Closet Film," "G.C.F" is a series of video content filmed and edited by Jung Kook himself. Record footage in the form of a vlog, it was largely produced and uploaded to the BANGTANTV YouTube channel between 2017 and 2019.

From what Jung Kook says, it seems that their concerns were materializing. However, it was Halloween at the time, and that gave them an unexpected gift. Jung Kook smiles and says:

———We went around wearing masks from the movie *Scream*, with black fabric covering our bodies, and black umbrellas. When people came over, we took pictures, it was fun. We went around people watching, and when we went to a restaurant, we took off our masks and ate.

Jung Kook discusses these memories, and talks about the joy that came from this simple experience:

———We were walking down an alley, there weren't many cars, there was the light from the streetlamps . . . It was really beautiful. And then Jimin said his feet hurt and so we walked slowly. Those simple things were so fun.

Jimin expresses his thanks to the fans for respecting the pair's privacy:

———Actually, we came across a lot of fans who recognized us. But they were considerate of us, and we could go around comfortably.

He then shares his thoughts on the trip:

———It was so much fun. It was so fun that I wanted to go again. But doing it once, I realized it wasn't a good idea (laughs). Too many people recognized us.

They were two guys in their twenties who had traveled to so many countries, yet couldn't comfortably go on a trip. Jimin and Jung Kook's trip allowed them brief moments to re-experience the simplicity of daily life, but also made the life they were living as members of BTS really hit home.

Jung Kook in particular felt huge pressure as an artist the whole world was watching:

—I can say that this was the time I was most overwhelmed. I loved performing, singing, and dancing. However, the occupation of a singer means being in the public eye. So lots of people already know my face, and it isn't easy to do everything I want however I please. Other than singing or meeting the fans, I sometimes have to do things I'm not too keen on . . . I'm well aware that I can't avoid doing these things. But occasionally it got really hard all of a sudden. If I had seen the time spent performing or working on music as precious like I do now, I wouldn't have thought like that, and I think it was because I didn't like music, singing, and dancing back then as much as I do now. So sometimes I told RM that I was struggling.

SUGA explains Jung Kook's position at the time:

—He especially began this work in his mid-teens. I also started out as a teenager, and you don't generally find what you want to do at that age. Jung Kook grew up to be someone who lives his life shattering every ordinary way of doing things. After all that working, I think he needed time to look back on what he was doing, what he was thinking, and what he was feeling.

For Jung Kook, who since his middle school years had given everything he had to become a singer at Big Hit Entertainment, it's fair to say that he experienced the world through the six hyoungs. The great success Jung Kook had achieved, and the increase in the things he "had to do" that came alongside that success, as well as the things he "had to watch out for"—having just entered his twenties, it was only natural he would find these things tough.

As RM reflects, all these complex situations culminated into a crisis for BTS:

————It was the group's first crisis. Not because of what was happening outside, but because of what was happening inside the team, the real crisis that we felt firsthand.

The problems that had begun internally for each of the members became bigger and bigger and started to rock the group. What was taking place in SUGA's mind and body was an omen for the upcoming crisis. Around when BTS's popularity had soared following the AMAs, given that SUGA had experienced so much success, he was paradoxically suffering from even greater anxiety because of a future he couldn't see. SUGA recalls:

————The way I felt then . . . 'The way people treat me is going to change now,' I didn't think this in the least. 'I just hope this scary situation is over as soon as possible.' I couldn't be glad in the moments I was supposed to be glad, and I couldn't be happy in the moments I was supposed to be happy.

SUGA, who went through day after day feeling like this, ended up getting insomnia, and continued sleepless nights ensued.

———— . . . Wow.

Recalling that time, when each of the members were struggling with their own problems, j-hope lets out a word that seems to encapsulate every one of their emotions. Before long, carefully, he continues:

————In a way, we spent more time together than with our families, and this was when we needed to support one another, and was the first time we'd spent so long in this kind of situation . . . It was frustrating and we began to struggle. About each other, we thought, 'Why's he being like that?,' 'Why does he see the problem that way?,' and those emotions had piled up, I think.

'I hope this scary situation is over as soon as possible.'

I couldn't be glad in the moments I was supposed to be glad, and I couldn't be happy in the moments I was supposed to be happy.

—SUGA

It was a single incident that sent all the members' problems bubbling to the surface. BTS's contract renewal.

To Do, or Not to Do

Korean idol groups' contract renewal is one of the most unusual things about the industry. As can be seen from BTS's debut process, in the case of most Korean idol groups, their companies invest a huge amount of capital and people power in production. It is also the company's job to bring together the members to form the group, and the members of course sign a contract with the company.

For idols that have debuted, the contract with their company generally lasts seven years. In 2009, the Korea Fair Trade Commission established a "standard exclusive contract for performers" so that popular culture artists, including idols, could protect their rights and interests when signing to a management company.

When one of their artists is just starting out, they are signed under contractual conditions beneficial to the company, and the company wants to maintain these conditions for as long as possible—exploitation because of this is not uncommon. The seven-year contract was one of the things that arose not only as a solution to this problem, but also a result of the search for contractual terms that allow the management company to expect a reasonable profit in the case that the artist is successful.

However, while the Korean idol industry was growing at a rapid pace, the issue of contract renewal in the seventh year became a drama that got everyone—the company, the group, as well as the fans—worked up. At the turn of the new millennium, large management companies like SM, YG, and JYP had all achieved a level of success that made failure of any of their debuted artists the exception. They therefore wanted to recontract their artists, even if that meant changing the conditions of the contract to a certain extent in order to benefit the artist. However, the artist may ask for even better conditions, and satisfaction with the financial terms is only the beginning. Even within a single group, each member may want different things depending on their personality, preferences, and style of working.

Most group members who were offered a contract renewal after seven years had been successful enough to have already achieved fame and fortune in their twenties. No matter how good the contract conditions were, they could very easily break away from the group and pursue a solo career, or even leave the entertainment industry entirely if they so chose. Or perhaps they had bad blood with the company or the other members and didn't want to renew. This is why it is uncommon for all members of a successful idol group to renew their contracts. Their love for the fans aside, the members can't help but consider their own lives before contract renewal.

Decision day came earlier for BTS. In 2018, around two years before their contract was due to end, Big Hit Entertainment offered to re-sign the members. The company's outlook was that, following the *LOVE YOURSELF* series, BTS would be able to do a worldwide stadium tour. Given that it was necessary to consider the schedule several years in advance, a decision needed to be made regarding contract renewal. In re-signing the group, the company could also offer the members conditions better than that of their first contract sooner rather than later.

In the end, not only did all seven members re-sign, but they also agreed to a seven-year contract, longer than their first contract, which had in fact ended up as five years. Considering that the period for renewed contracts is generally shorter than the first contract, this was a case almost unparalleled within the Korean idol industry.

RM, recalling the situation at the time, says:

——When we said we'd recontracted for seven years, the people around us said we were out of our minds. It was because we were still clueless, they said (laughs). I was told that a lot. No one does that, they said. They're right. No one does that. But at the time, where would we have worked if not for Big Hit? We had that kind of trust in them.

However, it was the period before the contract was signed that was the problem. It just so happened that the contract negotiations, between an artist and company who trusted one another, began during the most difficult time of the BTS members' entire careers.

Whether looking at BTS's popularity, the financial gains that both the group and company were set to make, or the relationship between the members, there was no reason for them not to recontract. Paradoxically, however, this "relationship" became their dilemma.

——At the end of the day, BTS has seven members. I believed the team couldn't stay together if even one of us left.

What Jin mentions is none other than BTS's identity. The rapper hyoungs playing music to the younger ones and teaching them hiphop, coming together and responding when one of them was slighted, discussing together in the tiny studio and creating song after song. The idea of one leaving the group, while the remaining members stayed together, had never even crossed their minds.

Jin expresses what BTS means to him:

————BTS is me, and I am BTS, that's how I see it. Sometimes I'm asked questions like, "Don't you feel the pressure with BTS's success?" but just . . . It's like this. When I go out, everyone goes, "Oh, it's BTS." I am part of BTS. So I don't think there was pressure exactly. For me, that kind of question is similar to asking someone going about their life, "You started out as the youngest in the company and then got a promotion . . . don't you feel the pressure living like that?" I'm just living my life as part of BTS, and lots of people are liking the fact I'm doing it.

However, their individual concerns as people, not one member of a group, did not stop.

SUGA explains their mindset at the time:

————We wondered whether we should quit.

He continues:

————The people around us said, "Everything's going so well, there's no reason not to." They seemed to think we were making a fuss over nothing (laughs). That was probably because they hadn't experienced our situation for themselves. But we were so afraid. At the time, I was a negative and avoidant individual, and so a big part of me wanted to run away. Every moment something would come at us, I'd have no time to reflect on myself . . . I think that was why I kept becoming more negative.

For SUGA, his welling anxiety was another dilemma that was inevitable given BTS's success:

————There's always a choice to be made, but I have to make the best one. And I believe that we have gotten here by making the best of the best choices. At times, we even made the second-best option into the best. If we were told to get "100," we were the kids who would go and get "120," after all. However, RM and I recently said a similar thing, "Our capabilities, I don't think they're enough to accommodate something as huge as this" (laughs). At the time, we didn't think we'd be able to do things like going around the whole world performing concerts in stadiums.

The group called BTS, the members' affection for one another, the weight of the name "BTS": anxiety about what they have to endure carrying all this on their shoulders drove the seven members into a complex emotion they couldn't put into words.

Jimin describes the atmosphere in the group at the time:

——We were having a really hard time emotionally, and everyone was incredibly exhausted. And in that situation, the conversation of contract renewal comes up . . . We were consumed by negative emotion.

V summarizes that time as follows:

——We were working on *LOVE YOURSELF*, but we couldn't love ourselves.

He adds:

——All of us got really on edge, and seeing each other like that, we ended up worrying about whether we should continue what we were doing. We all had so little space to think. That made it really hard.

As V explains, all the members had grown sensitive, and it was an atmosphere in which it was difficult for anyone to be the first to say "Let's" or "Let's not" recontract.

j-hope recalls the sense of crisis he felt at the time:

———It was hell. During our activities with BTS, this was really the first time there'd been such a serious atmosphere that we weren't sure if we could keep going. So when we practiced, we got so exhausted. There was a mountain of things we needed to do right away, and we couldn't concentrate during practice. This wasn't the kind of people we were at all . . . I really believed that time to be a crisis. At the end of the day, we had to go onstage, and we had to work. We were in a stupor.

Magic Shop

The problems rising to the surface alongside the contract renewal issue developed into a more and more extreme situation. Jimin explains how severe the mood among the group was at the time:

———The group itself was in a pretty dangerous situation. There was even talk of not making the new album.

Looking at BTS's history up until *LOVE YOURSELF* 承 '*Her*,' the idea of BTS not releasing another album was unimaginable. They had always released new songs and performed no matter the situation. This time, however, was different. RM even called his parents in advance to let them know there might not be another album. If the members ended up not renewing their contracts, Jin explains, he had even been considering leaving the entertainment industry entirely:

———My position was that, if anyone left, I would step away from the entertainment business and do something else for a living. I had planned to rest for a bit and think about what I wanted to do next.

However, what Jin was really struggling with wasn't the group's uncertain future:

———I felt really guilty about the fans. I hadn't been able to thank them or love them from my heart . . . I had the thought, 'Maybe my smile right now is fake?' It was the fans I felt most guilty about back then.

Between *LOVE YOURSELF* 承 *'Her'* and then *LOVE YOURSELF* 轉 *'Tear,'* which almost didn't make it out into the world, BTS did concerts, appeared on TV music programs and end of year award ceremonies, and updated the fans on their latest news through V Live.

Standing before ARMY, even when on the brink of catastrophe, worrying despite this that the emotion they are showing them might be fake: this was exactly what made *LOVE YOURSELF* 轉 *'Tear'*'s title song "FAKE LOVE"· "real."

For you I could pretend like I was happy when I was sad

"FAKE LOVE" is not, as the title would suggest, about fake, or false, love. As the opening lyrics convey, the song is about the intentions and concerns of a person hiding their pain before the one they love, trying to show them only the best of themselves. On the surface, these lyrics might appear to tell a universal story of the pain of love, but they also represent the BTS members' minds at the time, standing before ARMY.

LOVE YOURSELF 轉
'Tear'

THE 3RD FULL-LENGTH ALBUM
2018. 5. 18

TRACK

01 Intro : Singularity
02 FAKE LOVE
03 The Truth Untold (Feat. Steve Aoki)
04 134340
05 Paradise
06 Love Maze

07 Magic Shop
08 Airplane pt.2
09 Anpanman
10 So What
11 Outro : Tear

VIDEO

 COMEBACK TRAILER : Singularity

 "FAKE LOVE" MV

 "FAKE LOVE" MV TEASER 1

 "FAKE LOVE" MV (Extended ver.)

 "FAKE LOVE" MV TEASER 2

In *LOVE YOURSELF 轉 'Tear'*'s first song, "Intro : Singularity,"˙ the final lyrics go, "Tell me / Even if the pain was fake / What should I have done," while the next song, "FAKE LOVE," opens with, "For you I could pretend like I was happy when I was sad." These lyrics are saying that, no matter what pain the person is going through, they can show a happy face in front of the one they love.

Then, in the following song, "The Truth Untold" (Feat. Steve Aoki),˙˙ the lyrics go, "I'm afraid / I feel small / I'm so afraid / Will you end up leaving me as well / I put on a mask and go to you again." These lyrics tell the story of someone who is afraid that the one they love will turn away if they see their true face, and so, they wear a mask.

There are various possible interpretations of "mask" here, but from BTS's perspective, the mask could be the image they present as idols before the fans. Even in the midst of painful situations, if it was ARMY they were going to see, BTS worked hard to show only their best selves.

Jimin discusses his mindset at the time of making the *LOVE YOUR-SELF 轉 'Tear'* album, including the song "FAKE LOVE":

——Maybe our situation followed the album and became like that too, but it was always like that (laughs). Whenever we dealt with a dark topic, we really did end up going through that kind of thing. Or perhaps we went through it and that was why those topics came up.

It hadn't been planned for *LOVE YOURSELF 轉 'Tear'* to reflect this state of crisis. Of course, even since their debut when they sang about their lives as trainees, each of BTS's albums had reflected their present. In this respect, after BTS had success with *THE MOST BEAUTIFUL MOMENT IN LIFE* series and *WINGS*, with *LOVE YOURSELF* 轉 *'Tear,'* they had intended to express their love for the fans, and on the other side of that love, to reveal who they were as stars and as individuals.

However, no one expected that this "other side" would be a situation of psychological pain for all the members, in which the group was in danger of splitting up. Perhaps Bang Si-Hyuk had decided the direction for the album's production keeping all of this in mind. Ahead of the release of *LOVE YOURSELF* 轉 *'Tear,'* "FAKE LOVE"'s first teaser video˚ opens with the following sentence:

> *Magic shop is a psychodramatic technique*
> *that exchanges fear for a positive attitude.*

"A psychodramatic technique / that exchanges fear for a positive attitude." If we think about the problems BTS were going through, it even seems as if Bang Si-Hyuk was proposing the *LOVE YOURSELF* 轉 *'Tear'* album as a process of psychological treatment for the members. In fact, during the album's production, the BTS members had poured out their emotions without restraint. SUGA, who had fallen into a slump, became intensely immersed in his situation, and wrote songs in the midst of this:

————For songs I empathized with, I really did write them in thirty minutes. Thirty minutes to write one verse. Sometimes the recording was over within half an hour. Even when it was really difficult to write a song, when it came down to it, I went, "Pfft, whatever! Just do it!" Whether the song would get released or not, I decided to write it first and think about that later. Each and every moment was agonizing, writing it down line by line. It was so agonizing that I would drink and then go ahead and write while drunk, too . . .

One of the songs SUGA wrote through this process was *LOVE YOURSELF* 轉 *'Tear'*'s final song, "Outro : Tear":

————The song came out of the most difficult period in my life. We weren't sure if we could keep doing this work, and like that, my weight went down to about 54 kilos. "Outro : Tear" was the song I wrote for the members at the time. There are the lyrics, "'Cause there is no such thing / as a beautiful breakup," and I really cried a lot recording that part. After writing the song, I wondered if that had really been me . . . I played it to the other members.

Ahead of production on *LOVE YOURSELF* 轉 *'Tear,'* the members were seized by fear and confusion that this work might disappear. However, like how the resulting pain pushed SUGA into a situation in which he couldn't help but create, it was when the members' emotions hit an extreme that they poured their hearts into the album.

SUGA explains what *LOVE YOURSELF* 轉 *'Tear'* meant to him:

—It's an album that captures all the intense seesawing of my emotions. Sometimes the timing just works, really just . . . the heavens make it work. When making some albums, the situation [that the album talks about] always ends up happening.

RM also recalls how he felt at the time:

—At the time, I didn't think the album would get finished. It really was extremely tough.

BTS were all in crisis, but Jimin was in the process of breaking free from his concerns a little earlier than the others:

—We all wanted to work together, and now it was so much fun being together as a group, so I hoped everyone would quickly get back to the way they were before.

Jimin, who had isolated himself in a three-meter-square room at the accommodations, says that the videos he ended up watching became the clue to heal his heart:

—Inside there I drank alone, and while I kept spending time by myself . . . I watched through all the music videos we'd filmed since our debut, and I came across a video of our fans doing a "crowd sing-along" to our song "EPILOGUE : Young Forever." Watching that, I thought, 'So this is what we worked so hard for." And, "Why did I put this emotion to one side and just forget about it?' That was when I started to recover.

It was this emotion that allowed the BTS members to go all in when it came to *LOVE YOURSELF* 轉 *'Tear'*'s production. BTS always kept on practicing and writing regardless of the situation; in the same way, though the BTS members hadn't decided whether to recontract, they were determined to finish the album no matter what and poured all their emotions into the process. j-hope says:

I saw a video of our fans doing a
"crowd sing-along."
    Watching that, I thought, 'So this
is what we worked so hard for.'
    That was when I started to recover.

—Jimin

————It was really difficult, for sure. I started this work because I liked it, but it felt like it'd actually become "work"? During this period, we all came up against things like that. This was the music we loved so much, but it'd become work. This was the dancing we loved so much, but it'd become work . . . these feelings kept colliding.

We can guess at how the BTS members managed despite everything to complete work on *LOVE YOURSELF* 轉 *'Tear,'* from j-hope's comment below:

————Actually, we worked hard preparing while thinking of the fans who loved us. At the end of the day, all of the fans' love was an opportunity for us, and while we had this opportunity, even if I was finding it quite difficult, even if my body kind of hurt and I got injured, I thought, 'Let's do this.' The members were probably thinking exactly the same.

The first part of *LOVE YOURSELF* 轉 *'Tear'*—from opening song, "Intro : Singularity," up until "FAKE LOVE," "The Truth Untold" (Feat. Steve Aoki), and so on—tells the story of a person living their life wearing a mask, and feeling the pain of being unable to be sincere in front of the one they love.

"Love Maze"' located right in the middle of the album, talks about being trapped inside a dark maze, but the chorus soon reveals the intention of never separating from the other person:

A dead end in a maze blocked in every direction
We're strolling through this abyss

. . .

Take my ay ay hand, don't let go
Lie ay ay in this maze
My ay ay don't ever let me get away

After "Love Maze" comes "Magic Shop," in which BTS offer comfort to the other person. Next is "Anpanman," in which BTS say that, even if they are the weakest of heroes, they will live life as heroes to someone. Finally, the album concludes with a pledge in "So What."

On days when I hate myself and want to vanish forever
Let's make a door within your heart
Through that door, this place awaits you
It's okay to believe in the magic shop that will comfort you
—"Magic Shop"*

I'll fall again
I'll make mistakes again
I'll be covered with mud again
But have faith in me because I'm a hero
—"Anpanman"**

Don't just stand still and worry
It's all for nothing
Let go
There's no answer yet but
You can start the fight
—"So What"*

At the beginning of the album, the sound is dark and heavy; after this, the middle section contains melodies that fans can sing along to at concerts; finally, the latter part is one you can jump up and down enthusiastically to.

Even as they were preparing for the album, BTS still hadn't decided whether to recontract. In this way, if the earlier part of the album reflects BTS's reality at the time, then the latter part represents their intentions for the future—to remain a source of strength to ARMY no matter what.

That was the reason they could somehow practice, somehow write songs, and somehow do the "album, tour, album, tour" thing and have strength to finally release a new album while also getting through all their additional engagements aside from music. Perhaps as they were finishing up the album, BTS were once again coming to understand what lay at the foundation of their work, without even realizing it. SUGA says:

———For the fans we really just feel . . . gratitude, thanks, guilt, love, all of these emotions. These are the people who've walked along-side us. I can't begin to imagine how many people encouraged us and gave us strength to get through each day. I really can't imagine, but a big concern for us is to do everything we can for them.

Our Group

Discussions surrounding BTS's contract renewal were still ongoing up until the release of *LOVE YOURSELF* 轉 *'Tear'* and their performance at the 2018 BBMAs. Aside from their desire to remain as ARMY's "Anpanman," none of their concerns had yet been resolved. Even when they'd heard the news that they would be performing at the BBMAs for the first time, they couldn't be all that pleased.

Jimin talks of how he felt while preparing for the performance:

———The atmosphere in the group was chaotic and so . . . Even though
    it was incredible that we'd get to stand on that stage for the first
    time, to be honest, I didn't feel much emotion. This was because
    I'd never struggled as much as this my whole time in BTS. In this
    moment where I should have felt so moved and glad, I didn't feel
    any of these emotions.

However, from that point onward, a change that even the BTS members hadn't expected started to occur. In contrast to the weighty atmosphere within the group, the dance practice for *LOVE YOURSELF* 轉 *'Tear'*'s title song "FAKE LOVE" was going so well you could call it smooth sailing. j-hope says:

———I think we just did it "unknowingly." We worked hard, and even
    when we were on location, we kept practicing.

j-hope smiles, a quizzical look on his face, and reflects:

————Strangely, while struggling psychologically like that . . . the quality of our performances went up. Even as we went "Ugh, this is hard," we practiced, then the practice was over, and we did another practice, like that.

Jimin remembers the atmosphere within the team at the time:

————To be honest, up until then it was a disaster. We struggled when recording, we were sluggish during practice, but we pulled ourselves together, the atmosphere was just right, and we could concentrate. It must have been a month or two before standing on that stage.

Even the members themselves say they don't know how it was possible. However, unlike at the time of their performance at the 2017 AMAs, now they were suffering their own internal problems without the mental space to feel the pressure of the gazes watching them from outside. Though we can't know whether this actually eased the pressure on them, it's clear that they were able to concentrate more while rehearsing the "FAKE LOVE" stage performance. With the BBMAs' on May 20, 2018, this small change became something meaningful.

————Oh, before going onstage that day . . . I remember for the first time in ages shouting out the chant we do before concerts. "Bangtan, Bangtan, Bangbangtan!" like this. It's like, we do it to encourage one another.

This was how j-hope remembers the situation. He continues:

————Backstage was pretty hectic at that time. There was the crew, and the artists who'd finished performing before us were going past.

In the middle of all that, we shouted out the chant to mean, "Hey, this is a live broadcast, let's do this! Let's shake off all our worries!" before going onstage.

Then, once the "FAKE LOVE" stage performance was over, Bang Si-Hyuk, who was in Korea at the time, called them on the phone and boomed:

"You lot ****ing smashed it!"

According to j-hope, Bang Si-Hyuk couldn't hide his excitement over their performance, and even swore as he shouted out. It was a sign that, unbeknownst to them, all their problems were resolving themselves. During its first week of sales, *LOVE YOURSELF* 轉 *'Tear'* became the first ever Korean album to make number one on the Billboard 200. Meanwhile, the title song "FAKE LOVE" hit number 10 on the Hot 100—the fact that its music video reached 100 million views on YouTube in about eight days, breaking their record for "DNA" by a large margin, ended up being secondary.

The BTS members—who had always practiced regardless of the situation and had happily gone onstage even when they were struggling—put all their skills into action at the decisive moment, just like they had at the 2014 MAMA Awards. It was from there that they found the clue to solving all their problems.

Tilting his head, j-hope recalls the current of change within the group after the BBMAs:

———I'm not sure exactly, either. I don't know if I was the only one who felt this, but when we were onstage, it was like . . . it happened naturally. That day, we got Bang Si-Hyuk's phone call, and each of the members let out a little smile (laughs). After that, it was like something started to "gently, gently" untangle.

Before going on stage that day . . .
    I remember for the first time in ages
shouting out the chant we do before
concerts.
    "Bangtan, Bangtan, Bangbangtan!"
like this.

—j-hope

However, not all their problems were resolved by just that one performance, of course. In giving a performance they could be proud of, they discovered the meaning of what they were each doing as individuals, and the meaning of all seven members working together. One part of this process involved the six hyoungs listening to the youngest's story:

———I'm not sure the reason. I think just, there was something I kind of didn't like.

Here, Jung Kook opens up about what was a really difficult period for him. Perhaps we should say that Jung Kook, having debuted in his teens, faced adolescence later on in life. What the hyoungs could do was lend an ear to his story and stand alongside him. Jung Kook continues:

———One time after filming, I went to drink alone, and drinking alone it was like . . . I felt so hopeless. But that was the time I was really into taking photos of this and that on my camera. And so I set up my phone camera in front of me, and spoke to myself as if I was doing a YouTube stream . . . and I was drinking at the same time. But then Jimin suddenly appeared.

Jimin explains why he turned up in front of Jung Kook:

———I was a bit worried about Jung Kook, and so I asked the staff, and they said he'd gone out for a drink. So I got in the car, too, and asked them to let me out where they'd dropped off Jung Kook. I got out and looked around, and there was a bar right in front of me. Then when I went inside, Jung Kook was alone with the camera set up, drinking. That was how we ended up talking.

It wasn't through the conversation itself where Jung Kook found any answers. He says:

————I don't remember much of what we talked about. But I was pretty moved that Jimin had come. Because he'd come to comfort me.

Jimin recalls:

————Listening to what he had to say, I learned for the first time just how much he was struggling, and I cried a lot. I'd had no idea. Jung Kook had tried not to talk about it, but the drink kicked in and he talked.

Back then, neither Jung Kook nor the six hyoungs were sure exactly what it was they needed. But with the endless gazes from outside upon them, it seems that taking time to listen to how each other were really feeling had been important. Jimin says:

————I think that at the time we needed to do a certain amount of complaining and moaning . . . In some ways, I think by doing that we were trying to perceive reality in a more detached way. And the fact that, after all, the members are right alongside each other. I realized that, and from that point onward everything sorted itself out quickly.

Jung Kook also brings up another similar episode:

————It was me and . . . Jin and Jimin, I think, the three of us went to get something to eat, and the other members turned up one by one, too. They drank with us, and then someone threw up (laughs). It was a mess. We were there crying, these people . . .

Lost in thought for a while, Jung Kook then continues:

————We work together, and this is a business . . . right? However, it's more than that for us. I can't think lightly of them, they are so precious to me . . . and I'm thankful for these people, I came to realize that really strongly back then.

I'm Fine

The *LOVE YOURSELF* series came to an end, and in August 2018, BTS released the repackage album *LOVE YOURSELF* 結 *'Answer.'* The album opens with Jung Kook's solo song "Euphoria."* It was while recording this song that Jung Kook was finding his own voice as a vocalist:

———I don't know if I should call it a slump . . . It was like, in the vocal aspect, I'd come up against a wall.

Jung Kook explains the difficulties he went through:

———My method of practicing alone while continuously searching and searching for my voice, it wasn't the right way. There was a better way, but in practicing like that, I developed bad habits. That was when I needed to fix it, but . . . doing that, my throat, it felt like it didn't belong to me. But anyway, I still had to do something . . . so I did the recording.

"Euphoria" unfolds dynamically: Jung Kook's voice slowly cranks up the emotion, and at the appropriate point in the chorus, instead of his voice, a powerful beat stands center stage. Before arriving at the chorus, Jung Kook uses subtle changes to convey the delicate emotions captured by the lyrics: raising or lowering the key a little, or slightly speeding up or slowing down within the repetitive melody.

> *You're the sunshine that shone once again on my life*
> *The return of my childhood dreams*

I don't know what this feeling is
Could this also be a dream?

You might call the opening lyrics to "Euphoria" Jung Kook's story following his debut with BTS. Growing alongside BTS, Jung Kook went from a young boy who didn't understand his emotions, to a fully-grown adult and vocalist who could express emotions so complex they cannot be put into a single word. You could liken this to the young protagonist, Riley, from the Pixar animation, *Inside Out* (2015), who through feeling an emotion, a mix of happiness and sadness, cleanses her mind and grows a little more.

——It was.

Jung Kook replies, when asked if "Euphoria" was a turning point for him as a vocalist. He continues:

——I still didn't think my voice had cleared, but I felt I could express a greater number of emotions with it. Putting technical aspects like vocalization to one side, how much I captured the emotions that suited the song . . . I think those are the kind of things that naturally improved. But to be honest, it's still a struggle. It's difficult.

For BTS, the making of the *LOVE YOURSELF* series seemed to be a period of growing pains. Like Jung Kook says, the members had each kept their concerns bottled up inside, until finally these emotions came exploding out and impacted the members' closest relationships, those with their fellow group members. To resolve this, they sought a balance between the group and their inner lives, and between themselves and others. Jin says:

——Once that period had passed, I ended up with a pretty positive mindset, I think.

LOVE YOURSELF 結
'Answer'

REPACKAGE ALBUM
2018. 8. 24

TRACK

CD1
01 Euphoria
02 Trivia 起 : Just Dance
03 Serendipity (Full Length
   Edition)
04 DNA
05 Dimple
06 Trivia 承 : Love
07 Her
08 Singularity
09 FAKE LOVE
10 The Truth Untold
   (Feat. Steve Aoki)
11 Trivia 轉 : Seesaw
12 Tear
13 Epiphany
14 I'm Fine
15 IDOL
16 Answer : Love Myself

CD2
01 Magic Shop
02 Best Of Me
03 Airplane pt.2
04 Go Go
05 Anpanman
06 MIC Drop
07 DNA (Pedal 2 LA Mix)
08 FAKE LOVE (Rocking Vibe Mix)
09 MIC Drop (Steve Aoki Remix)
   (Full Length Edition)
10 IDOL (Feat. Nicki Minaj)

VIDEO

COMEBACK TRAILER :
Epiphany

"IDOL"
MV

"IDOL"
MV TEASER

"IDOL"
(Feat. Nicki Minaj)
MV

He also explains:

———I started to try and go with the flow. If I wanted to practice singing, I practiced singing, if I wanted to play a game, I played. When I had nothing on my schedule, I ate if I wanted to, and if I didn't, I went the whole day without eating. The people who know me are amazed by it. Asking how I can concentrate so much on something without complaining. And then I reply, "I think it's possible because I'm living without any thought at all."

Jin saying he was living without thinking shows us, in fact, just how much he had agonized over his way of life before arriving at this point.

———Because I live like that, there isn't anything big I want in my life, and I get a sense of accomplishment by doing the things I want to in the moment I want to do them. I can get a sense of accomplishment in any place. Through that process, I felt a lot of happiness, and found some mental space, I think.

The lyrics to Jin's solo song "Epiphany"* from *LOVE YOURSELF* 結 *'Answer'* begin:

> *It's so strange*
> *I'm sure I truly loved you*
> *I fit everything to you*
> *And wanted to live just for you*
> *But the more I did*
> *The less I could handle the storm within my heart*

I reveal my true self
Beneath this smiling mask

You always want to do your best for the one you love, but it's not easy to stand the storm inside your heart, and it feels as if you're wearing a mask in front of them. This is part of the complex emotion that Jin and the other BTS members felt while making the *LOVE YOURSELF* series. Once this period was over, at times Jin would accept the world he could do nothing about, and at times he would compromise and affirm himself. Perhaps it was through this that he learned to fully enjoy the happiness his work brings. Recalling his memories of "Epiphany," Jin says:

———The only part I don't remember from the *LOVE YOURSELF* 結 *'Answer'* album was recording this song. At the time, I was kind of out of it, and so I think that was part of the reason why . . . But performing this song has a bit more of a special enjoyment for me. When dancing you have to be thinking about the next move, and if you forget the choreography, it's a disaster, right? But if you sing this song standing in one spot, you harmonize with the situation and feelings captured by the song as they are. I'm the only one who can experience this enjoyment onstage, though.

j-hope talks about the series of changes taking place at the time:

———It really was a period of a lot of growth. For me, I learned a lot while making the *LOVE YOURSELF* albums, and I often thought about how I should express myself within this group called BTS. At that time, the fans also recognized those things. We were truly thankful during that time. I think the process of making these albums made up an incredibly large part of me. If it wasn't for that time, I don't think the j-hope of now would be here.

It was like that for all the members, but j-hope's role had always been in helping maintain BTS's signature close-knit atmosphere. When the members were struggling physically during dance practice, he would smile and drive the atmosphere so that they could try one more time, and then once more. j-hope gives the following definition of teamwork:

———We're a team, and the seven of us need to become one to do a good job at whatever it is we're doing. I'm not the only one who should do well, my belief is that all need to do a good job, and so I think I did my best in the parts I could do. Actually, when it came to making the *LOVE YOURSELF* series, or thinking about the contract renewal problem, the other members helped the group more than I did. In a way, they took on the parts I couldn't cope with, as well as the things I struggled with, and encouraged me.

Considering j-hope's mindset toward the group here, the role he played in the promotion of *LOVE YOURSELF* 結 *'Answer'* feels even more dramatic. A few days after the album's release, j-hope performed part of the title song "IDOL"'s choreography and uploaded a challenge video• to social media, alongside the hashtag "#IDOLCHALLENGE," so that lots of people could dance along.

j-hope, who has always been fully devoted to the group, plays the role of getting people to have fun and dance along to "IDOL." This was the j-hope the members and ARMY knew well, and he got a response right at the forefront of the promotion.

This challenge was an important moment of change for both Big Hit

Entertainment and BTS. Before the *LOVE YOURSELF* 結 *'Answer'* album, BTS would share the variety of promotional content the company had prepared for the new album, according to a detailed plan. Big Hit Entertainment's intentions were clear within all of BTS's activities—from the comeback trailer released first of all, to the stage direction at the end of year music award ceremonies—and these intentions were conveyed to ARMY and other music consumers. To give an example, for ARMY, guessing the concept for the next album based on the words that popped up on-screen behind the stage at an awards ceremony was an event in itself.

The "IDOL" challenge was therefore changing this trend. People's spontaneous participation and responses were an important part of the promotion, and this was something beyond Big Hit Entertainment's control. Of course, because it was BTS doing the promotion, you could expect the reactions to j-hope's challenge video to be good. However, it wasn't at all possible to predict how many ARMY would really dance along with j-hope, or how many of the general public outside of ARMY would take part in the challenge. It's likely that as a result of these fears, opinions would have been divided within Big Hit Entertainment about whether or not to go ahead with the challenge. It's clear, however, that *LOVE YOURSELF* 結 *'Answer'*'s "IDOL" challenge was something BTS needed to go through.

My, Your, Everyone's Idol

BTS are an idol group. However, for BTS, this brief definition contains countless stories. They trained incredibly hard to become idols. As soon as they became idols, they were rejected and denigrated for doing hip-hop and for being from a small company. Even once they'd become stars, with all the attacks fired at them, they had to comfort the fans. Following that, they suffered through all the concerns that came with being idols, and they worried that they were wearing masks in front of their fans.

For the group, being idols comprises all these things, as well as all the meanings of BTS that emerged after. BTS started out as idols. And even back when *LOVE YOURSELF* 結 *'Answer'* was released, they were still "idols." Despite everything.

Idols, particularly Korean idols, feel more and more pressure to become "artists" the further they progress in their career. By definition, the concept of "artist" can cover idols, musicians, entertainers, and so on. And so, an idol is also an artist, and one subset of artist is not superior to the other. However, in Korea, "artist" often comes to feel like an end goal that idols must reach. Phrases like "idol becomes artist," therefore, have come to mean that a given idol has a superior musicality, or more authenticity.

This is connected to the way idols are viewed within the Korean music industry, and also within Korean society as a whole. Idols were often belittled as having inferior musicality to other kinds of artists, for reasons including the fact that the company directs the production, that they don't write their own songs, or even that they're really good-looking or dance onstage. On top of this, there is also the highly misogynistic assumption that because fans of idol music tend to be women in their teens and twenties, the music must be of a poor quality.

However, since their debut, BTS have made music out of the stories of their lives as trainees, and within the *LOVE YOURSELF* series, they captured the pleasure and pain of living as idols. BTS's authenticity came from their stories of what they'd gone through as idols, and the group was inextricably tied to their internal struggles and growth, as well as ARMY fandom.

You can call me artist
You can call me idol
Or any other something you come up with,
I don't care

Just like these opening lyrics to "IDOL," for BTS, defining themselves as idols was a necessary part of "love myself." They had wanted the world to acknowledge their existence however possible, and once the glory they'd received alongside ARMY had piled up as high as a mountain, BTS climbed on top and defined themselves as idols. From extreme praise to extreme criticism, they were judged according to every kind of standard, and like that, flipped back and forth between glory and despair. Now, however, no matter what the world might say, BTS are BTS. They no longer need any other word to describe themselves. SUGA shares his thoughts about the word "idol":

———I'm well aware that people talk about idols as "seven-year singers" and "manufactured products." But it's just a difference in how much you express yourself, and on the whole idols have similar concerns. Thankfully, as a group we could talk about those aspects freely, and so we could express those thoughts as they were.

In this way, with the "IDOL" challenge, BTS were taking another step forward as self-defined idols. These idols, who had countless eyes on them, and who were defined in countless different ways, were encouraging not only ARMY, but anyone who wanted to, to give the "IDOL" dance a go. As a result, even someone who knew nothing of the context of BTS, ARMY, or the relationship between them could come across the "IDOL" challenge on social media and easily encounter the group.

The attitude of: no matter what you think of us, come give this a try and have some fun. This was a small yet important turning point in the history of BTS and ARMY. Since their debut, BTS had defended against outside attacks, and also sometimes wanted acceptance from the outside, but around the time they had come up with the "answer" to the *LOVE YOURSELF* series, they had started to create events that anyone could take part in, whatever people might say.

LOVE YOURSELF 結 *'Answer''s* title song "IDOL"* blends together a variety of cultural elements into a huge party. Musically, South African–style rhythms are blended with the rhythms used in Korean traditional music. In the music video, there are both suits and traditional Korean hanbok; backdrops reminiscent of the African plains; Bukcheong sajanoreum, a traditional Korean game; paintings created by the BTS members themselves. All these are mixed together within a video that emphasizes both the three-dimensional feel as well as the sense of a two-dimensional plane.

While combining so many elements that it can feel overwhelming, instead of the rock or EDM that is generally used in music with this type of festival vibe, the sound of Korean traditional music is what leads the song. In the part when everyone is most excited, the rhythm of Korean traditional music, "Bum badum bum brrrrumble," and the chuim-sae (a form of exclamation in traditional Korean music) "Oh yeah," appear in the lyrics.

"IDOL" is a piece of festival music, created by gathering a variety of elements together. For everyone in the world listening, the Korean traditional music becomes the sound of enjoying this festival. For Korean people, "IDOL"'s traditional Korean music is a special element you rarely come across in popular music, but also has universality as the highlight of this energetic song. With this, BTS reached a new stage in the *LOVE YOURSELF* series. BTS, who had always been tight-knit with ARMY, had become figures who could say to anyone, "Let's have a blast together," and throw a party.

In "Burning Up (FIRE)," BTS revealed their momentum, pushing on ahead without hesitation alongside a big dance troupe, while in "Not Today" they led dozens of dancers. And in "IDOL," with choreography that incorporated a variety of looks and all sorts of cultural elements, their role was to give everyone a good time. From their debut song, "No More Dream," to their arrival at "IDOL," they had received so much love, and were naturally changing their roles accordingly.

The change that BTS had revealed through "IDOL" symbolized that a shift was occurring not just within music but in the history of the Korean popular culture industry as a whole. In 2018, BTS had consecutive Billboard 200 number ones with the *LOVE YOURSELF* 轉 *'Tear'* and *LOVE YOURSELF* 結 *'Answer'* albums, and the following year *Parasite* (2019) became one of the most talked about movies in the world. Then, in September 2020, Billboard established a new chart called the "Billboard Global 200," which totaled figures from around two hundred countries and regions, including the US. It is fair to assume that the infiltration of music by K-pop and other international artists into the US Billboard chart played a role here.

And so, while new currents centered around a particular continent, country, or cultural region were forming, the face of the popular culture industry was also changing. Within this tide, Korean popular culture, seen as having an appeal different from the works of popular culture in the West, was beginning its meteoric rise. From the 2010s onward, Korea and Seoul emerged each as one of the newest countries and cities respectively to receive attention for their culture. As with "IDOL," Korea has given myriad cultural elements a modern interpretation and has thus began to capture the world. BTS were one part of this vast current and established their position as iconic figures.

BTS's performance* at the December 1, 2018, MMAs, held at the Gocheok Sky Dome, was a symbol of everything they were doing at the time. In the middle of a group of Korean samgomu traditional drum dance performers, j-hope appears wearing a hanbok and begins dancing. He performs not traditional dance, but street dance based on breakdancing. The overall concept is centered around Korean traditional arts, but the members' routines are based on the modern genres they are accustomed to. Jimin and Jung Kook, who appear after j-hope, are each inspired by buchaechum fan dance and talchum masked dance respectively, but the choreography has more similarity to the modern dance movements they had occasionally shown before.

The performance at the MMAs was a condensed version of Korean traditional arts and play culture, which BTS fuse naturally with modern popular culture elements as if it's nothing unusual at all. The members wear hanbok outfits distorted from their traditional form, and yell, "Bum badum bum brrrrumble / Oh yeah," from the middle of the stage, while the audience shout alongside at the top of their lungs. All of this happens so smoothly that it's as if everything is in its rightful place. These young people, who grew up experiencing Korea's traditions and popular music alongside one another, had created a new form that combined all these things naturally.

This was much like how, through "IDOL," BTS fused together the outside gazes with all the meanings that had been assigned to them. Combining inexplicably complex elements as one, BTS in fact made their identities both as Koreans and idols crystal clear.

For a long time, at end-of-year music awards ceremonies like the MMAs, the stage had been a fighting ground upon which BTS could prove themselves. There, they had to win against the other groups, as well as make ARMY who supported them proud.

However, after consecutive Billboard 200 number ones, and having overcome the chaos and conflict surrounding their contract renewal, in the end, BTS stood up again as one team, and there was no longer a need to prove themselves. They needed no explanation, and instead, the expectation fell on their shoulders: What kind of performance would they give this time? As idols, they had become icons.

SPEAK YOURSELF

Now they'd released another album, it was time to go on tour again. As in the album titles, BTS had passed through the "development" (seung, 承) and "turning point" (jeon, 轉) stages of literary composition, and drew the *LOVE YOURSELF* series to a close with the "conclusion" (gyeol, 結) stage. At the end of all this, on August 25,

2018, they kicked off the BTS WORLD TOUR "LOVE YOURSELF"·
at Jamsil Olympic Stadium in Seoul. A year-long world tour ensued,
which concluded with another concert at Jamsil Olympic Stadium
on October 29, 2019, BTS WORLD TOUR "LOVE YOURSELF:
SPEAK YOURSELF," and included songs from 2019 album *MAP OF
THE SOUL : PERSONA.*

As part of BTS WORLD TOUR "LOVE YOURSELF: SPEAK
YOURSELF,"··· they performed at world-renowned stadiums from America's Rose Bowl and the UK's Wembley to France's Stade de France. Before
they began production on the *LOVE YOURSELF* series, BTS had been
consumed by the anxiety that their success might come crashing down.
After the *LOVE YOURSELF* series, however, they were in fact flying to
even greater heights. Almost like an eternal flight that would never land.

———We do around forty concerts, right? And so sometimes I think,
  'What should I do today?' (laughs).

V speaks of how he presents himself during long tours. He continues:
———Before, when I did concerts, I had so many gestures I could
  express. But the same couldn't be said when I had "forty concerts" ahead. The things I'd present would have to be way more
  varied. I prepared quite a lot before we went. I had a lot of ideas,
  particularly when it came to songs like "Intro : Singularity." There
  were really so many that I thought my head might explode. Doing around forty concerts, I had the regret that, 'I should have
  used one idea at a time' (laughs). For example, at first, I came up

with about fifteen leaning poses. For each concert, I also thought up one to do in the middle of the performance, and a different one to do at the end, and for the dances, there were lots of new formations I came up with. But I basically used up everything I'd prepared in one concert, and so later my mind just went numb.

What V chose to do instead was to leave his body to the sensations that come naturally. He says:

——Onstage, I do it without thinking. No matter what ideas I have, I don't think things like, 'This time, I need to do this.' I do have a wider framework, though. I think what's most important is that it comes out naturally.

V's conclusion was perhaps a realization the BTS members made through the *LOVE YOURSELF* series. Facing life's unexpected problems, and mulling over and over every kind of worry, the answer is found in the simplest, yet most meaningful things.

Jung Kook sums up where his happiness now comes from:

——When I'm asked now what makes me happy, it's the fact of being able to have concerns like this. That's my happiness. If I was actually unhappy now, I don't believe I'd be able to think about what I'd call happiness. So, being able to think things like, 'Is this what makes me happy,' 'No, this is what makes me happy,' isn't that happiness?

Much like the message of theatrical play *L'oiseau bleu*—that happiness lies close at hand—BTS flew far and to great heights, before then returning to the values in their own hearts. Just like how Jimin, in making the *LOVE YOURSELF* series, once again came up with the "answer" of the members. Jimin says:

——There were a few things that happened, but in the end, I returned to BTS. I met up with my friends outside of the group, and spent time with them, getting things off my chest, but bringing the things that happened within the group into the outside resolved nothing, and I couldn't find the answers I wanted. And I think that's how I ended up relying on the members even more.

"Promise,"* released on December 31, 2018, was the first song Jimin made himself. The song opens with the lyrics "Slump down all alone," but Jimin realizes that he isn't alone, and the song ends with "Now promise me." Jimin began work on the song in spring of that year, but given the atmosphere of confusion within the group, he wasn't able to pick up any speed. Only once Jimin had put that time behind him was he able to complete the song with the title and lyrics it has today.

For the BTS members, *LOVE YOURSELF* was a process of discovering the values precious to them. In this regard, loving themselves was the process of finding out who they were. About this, j-hope says:

——I came to see myself as a genuinely bright person, who energizes other people. And someone who can express their unique charm accordingly . . . ? During the *LOVE YOURSELF* series, that's what I learned about myself.

j-hope explains this process of self-discovery:

——*LOVE YOURSELF*, while it has the message to love yourself, on the one hand I thought, 'What kind of person am I?' I studied myself a lot during that time. And I came to the realization that I had a bright energy, and that I was someone who could pass that energy on to others. Like that, coming up with a definition of myself that wasn't a definition, I put it into the songs, expressed it, and ARMY accepted it . . . Also, as I looked at ARMY, I came to think once again, 'That's right, this is who I am.' That was the journey.

For BTS, *LOVE YOURSELF* was not just the act of affirming oneself. Like j-hope says, it was actually a process to "know yourself" in order to find out if you can "love yourself." No matter who you are, this is a process that is inevitably ongoing, and there isn't one single answer, but through the *LOVE YOURSELF* series albums, the BTS members confessed stories from their lives and searched for the answer to the eternal question: "Who am I?"

As it so happens, following on from *LOVE YOURSELF*, the first line of the *MAP OF THE SOUL* series' opening song, "Intro : Persona," goes: "Who am I." Of course, like it says in the lyrics, "The question I had my entire life" is "The question I'll probably never find the answer to my whole life." However, it is in the process of answering this question, which comes around in every period of life, that a person learns what it is they have to do.

j-hope shares the answer that *LOVE YOURSELF* gave him:

———Thinking about it, I don't think I was that much of a bright person, but I changed a lot to become who I am now. I don't know what other people think of the expression "completion," but when I talk about the process of becoming complete as a person, I think I really wanted to tell people, "I also changed like this, and became this person," "You can do the same, too." I don't know how that message was taken by ARMY, but anyway, I hope it left a good impact.

On September 24, 2018, BTS attended the launch of UNICEF partnership "Generation Unlimited" at the United Nations headquarters in New York, where they gave an address.

I would like to begin by talking about myself.

As j-hope said earlier, by telling their story that day, they impacted not only ARMY, but many other people, too.

RM, who gave the address in English on behalf of the group, begins by introducing his hometown of Ilsan, and talks about his life growing up. He goes on to speak about the trying days that followed their debut, expresses thanks for ARMY's love and support which kept them from giving up, and then talks about living as himself. The key parts are as follows:

> *Maybe I made a mistake yesterday, but yesterday's me is still me. Today, I am who I am with all of my faults and my mistakes. Tomorrow, I might be a tiny bit wiser, and that'll be me too. These faults and mistakes are what I am, making up the brightest stars in the constellation of my life. I have come to love myself for who I am, for who I was, and for who I hope to become.*

He then recommends people go one step further in loving themselves:

We have learned to love ourselves. So now I urge you to "speak yourself."

Just as BTS WORLD TOUR "LOVE YOURSELF: SPEAK YOUR-SELF" followed on from BTS WORLD TOUR "LOVE YOURSELF," within the *LOVE YOURSELF* journey, BTS progressed toward their answer: *SPEAK YOURSELF*. No matter how the world sees you, and no matter what you've been through to get here, telling that world who you are and where you came from: this is the real BTS, that would remain even if they were to lose everything they have.

At the time, BTS couldn't know how long and how far up they would continue to fly. However, their address at the UN headquarters was a declaration—that if they were to reach even as far as the sun, they would still each stay connected to the ground from which they departed. In the address, RM also says that who you are beneath it all doesn't change and encourages those listening to talk about it and to connect with the world.

As seven young people who had only a few years before been ordinary boys in Korea, but were now traveling all over the world, perhaps this was the only thing they could say to ARMY, made up of all different nationalities, races, personalities, and classes.

——It was pretty important to me. I think it establishes one of the pillars of BTS.

RM briefly recalls the address that day, and then continues on, this time discussing art:

——When I read the critiques about painter Song Sangki, there was one part that touched me most. As far as I remember, it said, "I think that the greatest artists are the ones who can take their most personal experiences and distill them into the most universal of truths. Isn't this person art itself?"

RM explains how those sentences made him feel:

———"Someone who distills personal experience into universal truth." I felt that this was what I wanted to become. BTS also are probably somewhere in between personal experience and the universal. And it's saying that to head toward universal truth, personal experience must be prioritized, right? For me, these kinds of personal experiences are connected to the question of, "Where am I putting down my roots?," and that's at the beginning and end of our address. If the things that I like and so on these days are where my neurons have branched out all over the place, then the answer to the question of where I started from lies within the deepest roots of my whole identity, and within this complex world, it's the origin that allows the clearest recognition of my existence. To exaggerate a little, I think my identity and authenticity come from that alone. And so, when I express those things, I can be unashamed and speak the truth. Living as part of BTS, I think that will be evident, whether that's through my lyrics or my interviews.

RM then smiles, and does his own "speak yourself":

———It's not as if I'm the president, or John Lennon, right? Even so, I think I can introduce myself without being ashamed as follows. By saying, "I am a young person who is however many years old, lives in whatever place, and likes x and y." It's when I say these kinds of things that I feel I am just as good as them, I think (laughs).

Like that, a ray of light began to form. A light that would guide their endless flight.

CHAPTER 6

MAP OF THE SOUL : PERSONA

MAP OF THE SOUL : 7

THE WORLD
OF BTS

MAP OF THE SOUL : PERSONA | THE 6TH MINI ALBUM

MAP OF THE SOUL : 7 | THE 4TH FULL-LENGTH ALBUM

THE WORLD OF BTS

ARMY Time

When BTS released their new album *MAP OF THE SOUL : PERSONA* on April 12, 2019, at 6 P.M., a large part of their Korean audience on the music streaming platform Melon were unable to listen to it right away. Melon's servers had crashed due to the sheer number of simultaneous access attempts.

This was something unimaginable for anyone living in the Republic of Korea. In 2019, 10.28 million Koreans used music streaming services, with Melon boasting 4.1 million active monthly users. For an entire platform of this magnitude to go down because of the demand for just one album was like a pebble being thrown into the ocean displacing all of its water into space.

This had perhaps been foreshadowed about two months before the release of *MAP OF THE SOUL : PERSONA* by ARMYPEDIA,* a kind of treasure hunt hosted by Big Hit Entertainment as a special treat for ARMY. Jumbotron teasers were shown in Seoul, New York, LA, Tokyo, London, Paris, and Hong Kong, and ARMY around the world looked for 2,080 puzzle pieces scattered across the globe and the Internet to piece together. The number 2,080 refers to the 2,080 days from BTS's debut on June 13, 2013, to February 21, 2019—when ARMYPEDIA was revealed—meaning each piece of the puzzle was a day in the life of BTS itself.

ARMY assembled the pieces with breathtaking swiftness. Each puzzle piece had a QR code. Scanning this QR code brought you to a quiz question about BTS that when answered correctly would fill in a record of the ARMYPEDIA for that day. The ARMY who had answered correctly were free to upload their personal BTS memories in the form of text, photos, and videos. ARMYPEDIA showed that BTS by then had grown into a gigantic phenomenon that would draw a global response through something as humble as an event centered around the memories they shared with their fans.

A few weeks later, two offline ARMYPEDIA afterparties[40] of a sort were held in Seoul. At the time, the Korean media talked of these special events as "BTS events without BTS." While the members of BTS did appear in brief surprise video performances on the large screens set up at the event spaces, they did not attend in person. Still, the ARMY gathered in arena-audience magnitudes, singing along to their songs coming out of the large concert speakers, taking part in the proceedings prepared by BTS and Big Hit Entertainment.

ARMYPEDIA and the events that followed were a preview of what ARMY would show the world once the new album *MAP OF THE SOUL : PERSONA* was released. ARMY would now gather in large enough numbers to attract the attention of the media, even without the physical presence of BTS. Which is how, while *MAP OF THE SOUL : PERSONA* was a BTS album through and through, it was ARMY who became the star of the album.

---

40 "RUN ARMY in ACTION" was held on March 10 at Seoul City Plaza and "ARMY UNITED in SEOUL" was held on March 23 at Oil Tank Culture Park.

MAP OF THE SOUL : PERSONA begins with a story about "you," that is, ARMY. The concept behind this album was inspired by a recurring thought Jung Kook had as he promoted the *LOVE YOURSELF* series.

———I wondered what life was like for all the people who liked me.

Jung Kook's wish to know more about ARMY was not out of mere curiosity.

———I sometimes wonder, when I'm with people, whether I put on a mask in front of them. It's important to strike a balance between me as an artist and as a person, but I sometimes wondered if I'd begun to lose track of what I was doing.

BTS had always treasured their "one row" of fans who had come to see them in their very first TV music show performance, and now they were doing stadium dates with thousands of ARMY. This increase in their number of fans also meant an increase in the number of languages in which ARMY were expressing their love, support, and thoughts for the group from around the world, but why the boys were receiving so much love and what the lives of the people who loved them were like, they had no real way of knowing. Instead, there were countless cameras, or the interest of the media, or anyone who wanted to play the pundit about BTS trying to fill in the gap between BTS and ARMY. Jung Kook says:

———I think we got to where we were because we met the right era and the right people. But it was a lot of pressure. I didn't think I was quite right for this position, and there were things I had to do in order to become someone who was right for it. And there are

MAP OF THE SOUL : PERSONA

THE 6TH MINI ALBUM
2019. 4. 12

TRACK

01 Intro : Persona
02 Boy With Luv (Feat. Halsey)
03 Mikrokosmos
04 Make It Right

05 HOME
06 Jamais Vu
07 Dionysus

VIDEO

 COMBACK TRAILER:
Persona

 "Boy With Luv"
(Feat. Halsey)
MV TEASER 1

 "Boy With Luv"
(Feat. Halsey)
MV TEASER 2

 "Boy With Luv"
(Feat. Halsey)
MV

 "Boy With Luv"
(Feat. Halsey)
MV ('ARMY With Luv' ver.)

 "Make It Right"
(Feat. Lauv)
MV

always things we needed to put more effort into if we wanted to do the things we'd set out to do.

As Jung Kook says, the things BTS needed to do grew in proportion to their explosive popularity, and it was not easy to maintain the honest and candid selves that they wanted to show ARMY.

But BTS are a group that—long before "streamer" became a widespread word—had vlogged on YouTube about their travails as trainees whose debuts were imminent. Even after they had become an international sensation touring stadiums around the world, they would still, after a performance, switch on their V Live cameras and communicate with ARMY.

MAP OF THE SOUL : PERSONA was the product of a special relationship between a gigantic fandom and their beloved artists who had become global stars in the age of smartphones and YouTube. BTS, even in the midst of the idol industry, wanted to show their real selves as much as possible, and had become superstars as a result. And when they thought they'd reached the very top of what they could achieve, they wanted to communicate more with the fans who had come all this way with them.

From Saudi Arabia to America

Unless we were to ask every single ARMY personally, we would never be able to tell how far Jung Kook's hopes managed to reach. But after the release of *MAP OF THE SOUL : PERSONA*, it was clear ARMY wanted to pass on something to BTS.

On October 10, 2019 (local time), BTS were preparing for their performance of BTS WORLD TOUR "LOVE YOURSELF: SPEAK YOURSELF" that would be held the next day at the King Fahd International Stadium in Riyadh, the capital of Saudi Arabia. After the full rehearsal, Jung Kook and Jimin decided to practice one more time the part where they would perform a medley of BTS's hit songs.

"We're so sorry!"

The two begged the crew for their understanding. The temperature in Riyadh had soared to 40 degrees Celsius, and for any first-time visitor to the city, even walking the streets in this weather was an endeavor. The two were apologetic for asking the crew to stay on longer in the heat as their rehearsal time dragged on. Even though they were the ones who had to sweat the most.

But they weren't the only ones who were trying to overcome the heat. All throughout their rehearsal, there were endless cheers coming from outside the stadium. ARMY had surrounded the arena. From the outside, ARMY could only hear muffled sounds of the rehearsals taking place, making it almost impossible to tell the members' voices apart. Still, whenever the songs changed, ARMY sent up another collective roar and called out the names of the members. The sight of women wearing traditional niqabs that covered their forms and faces shouting the names of the artists they liked was surely an uncommon sight in Saudi Arabia. Jung Kook remembers what the concert was like at the time:

———Every country has their own culture, but I had hoped during our performances at least, our audiences would allow themselves to express everything in their hearts in that moment. Their traditional clothing must've been quite hot to wear, but they were having so much fun and being wonderfully loud that I felt incredibly thankful to them.

As Jung Kook says, the audience there, who were mostly women, were able to be as loud as they wanted as they enjoyed themselves despite the heat. Sure, it was only a brief moment, but BTS were showing a new way of how mainstream music was being accepted in Saudi Arabia, a kind of change. And that such a change was being led by over thirty thousand women of around the same age was in itself something to give pause.

America was the same. Every US media outlet commented on the women in their teens and twenties who had gathered to see BTS's shows. The group's *Saturday Night Live* performance on April 13, 2019, on NBC in particular was a milestone for them.

In teaser spots for the episode, that week's host, Emma Stone, and members of the *SNL* cast acted as stand-ins for ARMY where Stone says, "I'm camping out on this stage until BTS gets here." For some, however, this was not an exaggeration. NBC's *Today Show* was already reporting on ARMY who were camping out for days in front of the studio for a chance to get tickets to *SNL*.

This stage was also their first since the release of *MAP OF THE SOUL : PERSONA*, and *SNL* was, as the name of the show implies, live. The stage they had to perform on was also smaller than the average music show stage on Korean live television sets. Not even having the time to get nervous about appearing on *SNL*, the members were said to all have wondered how they were going to execute their performance for a wholly unfamiliar stage and audience:

———'The stage is so small. What do we do about our choreography?'

Careful of collisions and injuries, the members discussed and choreographed their movements right up to the moment they were live.* The members say similar things in their memories of the appearance:

———It didn't matter how big the physical stage was, the fact that it was *SNL* was what made it important.

Just as they had expected, this small stage became BTS's *Ed Sullivan Show* moment.[41] Not only did music journalism outlets like *Billboard* and *Rolling Stone* discuss BTS's *SNL* performance and the public's response, but the *New York Times* and CNN covered the story as well, and the very next day, BTS's Google search metrics spiked the highest for their entire promotional cycle for *MAP OF THE SOUL : PERSONA*.

And now, it wasn't just the Korean media but journalists around the world who were asking the question: "Why do fans love BTS so much?"

I'm Listening to You

The history of boy band fandom begins in the West. But bands like BTS with popularity that transcends national boundaries and can hold arena tours in Asia, North America, and Europe are decidedly few and

---

41 *The Ed Sullivan Show*, which ran from 1948 to 1971 on CBS, was the first American stage for the Beatles, who made their appearance there on February 9, 1964, when their album became a smash hit in the US.

far between. Not to mention bands that have vast fandoms holding the same official light sticks and calling themselves a single moniker (ARMY, in this case).

The Western media began comparing ARMY to Beatlemania, the fandom of the Beatles. ARMY was so sensational, Western journalists had to go all the way back to the Beatles to come up with an equivalent comparison. BTS also took almost six years getting to that *SNL* stage, six years of almost unprecedented growth in popularity both in terms of sales and geographic reach. And they were Korean artists, singing in the Korean language on the *SNL* stage, making American ARMY scream to boot. It was all truly unprecedented.

BTS's popularity cannot be put down to a single factor. One fan might've been attracted by their looks at first, another by their performances, and maybe another would've caught a fun video ARMY had made that made them curious about the band.

But more than all this questioning about where their popularity comes from, it's important to look at the answers provided by ARMY. For example, during the Generation Unlimited campaign event in September 2018 where BTS delivered a speech at the UN General Assembly, exhorting youth to "speak yourself," social media was flooded by ARMY expressing themselves and talking of their journeys of finding themselves and building up their self-esteem.

Through the music of BTS, ARMY learn of tragic events in Korean history such as the May 18 Gwangju Democratization Movement and the Sewol Disaster and express their condolences and offer solidarity to those affected. Not only that, when the COVID-19 pandemic began about a year after *MAP OF THE SOUL : PERSONA* was released, ARMY had donated up to 2 billion Korean won by September 2020, only counting the verified amount.[42]* The donations covered not only education and health, which were directly affected worldwide during the pandemic, but also human rights and the protection of animals.

While it was difficult to ascertain what made them interested in BTS in the first place, there is one clear theme that echoes through this fandom across the world. And that theme is that by being fans of BTS, they found new directions for their lives.

This wasn't, of course, something exclusive to ARMY when it came to fandom in K-pop. The K-pop fandoms that came before them were also proactive in their donating for all kinds of causes. But when BTS reached worldwide fame, other K-pop fandoms around the world began to echo this tendency. Through the particular form of unity that K-pop fandoms have, fans would express their identities and also speak out on various political and social issues outside of K-pop. And today, it has become the norm for any K-pop fandom to express their positions on not only the issues of the countries they live in but issues the world has in common.

As the *SNL* teaser described it, Western media's image of boy-band fandom is women in their teens and twenties who stay up all night to catch a glimpse of the groups they like and chat about their favorite members for hours. There is some truth to this, as it has been since Beatlemania. But as much time as BTS's fans spend on raving over their favorite band, they also each have lives they are living out as individuals.

---

42 *Weverse Magazine*. See article.

Which is why, perhaps, the question to ask ARMY and any K-pop fan, or any fan of any artist around the world, isn't "Why are you a fan?" but "What life, beyond being a fan, are you living now?" Only then can we get a step closer to the young Saudi Arabian women in their traditional clothes, gathered around a stadium to catch the faintest utterance of their favorite artists practicing inside, shouting their names in recognition.

Through the *SNL* performance, BTS took a decisive step toward ARMY. They performed "Boy With Luv,"* the title song of *MAP OF THE SOUL : PERSONA*, and "MIC Drop," originally featured in *LOVE YOUR-SELF 承 'Her.'* "MIC Drop" in particular is a song in the hip-hop genre that requires a dynamic performance from start to finish, and "Boy With Luv" is the opposite, one of BTS's most upbeat and cheerful pop songs.

The range between these two songs seems to encapsulate the relationship between BTS and ARMY. "MIC Drop" is a swagger of a song, a declaration of their golden era of success. This swagger is not just bragging but a message of victory: "Don't need to see you anymore / This is the last farewell / Don't got no words to tell / Don't even apologize." Contextually, the song is probably aimed at the haters who had harassed them since their debut.

On the other hand, "Boy With Luv" is about the small things that came together from the beginning into a massive upward force that made them soar. In other words, it was the story of ARMY. In the lyrics, BTS hope to meet ARMY at eye level through words like "I want you tuned in to my eyes" as they talk of their current success in "Now it's so high up here." And of ARMY, whom BTS are "curious about every-thing," they have this to ask:

> *Come be my teacher*
> *Teach me everything about you*

If "MIC Drop" was the process of proving themselves through their success, "Boy With Luv" (Feat. Halsey) is a declaration that they would let ARMY tell their stories first. It is the history of how an artist had come to put the voices of their fandom first, the fandom that had always been there to cheer them on.

BTS made their fans the main character of their album, and began telling the stories that their fans had wanted to tell. Jung Kook, compar-ing the influence of BTS member Jung Kook as opposed to the human individual Jeon Jung Kook, has this to say:

——Hmm . . . I don't think there's such a clear line dividing the two.
In any case, as Jung Kook of BTS, I am speaking to the fans who look toward me, which is why I want to tell them positive stories. Because I believe that I, too, have the power to give hope.

I'll Speak Very Frankly

RM's rap in "Boy With Luv" (Feat. Halsey) begins with the phrase "I'll speak very frankly." He speaks without filter of the realities faced by BTS and their thoughts as they achieved unprecedented success in the history of contemporary music in Korea.

Sometimes I was a little stuck up
Elevated sky, expanded halls
Sometimes I prayed let me run away

He captured in his lyrics the outpouring of feelings regarding their surge in popularity after the *LOVE YOURSELF* series, a surge so intense it was almost humanly impossible to handle. RM's expression "I'll speak very frankly" was written on the spur of the moment:

———When I write lyrics, I absolutely have to go inside the narrator's mind. Because I need to enter the world of the song. But when I write my rap part after having written the song lyrics, I kind of run out of things to say (laughs). I might write some song lyrics and forget about them for two weeks until someone says, "Hey, RM, you haven't written your rap yet." That's the hardest part. When the song is all written up and my rap is the last part that needs to go in. This was also a song where we were just wrapping up production, and I had a thought: 'I'll speak very frankly' (laughs). Still, if I were to ask myself, "Was this the best you could do?" then I would still answer, "It was the best."

In *MAP OF THE SOUL : PERSONA*, BTS's central intended message was that they would listen to the voices of ARMY, and as ARMY became the main character of the album, the narrator became the BTS we know today. RM says the following regarding the change he personally experienced through "Boy With Luv" (Feat. Halsey):

———I feel like I said, "I'll speak very frankly," because I really wanted to be frank. It's weird to think about now. Because when I wrote it, I thought, 'Are you really going to write it like this?' and couldn't

In any case, as Jung Kook of BTS, I am speaking to the fans who look toward me, which is why I want to tell them positive stories.

Because I believe that I, too, have the power to give hope.

—Jung Kook

believe what I was doing (laughs). I don't think I would've been brave enough to do that before. I would've changed the expression.

In that sense, "Intro : Persona,"* RM's solo song and the opening track of this album, was like a declaration of where this change in attitude would take BTS's music.

In this song, which starts with the line "'Who am I,' the question I had my entire life," RM wonders about where one is in life now with "How you feel? How you feeling right now?" and then confesses his honest thoughts on the fame that follows superstardom.

> *Actually I'm real good but a little uncomfortable*
> *I'm still not sure if I'm a dog or a pig or what else*
> *But others come and cast the pearl necklace on me*

On the lyrics of "Intro : Persona," RM says the following:

——To this day, when I see my name in the entertainment section of the news, I get scared. I sometimes imagine the kind of headlines that might come up one day: "Not Someone Who Deserves This Fame," "Not Really Talented, Actually Mediocre, Very Bad," "Look at Him as He Is," those kinds of fantasies.

This was why RM came up with the "persona" concept.

——I looked up a lot of things on the concept of the persona, and once I had done some thinking on it, I simplified the concept as "a social mask" and began to work on it. As well-trodden as it is, I couldn't help but bring up the question, "Who am I?" I was skeptical myself, thinking, 'Writing these lines is already so not cool' (laughs). But then the song wouldn't have made sense if I took them out.

Beginning with this question to himself, RM began writing the lyrics to this song as they came to mind. Working separately from the soundscape of BTS's music that was becoming more and more intricate, he wrote and recorded his lyrics on the spot as if doing a live performance, bringing out his inner voice as much as possible.

——When I received the beat track for the first time, I was a little surprised. There was just this repeating beat, a guitar, and really nothing else. So I was like, "What do you want me to do with this" (laughs). I needed a sense of an intro and a middle and an end to write the climax . . .

RM laughs as he says this, but the simplicity of the track he was given for "Intro : Persona" gave him the opportunity to be even more daring than before in telling his story. RM continues:

——Since the track had so little to it, the emptiness I needed to fill was that much bigger. So I could say a lot of things in the song and I wrote it pretty easily. It has the word "reveal" in it, I just thought, 'Let's just do what I want. Wasn't this what I've wanted to do all along? I know things are a bit confusing right now, but let's let it out a little.' I figured it would be all right to be a bit verbose.

RM was born on September 12, 1994. When he debuted in 2013, he was just shy of nineteen, and as mentioned before, other rappers would criticize him to his face or diss him. But five years later he was on top of the Billboard 200 and after releasing an album with the message to "love yourself," he was preparing an album full of messages for ARMY.

RM and the other members of BTS seemed to have completed their story. They had overcome the odds and reached incredible heights with the people who supported them. But as young men in their twenties, they were still in the process of finding out who they were as individuals. RM adds:

———What I wanted to say through "Intro : Persona" was, just, uh . . .

> An excuse, a confession, persuasion, a encouragement toward myself. Time is passing, I'm still standing here, and people are putting all sorts of labels on me . . . I couldn't avoid any of that as long as I lived, but maybe there was one last part of me that only I could define. And if that part joined another part that even I nor anyone else could ever define, then my yesterday and today can be created from there.

The sound that begins "Intro : Persona"ˑ is identical to the sound when RM begins the rap in the middle of "Intro : Skool Luv Affair,"ˑˑ the first song in the album *Skool Luv Affair* released in 2014. Also, the title of the song "Boy In Luv" in the *Skool Luv Affair* album is referenced by the title of the song "Boy With Luv" in the album *MAP OF THE SOUL : PERSONA*.

In "Boy In Luv," BTS were narrating the longing to be loved by someone else. And now, with "Boy With Luv" (Feat. Halsey), they are asking about the lives of ARMY and shifting to the position of *giving*

love. BTS convey their changing thoughts and emotions by looking back at their past, and in the process, discovering their present.

They had seemingly gone as far as they could as superstars. They no longer had to prove themselves to the world. But to these young men in their twenties, the task of drawing the "map of the soul" in search of answers to the question of "Who am I" was only beginning.

Surfin' USA

In 2017, BTS attended the Billboard Music Awards for the first time and won in the category of Top Social Artist. The following year, their BBMAs performance of "FAKE LOVE" (BTS's very first performance at the BBMAs) pushed them to the top of the Billboard 200. And in the 2019 event, the evening they performed "Boy With Luv" with Halsey joining them onstage, they not only won their third consecutive Top Social Artist Award but Top Duo/Group, one of the major awards of the night. Every time they took the BBMAs stage, their fame and the media's attention in America would take another giant step upwards.

On May 15 (local time), 2019, BTS appeared on *The Late Show with Stephen Colbert* on CBS.* In introducing BTS, the television audience was informed that precisely fifty-five years, three months, and six days since the Beatles debuted in America, a new star from overseas had made landing on the same stage. There at the Ed Sullivan Theater where the Beatles had made their American television debut, *The Late Show with Stephen Colbert* broadcast BTS's performance of "Boy With Luv" in black-and-white, just like the Beatles' had been fifty-five years ago. American mainstream media was now directly connecting BTS and ARMY with the Beatles and Beatlemania.

But BTS could not simply sit back and enjoy the fuss the media were making. The busier the world got, the more they knew for sure what they needed to be doing.

SUGA recalls their feelings from that period in time:

——When we won that major award at the BBMAs, we didn't have an emotion we could pin down like "greatness" or whatever. Our tour was beginning in a few days, there was no time to sit back and enjoy the moment. I really like that about the seven of us. No matter where we are or what situation we're in, we're always the same. We don't think too much about it (laughs). Not that we don't appreciate the significance of the award, I just think we make an effort not to dwell on it too much.

Perhaps to the US, the advent of BTS was an invasion[43] the likes of which had only been seen fifty-five years ago. But BTS had already been breaking unprecedented records in Korea since 2015. Only a year before they took the stage at *SNL* or *The Late Show with Stephen Colbert*, they were experiencing the dark side of glory to the point of thinking about breaking up. And so, the more they experienced ever-greater-by-the-year success in America, the more they had the chance to really look at reality

---

43 The British Invasion, spearheaded by the Beatles, denotes a wave of popularity of British rock acts in America in the mid-60s.

as it was. SUGA recalls the following in their exchanges with American artists at the time:

———Until then, my image of pop stars were just "pop stars." The people I grew up listening to and admiring. It's only right to be fascinated. I had this fantasy that they would be very different from me. But then, I learned they really weren't. On the outside, they ride expensive cars, wear gold chains, and have fancy parties every day. But a lot of it turned out to be just part of the business. It was "work" for them, in other words. And if they couldn't afford the cars or jewelry, they would rent them to show them off. There was, shall we say, a shattering. My fantasies were just shattered.

To BTS, their activities in America were not so much like the life of stardom often seen in movies, but more like something they needed to continue getting through. As they went through their list of things they had to do, they were coming to the realization that their souls were not aiming for more and more success but for something that was deep inside of themselves.

j-hope says:

———Standing on all those American stages gave us a kind of vibe that was different from what we felt in Korea. Because they're kind of freer over there. The more we got on television there, the more we felt affected by this vibe.

The freedom vibe j-hope felt then would influence his music later on. There is more to come on this, but his solo work like the single "Chicken Noodle Soup" and the song "Outro : Ego" from the album *MAP OF THE SOUL : 7* were the result of such sensibilities that he honed during their activities in America. j-hope continues:

———There was definitely an influence there. It was the kind of valuable experience money can't buy. I think that's why I feel so much affection for past moments like that. Because those were the performances where I learned something big, something I had never felt before.

MAP OF THE STADIUM

Jimin's inspirations from their American activities had a direct influence on BTS. As he attended the performances of various artists in America, he developed bigger artistic ambitions for BTS.

———I kept comparing their performances to ours. I think every performance we saw in the States made me do this. One group would have incredibly good dancers, another artist would have an amazing concept . . . For example, there was one performance where everyone is dancing like at a party, and then they suddenly coordinate so that the main performer is highlighted in the crowd, I loved that. There was even a performer who had really great staging and props.

Jimin wanted to incorporate these feelings into BTS's performances.

———I began thinking our concert staging could be better. Seeing the greatest artists in the world performing live . . . So we began asking more from our own concerts. I kept talking about the need to go beyond where we were, to change our repertoire and improve our sets and production.

The BTS WORLD TOUR "LOVE YOURSELF: SPEAK YOURSELF," which ran from May 2019, was a performance that realized all of Jimin's hopes. As an expanded version of the BTS WORLD TOUR

"LOVE YOURSELF," the new tracks from *MAP OF THE SOUL : PERSONA* were added to the setlist.

The BTS WORLD TOUR "LOVE YOURSELF: SPEAK YOURSELF" was the first BTS tour that was all stadium appearances. This changed everything from the BTS WORLD TOUR "LOVE YOURSELF" that had ended just a month ago. The stages were larger, which meant the members had to create a performance that could fill them and be able to convey their vision to a much larger audience. Not only that, the performance at Wembly Stadium, which was slated to bring in the largest single audience of the tour at sixty thousand people per date, was to be live streamed the globe on V Live.

Jung Kook remembers what they were determined to do as they entered these arenas:

———We were really nervous, but we went into these performances with the attitude of not being intimidated but thinking, 'We're going to completely destroy this place.' We kept our in-ear monitors out until the show began, listened to the audience scream for one moment, put in our monitors, and gave it our all for the performance. Honestly, I think it was thanks to the members supporting each other that we were able to do a stadium tour, and I've got to do my part.

BTS WORLD TOUR "LOVE YOURSELF: SPEAK YOURSELF" was not only one of the greatest moments in BTS history, but as Jung Kook said, it was also a time when they needed to show the world why BTS were BTS. The crowds of people were enough to fill these stadiums, but BTS needed to deliver the show of a lifetime to make a truly memorable impression on audiences. Jimin says:

———There aren't many artists who can perform in front of 50,000

It was the kind of valuable experience
money couldn't buy.
  Because those were the
performances where I learned
something big, something I had never
felt before.

—j-hope

people, and I wanted to really leave a strong impression on everyone who came. "We're really good," "We're a seriously great team," I wanted to show everyone that.

As Jimin had hoped, BTS WORLD TOUR "LOVE YOURSELF: SPEAK YOURSELF" delivered everything BTS were capable of. This performance begins with the song "Dionysus" from *MAP OF THE SOUL : PERSONA*. Two gigantic leopard sculptures appear on stage, and BTS atop a gigantic platform give a powerfully energetic performance as countless dancers fill the stage. This is followed by "Not Today," another song accompanied by the dancers in a large-scale spectacle. Around the middle of the show, the members leap around the stage singing a medley of their hits including "Dope," "Silver Spoon," and "Burning Up (FIRE)," while for the encore set that opens with "Anpanman," the stage is turned into a playground.

The magnitude of the stadium tour, the explosive performance of BTS, and the setlist that leads up to the bright and energetic "Anpanman" make the BTS WORLD TOUR "LOVE YOURSELF: SPEAK YOURSELF" setlist a chronicle of their journey thus far.

And after all those songs comes the finale, "Mikrokosmos."

Everybody's History

"Mikrokosmos" takes on an extra special meaning when being performed in a stadium-level arena. As in the lyrics "Shimmering starlight,"

"Peoples' lights / Are all precious," and "Starlight that shines even brighter in the darkest of nights," the lights held by all the people in the dark, especially from the official ARMY Bomb light sticks, spectacularly realize the intentions behind the song. From Korea's Seoul· to Saudi Arabia's Riyadh, the ARMY gathers in each city to shine a light in the dark.

As the final song of the setlist "Mikrokosmos" plays, it is ARMY that becomes the center of the performance, the true main character. And with the V Live live stream, ARMY all over the world are brought into the center of their life's narrative, connect with each other, and leave behind a collective memory. As the tour wound down, the vision of a stadium awash in violet light from ARMY Bombs became a distinct image that symbolizes ARMY.

Jimin, when talking about the tours from the *LOVE YOURSELF* era, seems especially subdued and thoughtful. He says:

———I think I cried a lot then. Because it was so great.

When asked what had moved him so much, he answers:

———I don't know. It's not just like it's a single moment . . . I was just, grateful and sorry and thankful and swept up in a thousand emotions.

The people Jimin feels grateful and sorry to are, of course, ARMY.

———Sometimes, when ARMY roars for us in unison, I could feel my soul blasting away behind me. That's when (all reason) just comes crumbling down.

BTS WORLD TOUR "LOVE YOURSELF: SPEAK YOURSELF"

was a BTS performance, but it was also a time, as in Jimin's recollection, when ARMY had managed to make BTS come "crumbling down."

It would not be an exaggeration to say that BTS's 2019, with the *MAP OF THE SOUL : PERSONA* album and tour, was the completion of a narrative. As the line in "Make It Right"· puts it, they were at a point of being "a hero in this world" when they decided to tell the stories of ARMY in *MAP OF THE SOUL : PERSONA* and finish off the BTS WORLD TOUR "LOVE YOURSELF: SPEAK YOURSELF" by putting ARMY in the center.

BTS had wished to prove their place in the world in which they found themselves. In the process, with the help of the people who loved them, they had created a universe where every person gathered possessed their own unique history. This was probably the reason behind the almost sacred mood of "Make It Right." SUGA's lyric in this song in particular is like the history of BTS themselves and a story of how they found salvation through ARMY.

> *The reason I survived the hell*
> *It wasn't for my sake, it was rather for yours*
> *If you know it please save my life*
> *The desert I've been struggling through without you makes me*
> *thirsty*
> *So hold me already*
> *I know that without you the ocean will be just like a desert*

A collaboration with the British singer-songwriter Ed Sheeran, the early version of "Make It Right" featured almost no rap and was mostly vocals. SUGA explains what happened behind the scenes:

———When the rap was added, the song got a little long. And Ed Sheeran's side suggested we might make the rap a little more melodious.

SUGA has this to say regarding the special advantages BTS have regarding rap:

———If, for example, you give the rappers in our group sixteen bars, the three of us can fill up those bars perfectly. Each of us three are distinct in style. What would otherwise take three or four songs to express, we can say it all in one. Concisely. That's an advantage that we have, I think.

Around the time *MAP OF THE SOUL : PERSONA* was being made, the members of BTS had developed a certain level of confidence in their music, and they could afford to make the daring choice of putting in a long rap in a fairly poppy song like "Make It Right."

In the changes he experienced around the time of writing this song, j-hope says:

———I think we began seeing a bigger picture. We were thinking of what kind of images and feelings we could inspire when the seven of us took to the stage with this song. We matured a little more in that sense, became a bit more refined.

j-hope has always been a team player who was vital in harmonizing the different voices of the group. But around the production of *MAP OF THE SOUL : PERSONA*, he realized what more he could express within the music of BTS. The method of singing with emphasis in parts like "everything is to reach you" and "The answer to my journey" in "Make It Right" was a way of satisfying his required role within the group and expressing his personality as an individual.

The pride and confidence BTS felt in themselves around this time were at an all-time high. As artists who had successfully pulled off a stadium world tour, what more did they find themselves wanting? Jimin answers:

———Doing this even better. And then doing better than that. No matter how fancy our staging gets, if we can't do what we do, none of that matters. To bowl the audience over with our performance, to make people shout, "Wow!" when they see us on stage. And to seamlessly convey the feeling that we are on the same wavelength as each other. Surely, that's what "doing this well" means.

Life, Art, Sleep

———I did feel a lot of resentment even then. I was way in over my head, how did I end up with all this . . . I couldn't put my thoughts in order.

This was SUGA's state of mind while writing the lyrics of "Make It Right." Since the end of the *LOVE YOURSELF* series, he was feeling the kind of anxiety that comes in the aftermath of great success.

———I could see it ending badly. The kind of ending that happens to successful people. There was this feeling that people were waiting for us below, thinking, 'When are they going to fall from there' . . . I hadn't realized that even when this situation was over, the anxiety would simply shapeshift into a different form. Hence the lyrics that emerged.

If "Make It Right" was a record of BTS's history of being saved by ARMY, to SUGA personally, this song was an ongoing story where he was still seeking salvation.

To say that the work surrounding *MAP OF THE SOUL : PERSONA* enabled BTS to accomplish all that they could as artists is not an exaggeration. Their album was a gift dedicated to their fans; BTS won Top Duo/Group at the BBMAs with it, and created a "microcosmos" with all of their supporters in stadiums around the world.

But SUGA fought constantly against the fear that comes from great success. Just as Jimin dreamed of doing better as he came off the stage, there would be no true happy ending for BTS even as they conquered stadiums the world over. Instead, the future they themselves had predicted in "Dionysus" was coming true.

> *Drink up (The pain from the creative work)*
> *One bite (The shout of the era)*
> *Drink up (the communication with me)*
> *One bite (Okay now I'm ready fo sho)*
>
> . . .
>
> *New records mean the competition, the competition with myself yeah*
> *Raise the glass and celebrate, one shot*
> *But I'm still thirsty as ever*

Just as the lyrics mention "pain" and "competition," hacking through the realities of their day-to-day lives was not easy.

———Ah, I thought I might die (laughs).

To Jung Kook, that was what the stadium tour felt like. No matter how they staged the performance, there was no way to avoid running themselves ragged across the huge stage.

———Every time we go backstage, we have to get changed and touch up our hair and makeup. But sometimes, we'd just lie down completely. Because we hadn't portioned out our strength to last throughout the performance . . . When you're on stage, your feelings run ahead of you.

As this problem of conserving enough strength to last the night shows, the stadium tour required an even stricter form of self-discipline than what they had been used to.

But the harder battle was waging outside the stadium. As the BTS WORLD TOUR "LOVE YOURSELF: SPEAK YOURSELF" was underway in 2019, Jin was beginning to discover something had changed in the world around him. He says:

———Even things like going to an amusement park in the middle of the tour gave me a lot of heartache. I might go with my manager or bodyguard or interpreter, but even if I tried to get them to enjoy themselves, this is work for them in the end which makes it impossible for them to to relax. I was basically alone in having fun.

By the time they began their tour, interest in BTS had increased to an unbelievable scale compared to the previous year. From crashing the Melon servers to their *SNL* performance and stadium tours, their popularity went from strength to strength, and Big Hit Entertainment had to do all they could to keep the members safe. It became extremely difficult to allow BTS to get some rest and relaxation even when overseas, much less in Korea. To be more specific, it became extremely difficult for them to go outside at all.

Jung Kook expresses a similar regret:

———During tours, we hardly ever go out. Before, we might venture outside every once in a while, but now there were all these things that we needed to do. And the people who worked at the company also found it hard to feel relaxed around us. Back when we could go about as we pleased, we would hang out with the staff and do shoots and it was fun. But now, it was hard to do little things like that.

The situation surrounding the tour deepened Jin's concerns regarding his place in BTS. He confesses:

———I love music, I really like it, but I thought I wasn't necessarily good at it. During our tours, the other members might spend time in their rooms working on a song for fun when they were bored, in other words, music was their hobby as well as work, but it wasn't for me something I did for fun . . . Because I didn't think I was the type who could make a song for fun. Which is why I think I lost a little of myself during the tour.

Since their debut, Jin had held the other members in awe. He explains:

———For example, when we practiced dance, some of the members would instantly master a move I would need several repetitions to get. I would get dejected. 'Wow, those guys are so talented. We're in the same classes, but how could they be so much better?'

So for Jin, he felt more of a sense of responsibility to do his best as a member of BTS than confidence in his abilities.

————I couldn't stand it if everyone else is working hard and I just become this "weak link" in the group. So I had no choice but to work as hard as possible myself.

But around this time, Jin's transcended his own expectations; he had composed the song "Epiphany" from the previous album *LOVE YOURSELF* 結 *'Answer'* on his own, and in the "Dionysus" performances that required a constant barrage of powerful moves, he tag-teamed with RM to lead the group. The fact that he and RM—who had once been so unsure of their dancing at their debut—would be pulling off this performance was proof of how hard they had worked since their earliest days.

But Jin only regarded such effort as part of the job, not as a special accomplishment. On this, he says:

————The old saying is that even the mountains and rivers change in ten years, so we must change, too. And whenever there is new choreography, I know it will take longer for me to pick it up compared to everyone else, so I always think, 'I've got to get this down as quickly as possible so there are no problems later.'

And when the fruit of all that practice was to successfully pull off a performance like "Dionysus," Jin has only this to say—something that sounds like his life's philosophy as much as how he feels about his work:

————I'm satisfied with it, like 'At least I held up my end.' That's really all it is. I'm so preoccupied with catching up to the other members that when I manage to get through it, I mostly think, 'I'm glad I worked hard enough this time to hold up my end.' I'm sure there are people who would hate this kind of thinking, but I can't help it if there are things that are beyond my capacity (laughs). I think it's a good thing if despite it, I keep getting better and continue to grow from wherever I happen to be.

It was important, clearly, for Jin that he had balance in his life. The life of constantly working at doing your best to be a member of BTS made going back to your normal life as an individual take that much more time. But with BTS WORLD TOUR "LOVE YOURSELF: SPEAK YOURSELF, the change in their circumstances took away almost all of Jin's transitional time.

————There was no balance in our lives at the time. And no one to really discuss this concern with. It was great to perform and meet fans, but there was almost no time to do anything else.

It became difficult to meet up with friends they had been close to since before their debut, and the stress was accumulating from having to change living spaces every time they moved to a different city during their tour.

————There wasn't actually much stress in the performance areas themselves. Everything is prepared in those places. We can ask for a doctor if we needed one, and there was always food available if we needed to eat. But it was the constant changing of the spaces that was always the problem. Whenever we moved hotels, our computers and everything else needed to be reinstalled, the room had to be rearranged to how we needed it to be . . . I'm not great at falling asleep in unfamiliar settings, but on tour, you're changing where you sleep every two or three days. And in Korea, if you're hungry in the middle of the night, you can just drop by a convenience store, but on tour, you can't easily do small things like that.

At the very least, Jin maintained some semblance of his previous life by talking to the anonymous people he met in online games that he would play when it was late at night in Korea.

SUGA, meanwhile, has this to say about the difficulties he experienced during the 2019 tour:

————I was just resigned. Like, 'What am I going to do, except accept it.'
Our schedule was so packed that it was a matter of, 'Is my body
going to break first, or my mind?' And my body was so tired, my
mind did not have the strength to be anxious, even. The problem
was, because of jetlag during our world tour, I would go to sleep
at night but then wake up around 2 A.M. That would drive me
up the wall. Finishing with our American tour and performing in
Europe was slightly better in terms of the time differences, but
before that was a month in the US where it was so hard to fall
asleep. It didn't matter if I was anxious or not, I needed to sleep
if I wanted to perform properly the next day.

To ensure they had the physical strength to soar onstage, the members battled through their sleep issues. And at the end of each performance, they had to battle with thoughts on whether they were living life properly, how they were going to do better as artists, or how they were going to process this surreal experience of having made it as far as they had. It was truly a moment that required a "map of the soul."

One Month

————I was such a mischievous boy. Even when we'd been selected to
debut, all I could think about was how to have fun (laughs).
Even at the trainee dorm I kept thinking things like, 'What if I
ordered some fried chicken and pizza and started a party?'
V continues to look back from his trainee days to the present.

——You know how people get all regretful and say, "I wish I made more memories as a school kid"? We talk about it a lot, too, but at least I managed to make a lot of memories. Because I got to spend a lot of time in school. That made me really happy. Because that allowed me to recharge, and I could pour all that energy into our practices.

V mentions this to explain what he means by the following sentence:

——I was, actually, a different person.

On what he was like as a trainee, V remembered himself less as a person who did his best unconditionally and more as someone who had to "like" something to do it. He needed, therefore, the leisure to recharge and take stock just as much as he needed practice to improve. He referred to this as "the adolescence of the mind," which could be interpreted as the determination to attain personal happiness over material "success."

——I tell myself a lot that I will become a better person. But I think I have to become happy myself first or somehow receive a kind of energy in order to take a step closer to becoming that better person. It's the same when I'm inspired. In the beginning of the pandemic, when our entire schedule was canceled and we could rest a bit, I suddenly had this craving to see the ocean at night. So I went with an old school friend to Sokcho in the middle of the night. We lit sparklers, recorded the sound of the ocean, and tried writing songs over the recordings of the night waves. Seeing the ocean at night when I really wanted to see it as opposed to when I really didn't was incredibly different. When my heart is satisfied this way, I take note of the emotions that come to me and write them down.

V's method of seeking inspiration from his lived experience is part of the secret to BTS's "magic."

By the time BTS were promoting *MAP OF THE SOUL : PERSONA*, the Korean idols and any artist falling under the category of K-pop were deemed cultural icons that represented the country overseas. The K-pop industry by this time, buoyed by BTS's success, had quickly grown into a true behemoth. The first week sales of *MAP OF THE SOUL : PERSONA* was about 2.13 million units, while *MAP OF THE SOUL : 7*, discussed in further detail later, reached 3.37 million in its first week only ten months later.

Another example is Big Hit Entertainment's boy group TOMORROW X TOGETHER, which debuted in March 2019 with the first album *The Dream Chapter: Star*, which sold 77,000 units in its first week, while three years later their *minisode 2: Thursday's Child* would go on to clear 1.24 million units.

The music industry around the world had to accept this new fandom-centric system developed by Korea's idol industry and fandoms like ARMY, and BTS were in the middle of this typhoon, if not the cause of it.

But just as the ability to go see the ocean at night when he wanted to was a prerequisite of happiness for V, it was important to allow the members of BTS the freedom to do as they wanted. Like having instant noodles together after a stadium performance, or playing online games with other anonymous Korean gamers before calming down enough to go to bed.

This was how even as the number of ARMY expanded tremendously across the globe, BTS were still able to approach ARMY in an emotionally meaningful way. To follow the heart—V discusses what this means in terms of their attitude in stepping onto the stage before huge audiences.

———Whether you're under pressure or not, what you really need to

I think I have to become happy myself
first or somehow receive a kind of
energy in order to take a step closer
to becoming that better person.

—V

prepare is your heart. Thinking about this and that will only make you too anxious to do even the things you're good at doing. Let go of the pressure, put behind yourself all that you've done before, and get up on that stage with just one thing, your heart.

The one-month break BTS took beginning on August 12, 2019, was a choice they made to find new ways to listen to their hearts through a little rest. With just two months before the opening of BTS WORLD TOUR "LOVE YOURSELF: SPEAK YOURSELF" in Seoul, they needed time to experience the things they genuinely wanted to experience, whether that was the ocean at night or online games or addressing their concerns on their music. Jung Kook explains the reasons behind the break:

———We were exhausted. The stages and performances were something we really wanted to do and now we were doing it, but our schedule was just so harsh . . . Afraid our affection for the work would diminish, that it would become simply "work," we all decided, "Let's take a little time for ourselves."

As RM would explain to their fans through various media several times over, the *MAP OF THE SOUL* series was supposed to be a trilogy of albums consisting of *PERSONA*, *SOUL*, and *EGO*. But with their break, production on their subsequent albums was delayed, which is how the trilogy was revamped into the duology of *MAP OF THE SOUL : PERSONA* and *MAP OF THE SOUL : 7*.

For BTS to cancel an album meant giving up on tens of billions of won in sales alone, and when including ancillary income from tours and other projects, at least 100 billion won in revenue. To those who regard the Korean idol industry purely from a business standpoint, this decision would probably not make a lot of sense. But no matter how big a company Big Hit Entertainment had become or what sales goals it set, some things simply took higher priority.

Perhaps to the members, a month was not such a long time. But it was a meaningful enough period to take pause to think about the direction of their lives. Jin describes recovering the psychological state he had lost:

———Even in the midst of our busy schedule, I would always have a moment of thinking, 'Am I allowed to do this?' whenever I paused for a break. I tried hard to rid myself of this attitude then. To rest without guilt, to do all the things I wanted to do without holding myself back.

What Jin had wanted was the small joys of ordinary life. He played games for whole days and met with friends. He even went on a fishing trip with SUGA. Jin recalls:

———We went fishing for a travel content shoot[44] one time and SUGA said to me, "Should we try catching a big one in the Han River when we're back in Korea?" And we ended up really going, and the fishing was fun, but it was also the hwe and the soju we had on the boat that tasted so good. And that led to other fishing trips.

Jin's attitude in enjoying and valuing such ordinary moments of life was a positive influence on the other members. Smiling, Jin says:

———SUGA said thanks to me, his mental health improved a lot and he was grateful for it (laughs).

To SUGA, fishing wasn't simply a means of having a relaxing hobby and taking a brief rest:

———I didn't really know what an ordinary life entailed. I think it was because music was both my favorite hobby and my job. It's the

---

44 From *BTS Bon Voyage*, streamed on V Live from 2016, currently available on Weverse.

same now, to be honest. I'd wake up, go straight to the bathroom, then go to the studio. Even when I read a book I would read it in the studio, play my games in the studio, and all those days would repeat themselves. But I have many other hobbies now. Like playing guitar . . . I tried looking for a hobby outside of music, but I just had too much fun playing guitar.

SUGA still considered music to be his whole life. But as he had the leisure time to take interest in other things, his attitude toward music also shifted. He remembers:

———My work methods changed with *MAP OF THE SOUL : PERSONA*. Before that album, I used to feel strongly that I had to do everything by myself, but with "Ddaeng,"[45] I happened to work with EL CAPITXN. We didn't have much time to work on it, which loosened up our methodology a bit. This allowed us to make more songs, and I began thinking, 'Even if there are slight imperfections, there's nothing to be done.' This freed me from a lot of stress and allowed me to keep working. But when I compared the results to my previous work created under huge stress, there really wasn't that significant a difference. That's when I realized, 'Ah, all my oversensitivity and worries, maybe they were because I was trying to attain some ideal that was never attainable in the first place.'

---

45 A "unit song" between SUGA, RM, and j-hope on a mixtape released in June 2018 on the BTS official blog commemorating the fifth anniversary of BTS's debut.

This experience would become the starting point of SUGA turning into a producer as well as a member of BTS, which for him was like going back to his own beginnings as an artist. SUGA says:

———I was a songwriter in Daegu, which was why I was so intent on producing. So I took on some outside work. After all, even if I wrote a lot of songs, I couldn't put them all on our albums. I wasn't really thinking of achieving something as a producer necessarily, but at the same time, there was no reason to say no to outside work. Because I was always writing songs, and if these songs were to see the light, I needed to work as a producer as well.

SUGA also remembers a certain conversation he had with Bang Si-Hyuk:

———Bang Si-Hyuk said to me, "You'll never quit music" (laughs). That I would never be able to quit of my own volition, that I would always return to it. I'm no longer tortured by music. Because I've accepted it. I'd hoped never to live always forcing myself and being worried all the time, and now it's come true, like, 'So what. This is fun in its own way, right?'

The Portrait of a Young Superstar

j-hope took the route of "working" to find himself over the break. He spent the month off putting together "Chicken Noodle Soup."* Just a few days after their break began, he flew to America to film the music video, and on September 27, not long after BTS resumed activities, he released the song.

In his typically reasonable manner, j-hope explains why he chose to work during that time.

———In a way, that was relaxation to me. And I'd always wanted to go overseas on my own at some point, so getting that chance to go and learn new things helped me to get back on my feet. It was "work" to me, of course, but experiencing something new overseas and sharing it in a vlog* and sharing it with ARMY was my own process of recuperation. To share, "these are the thoughts that I have about my work."

In his trainee days, j-hope had described the dorm as a "rap den" as he learned how to rap, and here he was now, writing his own songs and lyrics. Following up his first mixtape, *Hope World*,** which dropped in March 2018, j-hope released "Chicken Noodle Soup" (Feat. Becky G) in September 2019. A few years later, in July 2022, he became the first BTS member to release a full solo album with *Jack In The Box*.***

To j-hope, personal growth would always be entwined with the act of creation. A month before the release of *Jack In The Box*, j-hope speaks of the album's direction and his motivation for creating it:

———Because I knew all too well my own shortcomings and what problems I had inside myself, I thought I would be able to come up with more serious music if I brought them out of myself. After my first mixtape, it had been a long time since I released a proper album, so I had this idea that I wanted to show I had gotten a little better at what I do.

Looking back on his journey as an artist, j-hope says:

——It's true that my work took a while to develop because I started out in music through dance. I also admit that there are things I simply can't do. But I'm always on myself to learn quickly and grow and become a better artist. I still consider my growth as an artist as something that's in progress.

In this journey as an artist, "Chicken Noodle Soup" would prove an important milestone for j-hope. The experience of working with dancers of different races for his music video shoot would become an impetus to mix different cultures together in a single song to create a new whole. Recalling the shoot itself, j-hope says:

——Everyone on set was completely one with the atmosphere there. A natural vibe that hadn't been there before emerged, which allowed for a really fun shoot. Becky G, who featured in the song, freed me to do everything I wanted to do by saying, "Try whatever you want to try, I'll be right here for you." The dancers brought their own experiences and dances and vibes to the set. All these things came together into "a dance of one," a result that incorporated everyone's commonalities.

The act of collaboration had always influenced j-hope in an important way:

——If I'd had to find the answer to every question on my own every time, it would've been a really hard path to follow, but I think I was always influenced by the people around me. Who likes me,

I'm no longer tortured by music.
Because I've accepted it. Like,
'So what. This is fun in its own way,
right?'

—SUGA

whom I get onstage with, who will lead me, who will support me. These are what's really important to me.

This is perhaps the answer j-hope himself found as to the question of why he is the "hope" of BTS:

———I was having a drink with Bang Si-Hyuk, and it's a little embarrassing to say but he once said this to me: "To others you are hope itself, and without you, there would be no BTS" (laughs). I'd relied so much on him and the members of BTS, which I suppose meant a part of me had always sought his approval. So hearing him say that did put my feelings in order a bit . . . In any case, I'm surrounded by good people and beloved by our fans, so how could I ever fail?

To find their own answers was the task of not just j-hope but all the members. In thinking back on their stardom, BTS had looked to ARMY as their ultimate supporters through the years in creating *MAP OF THE SOUL : PERSONA*. And the question of what story they would follow that up with could only be answered by looking within.

RM found his answer through the lives of other artists. During his break, he immersed himself in art and visited art museum exhibits. RM says:

———After *MAP OF THE SOUL : PERSONA*, we had reached a new peak in terms of mainstream approval, and that happened to coincide with my growing interest in art. I had always liked going to places on my own and having time to think, and normally I would do that in nature, when suddenly I had a desire to see spaces others had created or something with a theme. At first, I dropped into exhibits without doing much research, and I went to a lot of photography exhibits. Then I remembered going to the Art Institute of Chicago while we were on our tour in 2018, so I thought of going to permanent exhibits in Korea. And that's how I got to see a lot of fine art.

Art exhibits were RM's way of conversing with himself. He continues:

———I think that's how I became conscious of how to think. As I began to have favorite artists, I found new ways of communicating with myself. A work of art is the visual result of an artist who had thought long and hard about things, right? With so much trial and error put into it. Which is why I feel such a catharsis in seeing the results of an artist putting out a piece of art as if they were saying, "This is what I think," after going through all that processing.

RM's own process of looking back at himself through art is also part and parcel of his interrogating the line between "artist" and "idol," something he had been thinking of constantly since his debut. He says:

———Fantasy is an important component of K-pop. 2019 was an endless repetition of thinking about this aspect, of me trying to close the distance. Between my persona as a member of BTS and the actual person that I was or wanted to be. To be honest, it's fine if I were perceived as just another member of BTS. Pretending I'm something else would require more of an effort, anyway. And whenever I meet my fans, I'm so grateful to them that I want to hug them all. Telling them, "Wow, thank you so much," "Thanks to you, I'm alive and breathing and making music." But what I'm wondering is, 'Can I do that and at the same time keep selling the fantasy?' I know there are people who think, 'You're not real people, stop pretending like you are,' 'But you guys make lots of money,' and all that. This makes me think we're on a bridge made of glass that lies across such boundaries. And we can see how far it falls below . . . So it's also scary. Because just one crack means we're going to fall.

7

MAP OF THE SOUL : 7, released on February 21, 2020, was perhaps the process of RM thinking through these questions. RM explains the structure of the *MAP OF THE SOUL* series through his roles in his solo song "Intro : Persona" and the unit song he did with SUGA, "Respect."·

———This series begins with asking, "Who am I," and ends with "respect."

The regular album *MAP OF THE SOUL : 7* includes the tracks "Intro : Persona," "Boy With Luv" (Feat. Halsey), "Make It Right," "Jamais Vu," and "Dionysus" from their mini album *MAP OF THE SOUL : PERSONA*. Everything from the sixth track, "Interlude : Shadow," onward is all new.

Beginning with the lyric "Who am I," the album describes a journey that leads to the outside world through "you," or ARMY, where in "Interlude : Shadow," they look down upon a shadow "as dark as the light's intense" that had followed their success. From that moment onward, each member sinks deep into their inner self.

Jung Kook thinks back hard to the time they were creating *MAP OF THE SOUL : 7*:

———There was a bit of inner confusion. I considered myself still lacking somewhat, but there we were flying around in airplanes doing concerts and winning awards, and people loved me, and I had to meet their expectations . . . I was dealing with all that chaos in my life with some awkwardness. I didn't know where I had gone wrong, and wondered how I could've done better.

Jung Kook, only twenty-two years old at the time of world superstardom and the production of *MAP OF THE SOUL : 7*, was going through some extremes. Through his solo song "My Time" in this album, he confessed this problem:

The younger me grew up without realizing
(Like a child who lost his way)
This got me oh just trippin'
This feeling of pacing up and down
Don't know what to do with / Am I livin' this right?
Why am I the only one in a different time and space?

Thinking back to that time, Jung Kook says:

———Jung Kook the singer's time and Jung Kook the individual's time were just not in sync. But I don't think there was anything I could do. No one can live exactly as they want. But instead, they might find a different kind of happiness in some other aspect . . . I think you have to endure and live through something like that if you want to step up to the next level.

With the album's predecessor, *MAP OF THE SOUL : PERSONA*,

MAP OF THE SOUL : 7

THE 4TH FULL-LENGTH ALBUM
2020. 2. 21

TRACK

01 Intro : Persona
02 Boy With Luv (Feat. Halsey)
03 Make It Right
04 Jamais Vu
05 Dionysus
06 Interlude : Shadow
07 Black Swan
08 Filter
09 My Time
10 Louder than bombs

11 ON
12 UGH!
13 00:00 (Zero O'Clock)
14 Inner Child
15 Friends
16 Moon
17 Respect
18 We are Bulletproof : the
Eternal
19 Outro : Ego
20 ON (Feat. Sia) (Digital Only)

VIDEO

 COMEBACK TRAILER:
Shadow

 "Black Swan" Art Film

 COMEBACK TRAILER:
Ego

 "ON" Kinetic Manifesto
Film

 "ON"
MV

 "Black Swan"
MV

 "We are Bulletproof :
the Eternal"
MV

where BTS had reached the pinnacle of mainstream popularity, whatever they put out next had been predestined to make waves in the global music industry. This was the point where BTS chose to fill the bulk of their subsequent effort with tracks containing their most personal thoughts and feelings.

Jimin describes his solo song "Filter" and the album-making process this time around as "a conversation I had with myself":

———I was thinking hard about whether I should separate myself from my persona as an idol or see them as one entity.

Jimin, around this time, had a lot of thoughts about what kind of person he was and was becoming. Through this period, he got to thinking of what the ideal Park Jimin would be.

———I think the most ideal kind of person is an honest person. In the past I tended to sweat the small stuff, and I would often hesitate in speaking out even when I had something to say. I wanted people to be smiling and have them near me, which is why I would sometimes resort to exaggeration. I'd be acting like someone else, in other words. Then, from 2019, I would stay silent when I wanted to be silent, and tried speaking out against things when I didn't like them. And that's when I began to see it clearly. It's not that I didn't want to be alone, I just didn't want to be left behind.

In an interview around this time with *Weverse Magazine*, Jimin describes himself as a person who wants to receive love.˙ That for reasons he couldn't understand, he had always wanted the love of others, and this desire had been a constant influence in his life. Jimin says:

———I don't know. I think I was just born that way (laughs).

He speaks from a very deep part of himself:

———It must've become rooted in me like some kind of obsession. That if I don't act the way people wanted me to, or if I didn't give as much as others wanted me to give, I would be a worthless kind of person.

Jimin's attitude also showed through the way that he lived his life as an artist. He gave his all onstage, vying for the love of his audience, and this took up a significant part of his self. Jimin continues:

———But thankfully, I think my idol self and true self are not that different. I've never really had to say to others, "I'm a person, too, please understand." Sure, there are personal things about me I don't necessarily want to reveal to the world. But the work I'm doing now is something I chose to do, and what you see is the way I really am.

A performer who achieves perfection onstage—this was Jimin's persona, and his solo song "Filter" reflected his desire to show his best self onstage to receive the fans' love.

Mix the palette's colors, pick your filter
Which version of me do you want
The one to change your world, I'm your filter
Color it to your heart

Jimin says:

———I want to show the fans a lot of different faces, show them how I keep changing. This song is like a story that portrays me very accurately, which is why I could approach it in a fun way when we started working on it.

RM explains how open he was with his story in the *MAP OF THE SOUL : 7* album, and at the same time how he expressed it in the music:

———For example, before, I would stop at saying, "These are my thoughts," or "I think I must be someone who's sometimes contradictory or hypocritical" but I've grown to the point of being able to express, "I've thought it over, and maybe I'm closer to being such-and-such person."

Just like the process Jimin went through to complete *MAP OF THE SOUL : 7*, this album shows how the members' self-reflection expresses itself in their artistic work.

The teaser song "Black Swan"· from *MAP OF THE SOUL : 7* is about how the members of BTS define themselves as artists. In this song, they ask themselves what would they live by if "The heart no longer races," "When hearing the music play."

> *If this can no longer resonate*
> *No longer make my heart vibrate*
> *Then like this may be how I die my first death*

Thankfully, I think my idol self and true self are not that different.
    The work I'm doing now is something I chose to do, and what you see is the way I really am.

—Jimin

If the song "Dionysus" was about their ruminating over what more they needed to do for their art, "Black Swan" was about going forward in their destiny as artists despite it all.

> *The waves go*
> *darkly by in a throe*
> *But I'll never get dragged away again*

In their choreography for this song, the hip-hop beats of "Black Swan" are enhanced with elements of contemporary dance, which combine with BTS's signature movements and dynamism, touch upon mainstream music and classical or commercialism and artistry, and without being wholly categorized as either, create a third, unique aesthetic. In their first performance of "Black Swan," broadcast on January 28, 2020, on *The Late Late Show with James Corden*, they danced in simple clothes and bare feet in a most symbolic gesture.[46]

Also, before the premiere of the MV,* "Black Swan" was released as an art film** that BTS do not appear in. The song was rearranged

---

46 In terms of its attempt to connect mainstream art with the avant-garde, the contemporary art project *CONNECT, BTS* by BTS and Big Hit Entertainment can also be understood in a similar fashion. This project, which transcends nationality, genre, and generations, brought world-famous artists and curators to feature pieces that extend into contemporary art the philosophy and message of the music of BTS, including "affirmation of diversity," "connection," and "communication." Premiering in London on January 14, 2020, *CONNECT, BTS* was also shown in Berlin, Buenos Aires, New York City, and Seoul.

as a classical piece, and seven dancers from the MN Dance Company from Slovenia put on a performance. To not feature the members of a band in a video ostensibly made to promote said band was a daring choice for a Korean idol group. But it showed how "Black Swan" moved freely between art and industry, erasing the boundary that divided them.

——This was a difficult song.

That is j-hope's take on the unique qualities of the "Black Swan" choreography.

——So I went about learning the choreography with the attitude of trying to learn as much as possible, and tried to discover what I could do for the song as much as I could. To the point where I wonder what everyone else was doing (laughs). Jimin, at least, is so specialized in dance that he can express anything he wants, but I do wonder what everyone else was thinking as they learned that choreography . . . That dance was not easy.

Jimin says of the "Black Swan" dance:

——Doing this song made me think, 'Why had we never thought of the songs we make, the music videos and performances we do for them as works of art?' "Black Swan" made me feel like we had truly created a piece of art.

To Jimin, "Black Swan" was also a song that opened his eyes to new horizons in his capabilities for performance.

——When we got our choreography, I was probably the most excited out of all the members. Because I thought, 'I can do this really well.' I felt it was something we had never danced before, it made me feel excited about it. And I loved the feeling of covering a wider range on the spectrum of dance. Maybe professional dance artists may not see what we do as real contemporary dance, but for us, incorporating elements of dance art helps us widen our range when it comes to expressing the songs . . . I was simply grateful that we could do that.

He had been a student of contemporary dance and learned hip-hop to debut as an idol, worked hard on countless stages to broaden the range of what he could do, and here at the pinnacle of commercial success managed to contain all that he had done until now in a single work.

The production of *MAP OF THE SOUL : 7* is the process of how each member of BTS, by looking back at the paths they had taken and their personas as idols, came to accept their lives as artists.

From this perspective, the song "Friends," which is also on the *MAP OF THE SOUL : 7* album, is the polar opposite of "Black Swan" and a kind of balancing force. A unit song between Jimin and V, "Friends" talks of the two meeting for the first time in "A particularly shimmering Seoul" and going through the thick and thin of "Best friends one day, enemies the next" until finally reaching the "I know all about you" level of friendship.

According to V, "Friends" was created from the very real friendship he had with Jimin. V explains the genesis of the song:

———I just wanted to do a song with Jimin. I really like him as a person, especially the Jimin who performs onstage. Which is how I got to think, 'If Jimin and I do a song together, shall I try being like him a little?' I thought of doing a song that required a dramatic performance. But Jimin said to me, "You and I have lots of stories together, and we're the same age, why don't we just make a song out of that, just as friends?" And he came up with some preliminary work on the track and I just really loved it. So I told him, "Hey, just finish it, why don't you" (laughs). Jimin got so fired up that he made it even better than it already was.

Considering their first encounter with each other, this was a surprising development. V had always thought of Jimin as someone who was the complete opposite of him.

———I'm so different from Jimin. When we were trainees, Jimin was really desperate for debut, and I was more like, 'If I get cut, I guess that's my fate.'

According to V, "Friends" is a song about how these two very different people came to accept their differences.

———I couldn't understand him at first. Sure, I was a little too young to be very understanding of others, and hadn't met many people then . . . But I was really curious and kept thinking, 'Why does he work so hard?' Because Jimin really, really gives it his all in every single song. And I came to realize, 'This kid is absolutely serious about being onstage. And he's constantly worried people will be disappointed by his performance.' I'd thought long and hard about Jimin this way, and it turned out, Jimin had also thought about me. And once I realized that I had things I was good at while Jimin had his things he was good at . . . I started to understand. It's just so fascinating to me. That complete opposites can be like, "Wow, we really don't go together," but once we saw how we made up for each other's deficiencies, we came to see each other with even more respect and admiration.

Two completely different people accepting each other's differences and becoming friends might come across as a cliché in a movie or a drama. But if the two happen to be members of BTS, then it becomes an epic narrative. This was how "Friends" became one of the most famous songs in the world that depicts the friendship between two specific persons.

The process up to the release of the song "Friends" was also one of Jimin and V rediscovering themselves as artists through each other. If it was Jimin's ambition to be the greatest artist he could be onstage, V wanted to immerse himself in expressing his emotions as an artist. V says:

———I don't need a studio. If I could only write songs in a studio, I would ask the company for one. But I can only write good songs when I really have the urge to, so . . . With melodies, it's the ones that came to me naturally that I like the best.

Of his solo song "Inner Child" in *MAP OF THE SOUL : 7*, V says:

———This song was supposed to be a "performance" song. Something to really show off to the fans in a live performance.[47]

---

47 The COVID-19 pandemic would make it impossible for "Inner Child" to be performed live for the fans. It was eventually performed online at the *BTS MAP OF THE SOUL ON:E* concerts October 10–11, 2020.

"Inner Child" also ended up being a story of the feelings he felt during the time of writing it. V says:

——I wanted to fill it with the hurt I felt. It's a very lively song, but the lyrics are really sad.

> *Yesterday's you*
> *Now I see it all*
> *So many thorns on a sprouting rose*
> *I want to give you a hug*

"Inner Child," depending on who is listening, can be understood as a song for ARMY who have faithfully supported BTS since the beginning, or as its title implies, be interpreted as a song about the delicate inner child that still exists within V. But either way, the song is V's way of extending his encouragement to all of his listeners.

Jin in his solo song "Moon"· wanted to express his feelings toward ARMY.

——I wanted a cheerful song, no matter what. With lyrics that spoke directly to the fans. So I came up with "I'll orbit around you / I'll be there by your side" for the chorus. When we were deciding on the lyrics, I insisted on this part being included. Because it contained my sincere feelings, I really wanted it to be there.

In the song, Jin describes himself as a moon that constantly orbits

ARMY, and he wanted to convey the joy of this song in his performance of it as well.[48]

——This is the song that made me think, 'I really want to dance on a solo stage for once.' So I prepared choreography and everything.

Jin had specific ideas about the choreography. Like the other members, he was exhausted from their never-ending schedule and from time to time was plagued with doubts. But he chose, one more time, the love of the fans, and to express his gratitude for their love.

RM constantly questioned the limitations put before him as an idol or superstar within the mainstream music industry. Jin worked hard to convey his sincere gratitude toward the fans. And this is perhaps who BTS are: they dig deep within themselves as both idols and artists, speak candidly about those issues, and at the end of it return to the relationship between themselves and their fans.

MAP OF THE SOUL : 7 uses the widest range in this spectrum and was the most complex and varied structurally in terms of its composition. "Intro : Persona," "Interlude : Shadow," and "Outro : Ego" served as signposts on the way to the members' self-discovery while the solo and unit songs, which contained their personal thoughts and stories, were confessions of where they were now and where they had come from, and the act of seeking answers to their life questions. The journeys of these seven idols and artists are as spectacularly varied as the genres of hip-hop, rock, EDM, pop, and combinations thereof that they express themselves through. At the same time, *MAP OF THE SOUL : 7* as exemplified in "Black Swan" is ultimately about

---

48 This song was also live streamed in *BTS MAP OF THE SOUL ON:E.*

bringing all of these disparate elements together into questioning what it means to live as an artist and the process in which the answer is drawn forth.

SUGA in "Interlude : Shadow" tells the story of a desire to succeed, but seeing "shadow at my feet" and realizing "I can leap in the air but also plunge." His fear was something that had haunted him since the success of BTS. But he confronts this fear in "Interlude : Shadow" and begins to break free of it. SUGA says:

———This song was written in the state of having completely accepted the situation. I wanted it to be a set of guidelines, almost. There are going to be other successful artists in the future, and I look forward to that, but they might feel what I'm feeling now. The anxiety I feel. But not everyone tells you, "Being successful is scary . . ." (laughs).

SUGA began to accept both the joy and suffering music gives and tried to reconcile the many emotions of life into music.

———The big reason I studied psychology was that it's very helpful for my music. There's a lot to be gained from learning about the formal definitions of emotions. I have two dreams, and one is to be an old, white-haired man still standing onstage and playing his guitar and singing, and the other is to become a licensed psychological therapist. Because I want to help the ones who come after me who do similar work as ours. I looked it up and it takes a lot of time so it won't be easy to begin right away, but I would really like to become licensed someday. And since I have these aspirations, it makes me think I won't be resting on my laurels anytime soon.

As in the final track of *MAP OF THE SOUL : 7* and j-hope's solo song "Outro : Ego,"* it all ends with nothing set in stone in the present moment. In the song, j-hope looks back on everything the group had experienced since their debut and says:

> *Now I don't care, it's all*
> *Choices by my fate, so we're here*

Having accepted the present, j-hope vows to not shirk the path before him. Even if it's impossible to know the answers in life, this determination to keep moving forward in step to the energetic EDM beat was exactly the life BTS had lived for almost seven years. Of "Outro : Ego," j-hope has this to say:

———I wanted to infuse it with my mood and vibe, to create a song in a way that only I could make.

j-hope's mood and method were also a part of how he had lived as a member of BTS. For example, before any dance practice, he always follows a routine:

———Now that I've clocked up some time in dance, there are things my body can become aware of on its own. And there are things I need to do for my body. I have to eat right to have enough energy before dancing, and then do my stretches. My legs tend to be a bit weaker, so I really need to warm them up. Because I know these things, I prepare for them with more care. And after practice, I soak the lower half of my body in a bath to relax. All these things have become routine.

j-hope takes these repetitions in life with the following attitude.

———That's not to say I know everything beforehand when I start out to work. The results are important, sure, but the process is also very important, and I try to maintain my own balance through direct experience. It's the same with dance. I think I tend to calibrate my moves by throwing my whole body into it. You've got to just hack through it.

ON, and . . .

The title song of *MAP OF THE SOUL : 7*, "ON"* seems to concentrate the lives of all the members into a single attitude. If the members with their individual thoughts, artistic paths, and solutions to the problem of what to do with their lives could be compressed into one song, this would be it. "ON" therefore contains that very state in which they carry everything on their shoulders and still manage to move forward.

———This song is basically saying, "Give us all the suffering, we'll withstand it all!" but the suffering in question, it can be a little hard (laughs).

j-hope laughs, but this is indeed the way the seven of them have lived their lives as members of BTS.

If we were to approach the album from a storytelling perspective, this song would've been enough if it had only been about conquering all their fears and promising to be heroes forever. But "ON" actually goes:

Where my pain lies
Let me take a breath

As the lyrics imply, the song is about their present, where for better or for worse, they must carry the weight of their own lives on their shoulders and keep moving on.

This was an important turning point for BTS. With the *MAP OF THE SOUL : 7* album and especially the title song "ON," BTS become not the heroes of some mythic quest narrative but a team that talks about the current situations they find themselves in.

As they had in the past, but especially with *MAP OF THE SOUL : 7* the story of the album became their realities. This method of conveying their message in a "speak very frankly" manner has allowed BTS to put the stories of their ongoing lives into their lyrics. Their later albums *BE* and *Proof* are also about the realities and emotions the members were experiencing in the moment of production, told in a manner both candid and frank.

"ON," therefore, does not make any conclusions about life either in the song or performances of it, only the determination that they will keep moving forward. To the beat of the snare drum, the members execute an energetic march replete with powerful dance moves from beginning to end.

The dance performance accompanying "ON" is an artistic challenge in that it further heightens and refines their ever-improving stage presence, and considering the song's message of endurance and determination, it almost feels like a ritual of sorts designed to send an imploring message to the heavens.

The *"ON" Kinetic Manifesto Film: Come Prima*˙ that was released a few days before the premiere of the "ON" music video was filmed not on a soundstage or a performance arena but wide plains. The scale is grand, but their performance as it happens against an endless horizon is not only an experience of perfectly executed choreography for the viewer but a true expression of BTS's message in this song that they are determined to live through whatever life throws at them.

———It was so hard (laughs).

That is Jimin's summary of the "ON" performance.

———We almost couldn't breathe by the end of it. "IDOL" before that
    had already been a new challenge for us. The motions were huge,
    there were a lot of jumps, and it was so elaborate. But this song
    was even bigger than that, with more blocking, and every gesture
    had to be razor-sharp—that was "ON." So it was hard, but I
    thought the results were pretty incredible and awesome. I was so
    grateful to our group for pulling it off.

As such, "ON" became a performance high point in BTS's career. As the scale of its choreography was too large for most music broadcast programs, BTS had to provide separate stages in order to showcase

"ON" unless they were performing it in a stadium. And this in itself was only made possible because of the group's clout in the music industry and indeed their proven capability of pulling off a performance of this magnitude.

The "ON" performance premiered on NBC's *The Tonight Show Starring Jimmy Fallon* on February 25, 2020. NBC had to rent out the entirety of Grand Central Terminal, the largest train station in the world and a symbol of New York, for this performance. BTS not only showed off their position in the American music industry but also how they came to stand on such an important stage.˙

When the performance was over and Jimmy Fallon came running toward them, the members of BTS were so exhausted they were barely able to keep standing. Jimin remembers:

———There's some discomfort dancing on bare floors. And I think there are spaces that are just about the right size for us, and when that's exceeded, I feel a bit overwhelmed by our surroundings. Which is why we put more strength into our moves and that exhausts us more.

Jimin goes on to explain why the Grand Central Terminal performance was especially difficult:

———It was so vast. We'd known beforehand how big it was and what it meant to perform there, but once we were physically there, we could see how huge and amazing it looked. We were intimidated. And the floor was very slippery. So we had to keep our guard up.

But every time BTS were met with such difficulties, they had always given their all in the performance and moved the hearts of those who watched them. As soon as they had finished, a cheering Jimmy Fallon came running to their side, introducing their new album and hugging each of the members as he continued to express his awe at what he had just witnessed.

"ON" was destined to become an iconic song in BTS's catalogue. It was the title song of their new album, and its performance overwhelmed all audiences. "ON" was a special event when it was showcased on television, and it made everyone look forward to its full impact when presented onstage in a stadium tour. Jimin himself was looking forward to performing it in concerts.

———"ON" was the kind of performance that I really wanted to show people. When we went to the Grammy Awards in 2020,[49] it was such a shame because I kept thinking, 'If only we could've performed "ON" for everyone here, we could have knocked them off their feet . . .' (laughs).

Jimin is about to say something when his expression changes—a look of calm comes over him, or perhaps it is one of ambivalence.

———But, of course, that became impossible.

49 BTS had been the first Korean artists to attend the Grammy Awards as nominees when they went the year previous in 2019, and in the 2020 ceremony, they performed onstage with Lil Nas X.

CHAPTER 7

Dynamite

BE

Butter

Butter

Proof

WE
ARE

Dynamite | DIGITAL SINGLE

BE

Butter | DIGITAL SINGLE

Butter | SINGLE ALBUM

||| | | | | WE ARE | | | | |||

"Chopped Off"

On November 30, 2021, V from a hotel in Los Angeles begins this interview in a state of excitement.

———The performance is *so* much fun!

This was in answer to the question of how the show was going. Two years since the 2019 BTS WORLD TOUR "LOVE YOURSELF: SPEAK YOURSELF," BTS on November 27 and 28 and December 1 and 2 held *BTS PERMISSION TO DANCE ON STAGE—LA,* a live show.[50] V, who normally speaks in a calm voice during interviews, sounds fired up on this day:

———It was like two years of being frozen in place and then shattering into motion again. Like coming back to what was "normality" to us. I'm so happy that we get to feel this again.

From the beginning of 2020 to the end of 2021, a period in which BTS could not meet up with their audience, their popularity and position in the industry only grew. Their digital single "Dynamite," released on August 21, 2020, topped the Billboard Hot 100 for three weeks, including two consecutive weeks, and "Butter," released on May 21, 2021, topped the same chart for ten weeks total and seven weeks consecutively. And the album *BE*, released between *Dynamite*

---

50 This concert was first delivered in an online format on October 24, 2021, in Seoul's Jamsil Olympic Stadium. While it had been originally designed to be an in-person live performance, Korea's pandemic situation at the time made it necessary to stage it online instead.

and *Butter* on November 20, 2020, became that year's second-highest-selling album on the Gaon Chart with 2,692,022 copies sold in just a single month. The highest-selling album was, of course, *MAP OF THE SOUL : 7*, which was released on February 21, 2020, and sold 4,376,975 copies.

————Aside from the opening, I think the screams were the loudest when we transitioned from "Dynamite" to "Butter."

What RM says of the *BTS PERMISSION TO DANCE ON STAGE—LA* event shows BTS's heightened positioning in the world of popular music since the release of "Dynamite" and "Butter." Not only did the worldwide success of these two songs cement BTS as the artists with the most passionate fandom in the world, they also made them the most famous superstars in terms of mainstream reach. This performance features surprise guest appearances from Megan Thee Stallion and Coldplay's Chris Martin,[51] garnering 210,000 audience members over the four days. Jin says of performing before a live audience again:

————I was thrilled! Maybe it's because I tend not to think of the past too much or dwell on sad memories, but this performance made me feel we were back to two years ago. Like we'd never left the stage. But meeting the fans was such a thrill. The members kept talking about that right before the first performance. We were worried we'd start crying in the middle of doing our opening number, "ON." I was really curious and wondering, 'Will these guys really burst into tears?' but thankfully, no one cried (laughs).

---

51 Megan Thee Stallion joined BTS onstage for "Butter" during the second performance (November 28) while Chris Martin performed "My Universe" with BTS during the fourth performance (December 2).

Jin didn't cry either, under a belief that an artist must have a certain attitude onstage. He continues:

———I tried not to get too sentimental while I was onstage. I was so glad to see the fans, but I needed to concentrate on performing first and foremost. And then the members started talking to the audience and I got very sentimental. 'Ah . . . This is so wild, like a movie. Yes, this is what I've missed.' But if I keep wallowing in that, I would never be able to perform properly, so I try as hard as possible to forget such feelings while I'm onstage.

But until the moment they returned onstage, the members had harbored the darkness of doubt with them at all times. Having begun in 2020 when they were prevented from meeting their fans, this doubt could not be dispelled just by looking at their phones to see their astounding chart performance. And beyond the pandemic, Jimin had always put store in encountering the audience through a live performance.

———Chart performance was something I couldn't fathom at all until we were with a live audience. And more than how well we did on the charts, I just . . . I just wanted to meet the fans in person the most. All I could think of when we finally got to perform was, 'I'm so glad we're seeing each other in person.'

Jimin also has this to say about the effect of the pandemic on his life:

———Well . . . I don't think I have a lot of memories of the pandemic. Like that time was "chopped off" my memory? I just felt like time was passing. It was hard at times, and we overcame it, but looking back at that time, I feel so wistful. Of course, we did well on the charts during that time, but we weren't in it for the chart performance to begin with. We were perfectly satisfied and grateful for the love and support we'd received even before then. Because good

Dynamite

DIGITAL SINGLE
2020. 8. 21

TRACK

01 Dynamite

02 Dynamite (Instrumental)

03 Dynamite (Acoustic Remix)

04 Dynamite (EDM Remix)

VIDEO

"Dynamite"
MV TEASER

"Dynamite"
MV (B-side)

"Dynamite"
MV

"Dynamite"
MV (Choreography ver.)

things happened then as well, I try to think, 'It wasn't a meaning-less time,' but I really feel like it's a "chopped off" part of my life.

200417 RM

———You want us to switch on the YouTube live feed and not think
about anything else? Do you really think we can do that? (laughs).
   Those are RM's words after his first ever live stream held through
the BTS YouTube channel on April 17, 2020.· Still under the mood
of the previous day's broadcast, RM notes how BTS have now entered
territory that's unfamiliar to them as well.
———When we warned Bang Si-Hyuk that we could end up saying all
kinds of stuff in the broadcast, he said, "Sure, go ahead." The
first episode was my turn, so I thought, 'Eh, whatever. Let's just
put something on the record,' and I talked about preparing our
album. And I got such a kick out of it.
   In this broadcast, RM promised two things to the people watching
him in real time. One was that for the time being, the members of BTS
would take turns at least once a week sharing their daily lives on YouTube.
The second thing was the eventual release of their new album, titled *BE*.
   This was unprecedented for BTS. The band was known for expand-ing on a theme in great detail for every album, organically connecting
all content including videos and photos, and their methods of sharing

I needed to concentrate on performing
first and foremost.
    And then the members started
talking to the audience and I got very
sentimental.
    'Ah . . . This is so wild, like a movie.
    Yes, this is what I've missed.'

—Jin

the message of their albums were concurrently ever expanding in terms of variety and scale. *MAP OF THE SOUL : 7* was at the pinnacle of such efforts. In this one album, BTS continue to look inward while connecting their work to outside projects like the global contemporary art exhibit *CONNECT, BTS.*

And now this same team was jumping into live streaming on YouTube without any set theme or plan just two months into the release of *MAP OF THE SOUL : 7* and making a surprise announcement about a new album. They were practically being extemporaneous. But it wasn't as if anyone could foresee what the world would be like after the pandemic. Promotional activities for *MAP OF THE SOUL : 7* had ground to a halt, the April premiere of the BTS MAP OF THE SOUL TOUR in Seoul˙ had been wiped off the schedule, and their international tour had been put on ice as well. They were grappling with the same issue that artists around the world were struggling with, which was dealing with an uncertain future. j-hope had this to say during the height of the pandemic:

———I wanted to spend each year after that being grateful for my life and feeling blessed but . . . Wow . . . I don't know why this year is so horrifying.

There was nothing to be done. Time seemed like it had stopped, but not the suffering, and there was no way of being sure about any plan for the future or what message to send to the world. All they could do was turn on their cameras and wait for their fans, wherever they were, to arrive. Just as it had been during their debut.

A Record of Mornings

The YouTube real-time streaming was a new experience for both BTS and ARMY. SUGA would turn on his camera and paint a picture* mostly in silence, and j-hope would show an entire practice session from beginning to end, including warm-up and honing his dance moves.** These broadcasts, hashtagged "#StayConnected" and "#CarryOn," allowed BTS to share their daily lives with their fans and show them what they were doing since the onset of the pandemic and what mindset they were trying to cultivate.

The routine j-hope undergoes before he dances was the product of someone who has taken a lot of time and effort to get to know himself, and sharing it was like telling others, without words, who he was inside. SUGA's painting was the same. He explains:

———'What should I be doing during a pandemic?' was the only thing I could think the whole time. A tour has a set schedule you just have to follow, but all that had shattered. I thought, 'If I were never able to set foot onstage again, then who am I?' So my answer to that was to just do whatever came to mind. Painting kind of makes you forget your worries. It was a device that allowed me to detach myself from whatever negative thoughts popped into my head.

The title*** SUGA put on the work at the time also symbolized what he had wanted to express and share with the fans:

434

————It's titled "Morning," but it was also titled "Worry." When I look back on my anxious moments, they tend to be at their worst around 5 A.M. in the morning. Which is why my least favorite color is that bluish shade right before the sun begins to rise . . . But when I drew, I didn't have a plan in mind. I just wanted to do what came to mind, and I had no idea I would end up with such a dark blue color.

To express the emotions one feels living their lives, to the point where not even the artist realizes what ends up appearing on the canvas— SUGA's painting and his method of revealing his process is similar to how *BE* was produced. During the pandemic, BTS prepared their album while making their discussions on the direction and methods of production public. The members' feelings as they lived through the pandemic were turned into songs, and the very best of these songs were chosen, and the members divided among themselves, through meetings, the various roles necessary to create an album. Just as they had in their Cheonggu Building days in the past, they put together their album as if engaging in a "cottage industry production."

The only thing that had changed was the reason they were making an album. What they had wanted as they gathered in that tiny studio and practice room in Cheonggu Building was the validation of certified success. They believed that once they succeeded, the world would show them who they are. But even when they had achieved such success, BTS had decided to do something else with their music. j-hope says:

————I'm sitting in the studio staring into space and thinking, 'Uh . . . what song should I write now?' I'd go back and forth between home and the studio wondering, 'What kind of life have I lived until now, and what were my thoughts as I lived that life?' and occasionally watched performances we had done for television. Then I would think, 'Ah . . . That's right, that's who I was,' or 'What was it like back then?' And a kind of determination arose from that process. That I should try to capture, like a diary, the songs and emotions that I can express only in this time of my life. 'Whether the results are good or bad, or mediocre, let's just do it. Let's try getting closer to the listener by showing and sharing the small parts of myself that have been in the shadows until now.'

Fly To My Room

> *Could somebody turn back that clock*
> *This entire year has been lost*
> *I'm still in my bed*

The song "Fly To My Room" in the album *BE* plainly captures BTS's feelings as they were experienced during the pandemic. Time keeps slipping away from them, but nothing seems to be getting better. Jimin looks back on that period when it was becoming clear the pandemic would not disappear anytime soon:

BE

2020. 11. 20

TRACK

01 Life Goes On

02 Fly To My Room

03 Blue & Grey

04 Skit

05 Telepathy

06 Dis-ease

07 Stay

08 Dynamite

VIDEO

 "Life Goes On"
MV TEASER 1

 "Life Goes On"
MV TEASER 2

 "Life Goes On"
MV

 "Life Goes On"
MV : on my pillow

 "Life Goes On"
MV : in the forest

 "Life Goes On"
MV : like an arrow

————I did a lot of thinking. I know this is a bit extreme, but I even had thoughts like, 'I worked so hard to be a part of this group, but what if the team disappears . . . ?' It was really hard.

But "Fly To My Room" is also about trying to change one's attitude at least, if changing one's circumstances happens to be impossible:

> *There's no other way / This room's my everything*
> *Whatever then / I will change this place / into my world*

The making of *BE* was a series of taking the endless challenges that would otherwise throttle the momentum of their lives and turning them into fuel to burn brighter. Because if they couldn't do that, things would really become unbearable. Like Jimin said, to live as part of BTS meant performing live and meeting ARMY. As the line "I can sleep all day now, no problem" implies in "Dis-ease,"˙ another song in *BE*, the pandemic did give them a little more free time compared to before. But by then, they had grown into a habit of work where not working actually made them feel a little anxious. Just as they say in the same song, "Feels like I should be working to the bone / But here I am, shoving down three meals a day."

During the pandemic, Jin had this to say about the complicated emotions during that time:

————All those things I've always wanted to do before, go fishing or play games all day or meet friends? When our schedule fell apart,

I spent about three weeks doing all that. But even then I felt pretty anxious, like 'Is it all right even if I keep doing nothing?' It was all too vague to really let myself sit back and take a rest. I kept thinking, 'I've got to do this, I still have to do that.' But on the other hand, the work I'm doing now, it feels different. Maybe it's because we're not touring, but even while we're working, it feels like resting.

Since debuting with *2 COOL 4 SKOOL* and reaching *MAP OF THE SOUL : 7*, BTS's accomplishments over those seven years followed the progression of what could almost be considered a classical hero narrative. A band of seven young men whom no one paid attention to, except the few who looked down on them, fighting through various difficulties and paying back with love all the people who came to love and support them along the way. But not only did their story keep continuing after they'd triumphed as heroes, reality kept throwing all sorts of obstacles no one could ever have imagined. *BE* is the story of how "Life" as an artist and individual "Goes On" in all sorts of unexpected ways.

⸻I kept saying how hard things were. Of course, I had so many people to be grateful for, like ARMY and the members, and the hyoungs who stayed by my side even as I was feeling blue. I was so grateful to them that there's a song written for them. But as for the really sad one, we put in *BE*.

The "sad" song V is referring to here is "Blue & Grey."ʼ V had been working on his own mixtape during the production process of *BE*. Of the many songs he was working on during this difficult period, "Blue & Grey" especially looks deep into what he had felt since his debut with BTS and the pandemic:

> *Everyone seems happy*
> *Can you look at me? Cuz I am blue & grey*
> *Tears reflected in the mirror mean*
> *My colors hidden behind the smile blue & grey*
>
> *Don't know where things went wrong*
> *Since I was little, a blue question mark in my head*
> *Maybe that's why I lived full-on*
> *But looking back standing here by myself*
> *That menacing shadow devours me*

The feelings V captured in "Blue & Grey" were no doubt what he had felt during the making of *BE*. He adds:

———You know, my thoughts . . . through the song I wanted people to understand us better and how deep our feelings were running. Everyone has it hard, of course, but I really wanted to capture and share the pain and thoughts we experienced in our growth or our path to success. I guess you can say, I wanted to make it obvious a bit. To make my feelings known. I'm not the type to talk directly about my feelings, but it occurred to me that I could still talk about them through song.

"Blue & Grey" serves as a dividing line within *BE*. The determination to let go of the pandemic in "Life Goes On"* is only possible after changing one's perspective of the pandemic in "Fly To My Room." And "Fly To My Room" is only made possible after an experience of looking into one's sadness as in "Blue & Grey." The three songs—"Life Goes On," "Fly To My Room," and "Blue & Grey"—that comprise the beginning of *BE* go deep into the dark emotions and events experienced by BTS since the onset of the pandemic. And once the bleak loneliness of "Blue & Grey" passes like a dark night, the first words of "Skit"** can be heard:

> *Congratulations!*
> *Billboard's number one artist coming through!*

Be Dynamite

If it weren't for the pandemic, perhaps BTS would never have sung "Dynamite." The last scene of the music video for "ON," the title song of *MAP OF THE SOUL : 7*, is a title card with the words "NO MORE DREAM" where the words "NO MORE" slowly fade away, leaving behind "DREAM."*** Just as the song "Boy With Luv" and "Boy In Luv" or "ON" and "N.O" are connected, "DREAM" was supposed to be the answer to "No More Dream," the title song of their debut album.

The young men who in their debut had searched for love and shouted

"No!" to a world that tried to make them live other people's dreams had now reached a superstar status so high they could barely see the ground, just as they found themselves at the end of the "ON" music video. And it was in that moment BTS had been planning to sing the song that encapsulated the weight of the past years of building up their name.

But just as it had been for everyone else in the world at that time, BTS's history pivoted toward an unexpected direction. If *BE* is a record of their changed situations and feelings during the global health crisis, "Dynamite" was the first major challenge presented to them during the pandemic era.

It began with what Bang Si-Hyuk would only call "a feeling." Bang Si-Hyuk was thinking about everything that would change for BTS because of the pandemic, and the core of his concerns was "jetlag."

By the time of *MAP OF THE SOUL : 7*, BTS had become a band that toured stadiums around the world. Seven years since their debut, they were at the peak of their powers, and their artistry had matured. But at the same time, BTS were creating another sensation. The media was focusing on ARMY's passionate response to the *LOVE YOURSLEF* and *MAP OF THE SOUL* series, and this had led to their unprecedented levels of exposure in the US mass media such as their *SNL* performance, which in turn meant people around the world were now paying attention.

To those who already followed K-pop through YouTube content and the like, BTS were already superstars. But to those who had first seen them on television through shows like *SNL* or read about them in mass media articles, BTS were something completely new that had sprung from South Korea.

If it weren't for the pandemic, this "jetlag" in exposure might've been resolved fairly easily. Putting out albums and doing more stadium tours would go far in justifying their popularity through the scale and artistry of these efforts, and the explosive response from fans in each touring city would've provided ample opportunity to show the world just what kind of group BTS really were.

But because of the pandemic, BTS could not go forth to see the fans who were waiting for them, and the chance to let the world know of the group's renown, talent, and history disappeared. No matter how much they racked up the hits on YouTube, they wouldn't be able to appeal to an even greater audience without live performances. Especially for an act that already had a large, worldwide fandom like BTS, who needed something more to break into the next level.

Bang Si-Hyuk, intuiting this problem, made two decisions. One, to step back a little in the role of producer of *BE* and have the members of BTS take greater responsibility in deciding the direction of the album. Instead of following an extremely detailed plan, the album would consist of what the members had experienced and felt throughout the pandemic. Two, that a "Dynamite" would be thrown at everyone who was beginning to discover BTS. That at this moment in time when BTS attracted more attention around the world than ever before, they would throw at the audience a song that everyone everywhere would love, giving them the chance to become new fans.

Singing in English

———When we first heard it, the song sounded great. But it was going to be the first English song we released, and someone from the outside had written it, so we did worry a little. 'Will the song grow up nice and strong?'

RM had been a little worried about "Dynamite," released on August 21, 2020. Aside from their activities in Japan, BTS had always released songs in Korean, and the fact that they had achieved worldwide fame with Korean-language songs was a point of great pride for them and ARMY. While there was no law against singing in English, trying out something so new was bound to give anyone pause. But it was also clear why BTS had to release "Dynamite." On the global response to the song, RM says:

———The fandom must've craved it more than we'd thought. It was back when everyone's emotions were extremely suppressed by the pandemic, which is why people responded so ardently online. And there was probably a lower barrier of entry thanks to it being an English song. It made me think, 'I worried over nothing.' ARMY are always more awesome than we think.

Seven months after entering production, *BE* was released on November 20, 2020. If BTS hadn't released "Dynamite" that summer, they would've had almost no opportunity to perform during those seven months. With the pandemic making most nonessential outside activities impossible all over the world, the deprivation fans would've felt from the lack of live performances would've been even more acute. Jin thinks back on that time:

———Before we started promoting "Dynamite," there was a three- or four-month period where we didn't get to go on any stage. It almost made me think, 'That kind of thing is not my job.'

"Dynamite," while essentially the emotional opposite of *BE*, was also the capstone that completed it. With *BE* being a candid record of their experiences and thoughts surrounding the pandemic, "Dynamite" was a fun disco-pop song that described looking forward to an outing as if the pandemic were over. At the online press conference for "Dynamite" held on August 21, 2020, Jimin explained:

> We really wanted to stand on stage . . . As a group who must meet and communicate with their fans, I honestly think we felt very empty and helpless. We needed a way to overcome this emptiness and helplessness, and also thought it would be a good opportunity, a new challenge.

BE was the pandemic's reality while "Dynamite" was the dream of everyone hoping for the end of the pandemic. While "Dynamite" was indeed the opposite of BE, it was a kind of pandemic song as well, and this digital single was included as the final track of BE, giving BE a twist at the end of its narrative. From the first song, "Life Goes On," to "Fly To My Room" and "Blue & Grey," the mood quickly turns with "Skit," which contains a boisterous moment congratulating BTS on their Billboard Hot 100 number one, followed by "Telepathy"˙ where SUGA captures his longing for someone he could not see and his hopes they would meet again, shining a light of hope through the dark. j-hope has a lively moment in "Dis-ease" where he lets loose about his complicated feelings about not having to work because of the pandemic, and Jung Kook's "Stay"˙˙ imagines a moment in the future where BTS and ARMY would meet again in concert, infusing *BE* with hope and determination. With the final addition of "Dynamite," *BE* becomes a record of life under the pandemic and the process in which we overcome its challenges.

> *Since it's BTS's music video and not just mine, I wanted it to capture not just one member's thoughts but everyone's situation, to put in all of our situations and show them directly. That while everyone watching may have their own thoughts, we also feel what others are feeling and are in the same boat as everyone else.*

That was Jung Kook's intention as stated in *Weverse Magazine* on the direction of the "Life Goes On" video. Interestingly, both the video for "Life Goes On" and "Dynamite," the first and last songs of *BE* respectively, show the inside of Jung Kook's room." "Life Goes On" has a heavier mood, reflecting the onset of the pandemic situation, while in "Dynamite," Jung Kook dances joyfully in the same space in a much lighter atmosphere.

BE also moves from the reality of "Life Goes On" to the hopeful dream of "Dynamite." As Jung Kook implies, BTS created their songs with the understanding that what they were going through was probably not that different from what the rest of the world was going through and chose to end the endeavor with the hope shown in "Dynamite." These duetting lines of emotion were BTS's record of the first year of the pandemic.

Fireworks Shot Up in a Silent World

Regardless of what the response to "Dynamite" would've been, BTS had worked on the song a little differently from their previous work, adopting a more lighthearted approach. Jin describes what the mood was like working on the song:

⸻In other times, we worked with very strict discipline, but "Dynamite" was more like working on a bonus track.

The members had been working on *BE*, and this unwarranted rest period had given them more time to prepare "Dynamite" for release. It was an ideal situation of sorts where they felt lighter than usual while having more time to work on something to get it absolutely right.

⸻Everyone was so great then (laughs).

j-hope, who often sets the tone for BTS's dance practices, thinks back to when they were practicing the "Dynamite" choreography:

⸻We'd grown that much more by then. Everyone knew very well how to pick up choreography and put their own spin on it. Everyone had truly become champions of the game (laughs). Which is why we didn't really have any difficulty performance-wise. The dancing looks light and easy but the perfect execution of every movement was make-or-break for this song, we tried our best to be as precise as possible.

The "Dynamite" video overlays disco moves over the song's upbeat disco rhythm.* It was a choreography anyone could have fun following.

But BTS, amid the fun and free atmosphere of the visuals, infuse a feeling of dynamism in the performance through perfect synchronization of movements in different points of the video. The chorus especially is composed of rousing disco dance moves, but from the moment they step forward as one to execute their razor-sharp group dance, they stamp the performance with their powerful trademark.

"Dynamite" was the perfect introduction to BTS for those who were just becoming aware of the group. The song was a new starting line for the group that had already amassed a huge following over their seven years of activity.

————We had a feeling fans would love "Dynamite." But we were curious as to whether people who were not ARMY in America and other places overseas would also like the song.

As Jung Kook implies, no one could've predicted the general audience's response to "Dynamite." *MAP OF THE SOUL : 7*'s "ON" had entered the Billboard Hot 100 at number four in its first week, which made it fairly reasonable to assume the newer song would do at least as well. "ON" was a Korean-language song and meant for a giant stage, which meant there were limits as to its viability as a listening-only song. But it had still made number four, which bode well for the reception of "Dynamite." But there was simply no guarantee for how well the later song would actually do.

The night "Dynamite" was scheduled to debut on the Billboard Hot 100, j-hope had gone to bed early without bothering to stay up to see what position it would chart. Only when he woke up the next morning did he realize the whole world was different.

————I was actually asleep when it was announced (laughs). So I didn't see it right away, and when I learned of it waking up, I was surprised. 'We made number one. We did something absolutely grand.'

V recalls the members' reactions after the news of their number one:

———We were overjoyed together. Someone was laughing and someone was crying and it was all . . . how do I say this . . . 'Ah . . . we weren't going down a dead end this whole time.' That our path had actually been going somewhere, that we hadn't been trying to do something that was simply impossible. I realized, 'All along, we'd had the opportunity and a tiny bit of possibility.'

But they didn't have long to enjoy their triumph. The pandemic had created a completely new work environment for them. j-hope explains what happened that day:

———As soon as we learned we got a number one, a whole schedule was set up (laughs). As soon as we heard of a schedule we went, "All right, we're coming!"

Topping the Billboard Hot 100 was an event of such magnitude that the members had cried upon hearing it had happened. But because of the pandemic, they were unable to go to America or perform "Dynamite" on a live stage. This was why even the members themselves found it difficult to really believe it was true.

———We'd dreamed a lot about making it to the top of the Billboard Hot 100. Imagining, 'What will it feel like when we make it to that level?' But making it to the top during the pandemic made it a little too surreal. We were happy, but after a while it was like . . . 'That's how it is,' you know?

Jin compares the feeling to when they won their many awards:

———Of all our awards and rankings and such, this was the one that felt the least real. All of our awards like the BBMAs felt very real in the moment, but not this event. To the point of thinking, 'Is it all right if we accept this?' It was probably because we were so physically isolated from the outside world.

A Korean group had scored a Billboard Hot 100 number one song while still in Korea. The popularity of the song continued. "Dynamite" went on to have a second consecutive week at number one, and retook the top position on its fifth week, spending thirteen weeks total in the top 13.

Korea's idol industry utilized in various ways their knowledge of online-platform promotional channels like YouTube to great effect. This was also how BTS could return to a busy promotional schedule, as j-hope mentioned. Only the method of this promotional work was very different from how they had gone about it before, and it was beginning on a global scale.

———It was like being a new group again. Because we had to work for a very long time.

RM remembers the work surrounding the release of "Dynamite" as a unique experience in BTS's career. From the moment the song was released, they were in promotional mode for two whole months. This was the longest promotional period they had ever had where they didn't have to do any live performance work. But they still had to perform, creating recorded performances for every presentation of the song as if filming a new music video every time, using different settings and staging. These presentations were broadcast through various media and YouTube.

In the one for *America's Got Talent*, a popular American audition program, they performed the song retro-style in a theme park in Korea.·

For NPR's music channel on YouTube, they filmed for that outlet's Tiny Desk Concert series—titled "Tiny Desk (Home) Concert" on this occasion—in a record shop in Seoul.· For the 2020 MTV Video Music Awards where they premiered their stage-performance version of the song, New York City and Seoul came together as one city through the magic of special effects,·· while the 2020 BBMAs performance was filmed at Incheon International Airport.···

That these were all recorded performances with no live audiences was a constraint, but on the other hand, the constraints forced everyone involved to try things they never would've tried in previous television programs or award shows. While it was regrettable they couldn't perform live for the fans, BTS still managed to put a different twist on their performance of "Dynamite" every time.

This approach of recording a different stage presentation every time for different occasions was in itself quite an adventure. The MTV VMAs appearance involved two months of discussion between BTS and MTV as they came to an understanding on this new kind of performance. With the BBMAs, it took a month to fine-tune the visual concept where a video of the instrumental band, playing in New York, could be inserted behind the BTS members singing the song in Korea's Incheon International Airport.

The pinnacle of the "Dynamite" performances was at "BTS Week" in *The Tonight Show Starring Jimmy Fallon* where BTS would perform on a different stage every episode from Monday to Friday for this extremely popular American late-night show, a feat that cemented BTS's status in America.

For "BTS Week,"* "Dynamite" was performed in two versions, one where BTS, Jimmy Fallon, and the Roots (the live band for *The Tonight Show Starring Jimmy Fallon*) did an a cappella version mixed with various sound effects, and another that was more of a retro vibe, filmed in a roller-skating rink. They also performed "HOME" from *MAP OF THE SOUL : PERSONA* and "Black Swan" from *MAP OF THE SOUL : 7.* "IDOL" was performed in Geunjeongjeon Hall of Gyeongbokgung Palace, and "Mikrokosmos" in the Gyeonghoeru Pavilion of the same historical site. The Cultural Heritage Administration of Korea, which supported BTS in their filming these performances on palace grounds, stated through their social media that it was a meeting between the crowning glory of Korea's cultural heritage that was Gyeongbokgung Palace and BTS, a group of artists beloved around the world. The performances also left a big impression on Jung Kook:

———We did so many performances for "Dynamite," but the most memorable were the ones at Incheon Airport and Gyeongbokgung. Because these are, it must be said, iconic locations.

Their activities were making the rounds in the music industry for their innovative presentations, and their stature rose higher with every performance. Form followed function to perfection as BTS performed in the very airport that would've connected Korea and the world if not for the pandemic, using mass media instead to connect artist and fan.

BTS and "Dynamite" encapsulated what it meant to do mainstream music in the pandemic era. Artists and fans could not meet, but it became possible to have a global hit solely through online performances beamed to local TV programs or online streaming platforms like YouTube and Netflix. A song like "Dynamite" could reach the top of the Billboard Hot 100 despite all of its promotion being physically executed in Korea. The promotional cycle of "Dynamite," and the other Korean global hit *Squid Game* that was released a year later, seemed like heralds of a new era.

———We recorded that wearing hanbok, and I thought it would be cute if I did the traditional bow in it (laughs).

This was why Jimin and the members did a few such bows during their performance at Gyeongbokgung,· perhaps as a tribute to the fans whom they couldn't meet in person. Despite the vociferous praise coming in from around the world, it was still a point of frustration for Jimin and the other members that they couldn't breathe the same air as their fans.

———In some ways, "Dynamite" was our way of overcompensating in that situation. Because we couldn't show the fans something they could see with their own eyes, we tried to make the best of it. It's actually harder to record things without an audience than it is to do a live performance.

The two months of promoting "Dynamite" were an unprecedented experience for BTS in the sense that they had a global hit but were unable to really feel it in their bones, but they still had to work every day to show themselves to the world. Their "album, tour, album, tour" schedule had turned into "album, recordings, album, recordings."

As "Dynamite" wound down, Jin was having the following thoughts:

———We had worked so hard and done such a variety and quantity of things this time, but oddly, it didn't feel like we were really out there being "active." I was watching TV one day and there was an idol group saying, "We debuted this February but we've never performed for a live audience." It made me think, 'I wonder what that feels like for them?' We also filmed our performances for many different broadcasts, but it felt like we were doing a V Live. Since many people were watching them on their phones, it felt a little less like we were meeting our fans, and that's how we did "Dynamite." We put in a lot of effort and the results were really great, but there was a lack of that thrill you'd get. Which was why when I saw the artists who had debuted during the pandemic, it made me think, 'How sad they never got to experience that wonderful thrill.'

Even with "Dynamite" clocking three weeks at the top of the Billboard Hot 100 and being a hit all over the world, the members were less enjoying the enthusiastic response to the song and more concerned with how to understand these fruits of their efforts. SUGA says:

———I think we all had the same thought. They were results the likes of which we had never achieved before, but we're so well-trained in coming back down to Earth for all that . . . Not that we deliberately trained for it, but anyway (laughs). It wasn't like we felt nothing, it was more like . . . 'I'm happy, but let's get what we need to do over with.' There were so many great moments, and as a musician, it was so important to fully experience all of them, but as I experienced them, I realized it would be wiser to

In some ways, "Dynamite" was our
way of overcompensating in that
situation.
    Because we couldn't show the fans
something they could see with their
own eyes, we tried to make the best
of it.

—Jimin

get back down to Earth as quickly as possible. There was no need to be floating in the air like that, and the other members weren't ones to float, either.

As SUGA put it, BTS did their jobs no matter how the world responded to their labors, going to work in the studio every day as usual. As "Dynamite" was followed by "Savage Love" by Jawsh 685 and Jason Derulo where SUGA and j-hope participated in a remix* and "Life Goes On" from *BE*, both of which went to number one on the Billboard Hot 100, BTS became the hottest musical act in the world. In addition, "Dynamite" went to number two on the first week of both the new Billboard Global 200 and Billboard Global Excl. US charts. BTS presented a new paradigm for the American music industry that was finding it difficult to ignore the global music market. This was probably why the International Federation of the Phonographic Industry presented BTS with an award for Global Recording Artist of the Year. A prize given for the musical act that sold the most units in the world, it was the first time a non-Western artist had won. j-hope summarizes the year 2020, a chaotic time for the whole world, as follows:

————Really, it was like being showered with prizes. We were so honored, and we had done new things, and while in general it was dizzying, I think the year had many meaningful events. And as a person, the pandemic was a time where I looked back on everything I had done so far and realized, 'This work was valuable after all.' And I made a song that captures that. So while there were stumbles, I think for BTS it was a year where BTS took another giant step.

People Who Pray

On November 3, 2020, SUGA underwent shoulder surgery. It was to treat his left shoulder, injured in a traffic accident during his trainee years.
——I worried a lot after that surgery. It wasn't easy moving that arm in the days right after surgery. I thought that I should concentrate on physical therapy before going back to work.

SUGA was right in that he needed time to heal, and he stepped back from BTS's activities at the end of 2020 to undergo physical therapy. In terms of time period, this stretched from the beginning of November to the end of December, which meant it was a little less than two months. But for SUGA, this happening was a key turning point. SUGA's shoulder injury symbolized a period in his life, a trace of those pre-debut years where he had slogged hard under the uncertainty as to whether he'd be given a chance to do the work he loves. His surgery and treatment thereafter were a goodbye to those years. A thing that had gripped him for a long time was slowly beginning to loosen its hold.

SUGA discussed his shoulder injury in detail during an appearance on tvN's *You Quiz on the Block*. The fans had known about it to some extent, and SUGA had briefly addressed his injury in his song "The Last" on his mixtape *Agust D*, but this was the first time he had discussed his injury at length in public. Jimin also talked about the precarity of their time up to the moment of their debut where they had to prove their worth. Jimin explains of the reasons they were so candid in their *You Quiz on the Block* appearance:

———When we were trainees, someone who now no longer works in the company told me, "You might have to get ready to pack your bags." Now what could have been their reason? (laughs). In any case, I'd come up to Seoul with nothing but it looked like I wouldn't get to debut in BTS, the company was preparing a girl group instead right next to us. 'What's going to happen to me . . .' I worried a lot. But everyone was so nice to me in the dorm, and I kept asking them questions. So I said to RM, "Hyoung, how do I get charisma?" (laughs). Then he'd say, "Hey, it's not like I have it either. I think that kind of thing requires a bit of growing up first" (laughs).

When asked whether he'd be able to explain to the Jimin of the past how to get charisma, Jimin laughs and says:

———I have no idea. I'd tell him to stop thinking silly thoughts and to concentrate on his training (laughs).

Jimin could now think back to the group's past and laugh about it a little. Over the pandemic, they had garnered even more success than before, and had as artists and as adults begun to think about a brighter future. Just as SUGA began to think about what he wanted to do in the future as a musician:

———In fact, I wonder if talking about goals and such has become somewhat meaningless. 'What more do I have to do,' I'm almost thinking. My biggest goal now is to work as a BTS member for a long time. I think the whole group has working together even as we grow older as a common goal. We're thinking a lot about how we could perform with more fun, with more happiness.

During the 2020 MAMA Awards, BTS presented "ON" in the World Cup Stadium in Seoul.· As befitting the scale of the arena, they performed with even more dancers than "ON" usually requires, putting on a show with a marching band concept and adding new choreography to fit.

This version of "ON," one they were showing to a non-live audience and otherwise would've performed during a world tour, was less like a performance and almost like a prayer. A hope that at some point in performing like this, the pandemic would end and we would all be able to meet again. This was perhaps, like SUGA said, the first step as a group in performing "with more fun, with more happiness."

That spring of 2021 when no one knew how much longer the pandemic would last, Jimin had this to say about what the group had wanted to share with others:

——That they would listen to our songs and like them and enjoy them with us . . . Wouldn't that be it? Success and fame and the money that follows are not the biggest meanings in our lives. I just want to do one more performance, to converse with more people. Even if we can't have a long and deep conversation with each and every individual, at least a conversation where we look at each other and shout together and exchange glances, that kind of conversation. That's what's more meaningful.

Finding Hope

BTS's work since the worldwide success of "Dynamite" was a list of all the things they had to do and did to make Jimin's wish come true. The digital single of "Butter," released on May 21, 2021, entered the Billboard Hot 100 at number one and stayed in that position consecutively for seven weeks for a total of ten. And that was how BTS became, along with the Beatles, one of only seven artists in Billboard history up until then to chart at least four number one hits within one year.

Chart performance was not the only thing that made it clear BTS had become a phenomenon unto themselves. Just a few days after "Butter" was released, McDonald's also released the BTS Meal, sold for four weeks from May 27 to their stores in fifty countries, making the group one of the very few that could put their name on a meal of this global franchise.

It was the follow-up to "Butter" that completed their successful streak that year when "Permission to Dance" dropped on July 9 and also topped the Billboard Hot 100. This song, which from the very title itself managed to embody everything that BTS represents, is an ode to the days gone past and infused with a determined spirit to overcome the pandemic:

> *We don't need to worry*
> *'Cause when we fall we know how to land*

Butter

DIGITAL SINGLE
2021. 5. 21

(Hotter Remix)

"Butter"
MV TEASER

"Butter"
(Hotter Remix)
MV

"Butter"
MV

"Butter"
(Cooler Remix)
MV

Butter

BTS

TRACK

01 Butter
02 Permission to Dance
03 Butter (Instrumental)

VIDEO

 "Butter"
MV TEASER

 "Butter"
MV

Don't need to talk the talk, just walk the walk tonight
'Cause we don't need permission to dance

As the lyrics show, BTS knew that even if they were to come down from their height, they knew how to land and not fall. This was the result of resilience and hope earned through coming through countless struggles. They put this mindset into a melody anyone could easily enjoy, portraying the lives of people who continue to move forward despite the pandemic. The performance included messages conveyed in International Sign, and through the *BTS PERMISSION TO DANCE ON STAGE—LA* concert at the end of 2021, they were finally able to do it before a live audience. Jung Kook shares his thoughts on that day:

———We are ecstatic. And also exhausted, my legs could barely keep me upright during "Permission to Dance," but I kept laughing. 'What a great final song for this concert,' I thought. And everyone singing together at the end, that was so great.

The message behind "Permission to Dance" could be completed only after it had finally been performed in front of a live audience. This song was a consolation not only to its listeners but to BTS as well, a consolation most palpable to anyone who had gone through what they had gone through even before the pandemic happened. Jimin explains his feelings performing "Permission to Dance":

———It's such a bright song, but . . . My eyes kept brimming over in tears. We did this song and stood in a row for our final bow, and I really sobbed. I think it was because the emotions of the song were truly being felt in me then. It's such a great song.

As BTS worked on *BE* in 2020, they had put into the album their thoughts and feelings on their abruptly stopped lives while with "Dynamite" had pushed a message of hope. And the summer of the year after that, they sang of the fun and hope one could still have in the pandemic era. These songs, released over a period of two years, charted the feelings of countless people around the world, who in turn responded to their message. A message whose sender was BTS.

Smooth Like Butter, Firm Like BTS

The string of recent hits comprised of "Dynamite," "Butter," and "Permission to Dance" introduced a slew of new challenges for the group. The first challenge had to do with how they sang and danced. Jimin elaborates:

———When we were recording "Permission to Dance," I just got the feeling it wasn't easy conveying my emotions. I was also worried my intentions wouldn't quite come through singing in English. Even if I ended up really liking the song once it was finished.

While "Permission to Dance" is a light and carefree track, the members had to put in much effort to make it sound the way they wanted it to sound. The English aspect also meant that RM, SUGA, and j-hope would need to focus more on singing than rapping. Clearly, the song presented a variety of challenges to the whole group.

"Butter" especially shows what BTS chose to focus on as they switched to completely English lyrics. When it was first being written, the song had no rap part. But in the recording process, RM inserted a rap and created what we know as the current version. RM spoke of this decision later on in *Weverse Magazine:*

> *It would've felt incomplete otherwise. I thought we really needed a rap section. In the end, parts of us differ from American pop stars. Because our DNA is just different.*

RM's added rap includes the following:

Got ARMY right behind us when we say so / Let's go

While "Butter" is a classic summer smash on one hand, conveying the feel of joyful dancing in the sun, the lyrics including the rap show how indeed BTS have managed to gain the affection of their fans the way they have. With the rap, "Butter" became not just another summery moment but a point in the group's history reached during a time of strife and change. The rap also adds the group's trademark toughness to a song that is otherwise "smooth like butter."

From 2013 to 2021, BTS was a restless juggernaut that even time seemed to have trouble keeping up with. BTS found themselves reacting to these rapid changes while at the same time trying hard not to lose themselves in the process.

The performance video j-hope, Jimin, and Jung Kook—dubbed "3J" for their initials—made with a rap contributed by Megan Thee

Stallion* was a part of such efforts. Jimin says this performance began as one of j-hope's ideas:

———j-hope suggested, "Wouldn't it be cool if we made a special event for the fans?" and Jung Kook proposed I join them in it. He said, "Let's throw ourselves at it like we used to and show the fans what they didn't get to see in a while," and we were game.

Jung Kook says of the performance:

———When j-hope made the suggestion, I just had this urge to do it. It's always when we really want to do something when we get the best results, and the premise of this plan was great, and the whole thing sounded fun. We practiced, and it felt like we were trainees again. Like when we practiced our moves and learned to dance. It was a different feeling from preparing for our albums.

As it was an almost spontaneous project, they did not have a lot of time to put the performance together. But the three of them practiced hard, almost to the point where it felt violent. Reminiscing of that time, j-hope says:

———We had to do it in the extra time we had after our regular schedules, we just didn't have a lot of time. I hated to do this to them, but I told the younger two we needed to rehearse every moment we had. But because we'd volunteered for it, the mood was very different. Every little part of it, our passion just overflowed.

As we could see from the behind-the-scenes footage," the three of them managed to find another day to reshoot after completing the performance shoot. Jimin explains what happened:

———We hadn't managed to practice a week for it. But then . . . I guess it's the same every time, but you know how the more you do something, the more obsessed you get about it being perfect? "One more time," "Just one more time," and we ended up adding a whole extra day to shoot. If the three of us are dancing and one of us happens to not look as good, we'd have to reshoot the whole part. Or we would like the choreography in one part but not the next one and need to reshoot that one.

The short performance was indeed produced on a voluntary basis, but that didn't make it all fun and games necessarily. Jimin says this particular video, the practicing and filming of it, was a great help in assuaging his anxieties connected to the pandemic:

———Over the pandemic, I was worried that instead of having an exchange of emotions with our fans . . . That it could end up being one-sided. Because we were doing this one-sided thing of making our songs and putting out the video performances. So this was such a precious opportunity for me, and I was incredibly grateful to j-hope. If he hadn't brought it up then, I probably would've just done nothing about it as usual. But making that performance really motivated me.

The more they shot, the more the three became immersed in dance again and found direction in their art. Jung Kook was able to analyze his artistry in more detail thanks to this work:

———It was fun, and at the same time I was like . . . 'Ah . . . is this all I can do?' (laughs). It just wasn't easy learning the choreography and going right into the dancing. My head would understand it, but I could see myself creaking along in the practice room mirrors (laughs). So I went, 'I really need to practice more.' We'd done all sorts of choreography until then, but I never focused on a particular style of dance. But this experience made me realize, I needed to be serious about learning dance. Because our bodies kind of get used to our group's choreography after a while. If I wanted to be able to pick up a new dance and master it quickly, I needed to train my body so it could step up.

Jimin was the same. Praising Jung Kook's strongpoints, his only criticism is reserved solely for himself:

——It was hard, doing that. j-hope is already an above-average dancer of many different genres of dance. And Jung Kook is so great at this choreography. Jung Kook picked up immediately what took me three days to learn . . . (laughs). Since it was different from the kind of dance I was used to, it was hard for me to the point of not liking how I was doing it. The choreography requires flexibility and lightness and strength at the same time . . . It really wasn't easy.

The reason they put so much work into a choreography that was barely a minute long is explained by Jung Kook, in a way that shows how far BTS had come by then in their artistic development:

——We had decided on the final version and finished the shoot, but I kept feeling dissatisfied with the results. There were all these little things that just didn't fit right. 'We can't just release it this way,' I thought. So we made time in our schedules to practice it a bit more. Because I thought I would regret it otherwise. Because if we put in just a little more effort, we could come up with something better.

BTS no longer did anything for the sake of outside approval or to prove themselves. They were now more focused on evaluating themselves and trying to reach a point of excellence where they could feel satisfied with their results.

This was also the only way they could overcome their particular difficulties at the time. The pandemic had taken away the opportunity to empathize with a live audience and gauge the effectiveness of their performances. They could look at online responses, but it was hard for them to be deprived of sharing the live experience onstage.

The online concert *BTS MAP OF THE SOUL ON:E*, held October 10–11, 2020, made this feeling as acute as ever. At the time, Jimin spoke of the fundamental conundrum of having to perform to an invisible audience:

———I actually learn a lot during tours. I collate all the feedback from fans and my own performance notes and gear my practice to this. I ask the other members for advice, I monitor my singing parts . . . But there's no way to do that now. We're practicing a lot, and I'm having fun when recording as I think about things like, 'How should my voice sound when singing in English?' but there's just no feedback.

It was initially hard to judge their own work and measure their progress on their special performances of "Dynamite," "Butter," "Permission to Dance," and "Butter" (Feat. Megan Thee Stallion) as well as the online concert *BTS MAP OF THE SOUL ON:E*. Despite this, they tried hard to see themselves as objectively as possible and try to redefine what it meant to interact with their audience in an era where artists and fans were no longer able to meet in person. V's words, spoken around this time, are proof of why BTS can be BTS:

———We just tried to overcome it. Because we couldn't stay mired in negative feelings forever. These days I'm like . . . If I pour these feelings into something, if I take the things I've felt or my mood and make it into a song, then I feel a bit better. You might ask me if I wish I could get to share more with our fans, but I'm fine with that now. It's all right if we don't show everything, all I want is just . . . The biggest thing for me is that ARMY and we survive this to see each other again in our next concert. I think I can wait without breaking until then.

BTS UNiverse

The global BTS sensation sparked during the pandemic raged on beyond the summers of 2020 and 2021 into fall of that latter year. Even bigger things were happening around the end. On September 20, 2021, BTS spoke for the youth and future generations at the United Nations for the SDG Moment event,* and a few days later on September 24 released "My Universe,"** their collaboration with Coldplay. This song also went to number one on the Billboard Hot 100. Not only had BTS become artists who could collaborate with veritable living legends like Coldplay, they had also the status to be appointed Special Presidential Envoy for Future Generations and Culture by the Korean president and speak of hope and vision for young people everywhere at the UN.

BTS no longer needed any adjectives or other qualifiers to be identified, the juxtaposition of the three letters of their name being powerful enough now. Their smallest throwaway comment on V Live (now Weverse Live) was enough to send a ripple through the Korean press and into overseas newsrooms.

The UN event and collaboration with Coldplay" were meaningful events to them in that beyond the public's response to their work, these two things had helped them find meaning in the work that they were doing after the pandemic period of growing as artists and people.

———Chris Martin is one of the most sincere overseas artists I've ever met.

RM shares his impression of the lead singer of Coldplay and working on "My Universe" with him.

———We run into several kinds of artists overseas. There's the kind who're like, "Oh, you guys are famous these days, good job, I guess? Go for it," and seem to look down on us a little, and those who're all business and go, "I really want to do a song with you!" And there's a third category of people who're oddly positioned between those two. But Chris Martin was none of these three. He was an exception.

The members of BTS had always enjoyed Coldplay's music with Jin even naming them as his favorite group. V also looked up to Chris Martin as a role model. When Coldplay proposed to collaborate on "My Universe," BTS could not say no. But the actual collaboration process with Martin exceeded the members' expectations. RM adds to his impressions:

———It was the pandemic but he insisted on coming. Saying he had never collaborated on anything virtually. He said, "So you guys can't come? Then I'll go to you," just like that. We were so surprised. You had to go through quarantine when you entered Korea back then, and that would've been a significant time commitment for him, but he really came. And when we finally got to meet after all that, he was much more down to Earth than we'd expected.

Jung Kook was also deeply shocked by Martin's attitude. He describes it as a chance to rethink his attitude as an artist.

———I was so bowled over when he said he would come to Korea himself to direct the vocals. I thought, 'Wow . . . Think of how much you'd have to love music to do that! Have I ever put that much passion into something myself . . . ?'

Not only that, Martin also rehearsed and performed with the members for the *BTS PERMISSION TO DANCE ON STAGE—LA* concert, dedicating himself to every aspect of the collaboration. The next year in 2022, Coldplay also participated in Jin's solo song "The Astronaut"· and Jin flew to Buenos Aires in Argentina to take the stage with Coldplay on their MUSIC OF THE SPHERES WORLD TOUR to sing this song.··

Regarding Martin's influence on him, Jimin says:

———He was already a legend but still doing all this for us . . . That positivity was so overwhelming. And since he has so much more seniority in the music industry, we learned a lot from him. Things like, what attitude to have as artists when approaching fans. He's a great singer, of course, but it was also the way he was onstage and how he felt toward the members of his band that was so awesome.

In a conversation between BTS and Chris Martin on some original YouTube content, RM mentions that he sometimes asks himself, "Can a song like this change the world?" BTS were thinking about what meaning their artistry might have in the world, and their encounter with Martin would become one of the things that helped them understand the possibilities more. On the reason why they spoke of such things then, RM says:

———This music . . . I wanted to believe that the music in this file would be valid for a long time, but the world changes so fast that I kept thinking, 'What if it's thrown away in just a year or two?' So I switched to the side of trying to be more universal and long-lasting. My music can be meaningful to someone, or not . . . But I thought it would be good if it were more, just a little more timeless.

If working with Chris Martin had been an opportunity for them to think about their attitude as artists, the UN event on the Sustainable Development Goals was a chance to consider their thoughts on world issues as young people living through the current era. In their presentation, they talked of the need to become not the Lost Generation that had missed many opportunities for growth and progress but the Welcome Generation that believes in possibility and hope, discussing environmental issues and urging the public to get vaccinated for COVID-19.

Jung Kook has this to say about this visit to the UN that came three years after their first:

———It was a lot of pressure to be honest (laughs). A great experience, and it's not like you get to stand at that podium just because you want to. I was mostly thinking, 'My thoughts could just be pretty ordinary, is it right for me to take this opportunity just because it's given to me?'

But Jung Kook's words precisely show how there were things only BTS could do and what they learned from this experience. Jin explains their approach to the presentation:

———We didn't try anything fancy. Our wish was just that people would become more interested in these issues through us. That they were issues with high barriers of entry, and maybe we could help make it easier to talk about them.

The fact that they were the hottest idol group in the world, were in a position to collaborate with Coldplay, and were invited to talk at the UN meant the group could become an entry point to pretty much anything in the world. The UN presentation was an example of how BTS might use their influence for positive purposes. On this, SUGA says:

———It's a lot of pressure to speak for the youth of the whole world. How could we possibly do that? We also live very differently from the great majority of youth around the globe. I hadn't thought about climate change or the environment a lot, my thoughts were just a vague, 'Oh, technology will solve that someday.' But I learned these were very serious problems. Then wouldn't I be able to help people become more familiar with them . . . So if people can get even a little more interested in these issues through us, didn't our fame make it our responsibility to take that on?

Regarding his feelings as he prepared for the presentation, Jimin says:

———I did feel a little strange. Maybe because it had been so long since the onset of the pandemic, but there were things where I was like, 'Eh, whatever,' and had to ignore. Which made me pay less attention to the many things of the world . . . But in preparing for the speech, I was quite shocked that people even younger than I was were extremely interested in environmental issues. The material made me think, 'Really?' and I looked things up on the Internet, and it actually really surprised me. I was embarrassed for myself. 'Here are these other youth who're working so hard to make all of our lives better, how could I just coast like this? When everything we have now was made possible by someone else.' It was honestly a shock, and I am grateful for it.

The "Permission to Dance" performance where BTS shows the UN General Assembly and other parts of the UN Headquarters building* was a chance to show their inner growth. Not only was performing within the UN Headquarters a rare occasion but the process of filming it was also not easy. Because they needed to film it at night when the General Assembly hall was empty, BTS had to go straight to work as soon as they landed at the airport. Their shooting schedule continued from 1 A.M.

until morning. On the second day, they mostly did outdoor shoots, but there were many rules to follow regarding disease prevention. Of the difficulties they had during that shoot, Jimin says:

———It was not a great shooting environment, to be honest. The microphone kept going out mid-song, and we had to adhere to strict COVID-19 rules, which meant we weren't even allowed to drink water inside. So we worried a lot about how it would come out in the end, but the next day, when we were shooting outside with the dancers, it was really fun. The dancers looked so cheerful that I felt cheered up myself, it was a big lift. Even when this song was our song (laughs).

The UN performance was BTS's first overseas stage since the pandemic began, and that alone was reason enough for the members to enjoy this experience. They were already trained to focus on the fun of a performance rather than the constraints of their environment. As j-hope says:

———It was clear what we wanted to show in that performance, and we had faith in that if we followed the schedule and did well in the shoot, a really nice picture would emerge. So we worked very hard each in our different parts to capture on film the best footage we can. I think we managed to come up with good results because we knew all too well the significance of this performance.

As implied in j-hope's attitude, BTS had grown into artists who thought deeply of what they wanted to convey in their work and knew what they had to do to achieve the best possible results. Having reached a point where their every move affected the direction of the global music industry, BTS knew how they needed to act in accordance to such influence. On their YouTube channel, the United Nations posted the "Permission to Dance" performance and wrote this in their caption:

K-Pop sensations BTS perform their hit song Permission to Dance in a video produced at the United Nations. The video accompanies the bands remarks at the SDG Moment and is meant to draw their audiences attention to the importance of Keeping the Promise of the Sustainable Development Goals and to inspire action.

In the video, the members of BTS sing and dance in the General Assembly hall and the park outside the building, realizing the almost surreal content of this caption as they use their influence for the sake of raising awareness on important issues, a laudable use of their status as "sensations." And just when they had reached a new high in just how sensational they were, the world finally began opening up again.

Artist of the Year

On November 21, 2021, at the AMAs held at the Microsoft Theater in Los Angeles, BTS were awarded in the categories of Favorite Pop Duo/ Group, Favorite Pop Song, and the greatest honor, Artist of the Year. SUGA recalls how he felt that evening:

———Our American debut had been on this very stage, but now we were receiving Artist of the Year . . . ? I was thinking, 'Did they make a mistake?' or 'Was the world playing a prank on me?'

But more than that, for SUGA, was this:

———It was almost fascinating to see a live audience again. We learned later that many in the audience had come just to see us. Which was the case four years before as well, but nevertheless it felt different somehow. I was like, 'Did something really change in the interim, or has it been that long since I'd seen crowds in person . . .'

BTS were finally able to perform for a live audience at the 2021 AMAs for the first time since the start of the pandemic. On the very stage, no less, where they had made their American debut four years ago, accompanied by even more screams than before. They were the de facto stars of that year's AMAs.

That BTS were given this honor was not only because they performed "My Universe" with Coldplay and "Butter."˙ The AMAs had also invited New Edition and New Kids on the Block to perform, and with the awarding of Artist of the Year to BTS, that year's ceremony had shaped up to be a tribute to boy bands. The ceremony had in effect been the passing of the baton from the American legends to BTS.

This cemented their place in music history not only in Korea but the US as well, and the fans who had gathered there to witness this coronation had been behind the band in their ascension, the very reason BTS could take the stage on that day. RM says of the mood in the States then:

———I felt like we'd been outsiders or outliers until then, but now it felt, not like we were in the mainstream necessarily, but we were being welcomed more.

When BTS won their first major award at a Korean ceremony in 2016, they had almost lost their minds with joy. But now, even as they rejoiced in their honors, they'd matured enough in their attitude to think deeply on what such accolades meant for them. Jin explains:

————We were as happy to win Artist of the Year at the AMAs as we had been for any grand prize in Korea. But this time, we did have a slight expectation that we might win (laughs). Because I had this thought, 'What should we do if we win?' If previous prizes gave us uncontrollable joy before, now we could feel happy but also handle our emotions a bit better.

The *LOVE YOURSELF* series had unleased a chain reaction that had taken them to the stratosphere, and in that process, they had learned how to maintain altitude. Even around the time they had scored big at the AMAs, they were thinking of next steps. V discusses the meaning given to them through their AMA wins:

————We need to take in what a heavy and wonderful thing this award is to us. We'd always run forward without stopping, became a much-awarded group in the process, and it would've become easy to forget the value of these prizes. We have to be careful about that. To really feel the value of these prizes, to know where we are. More so because during the pandemic, our popularity had felt so abstract.

Jung Kook in the group's acceptance speech for Artist of the Year called this award a "beginning of our new chapter." BTS had to think what that new chapter would entail. Jung Kook elaborates on his acceptance speech:

————Who would've thought we could win Artist of the Year at an American awards ceremony? It was so shocking. It sent chills down my spine. I said it was the beginning of our new chapter, and in that moment, I really felt like it would be that. A moment where I couldn't quite see what exactly it would be like but felt, 'There's going to be something more after this.'

BTS PERMISSION TO DANCE ON STAGE—LA, held only a few days after winning Artist of the Year at the AMAs, felt like the beginning of this new chapter where they were reunited with a live concert audience for the first time in two years. The concerts allowed them to show ARMY how they had grown during the pandemic and also herald the beginning of a new era. If BTS indeed had anything left to prove, it was to show the world what they could do on a live stage. RM describes the direction of the concert:

——Since we weren't able to perform in front of an audience for two years, we wanted to make a kind of giftbox of a concert. To show everyone the things we couldn't show them before, to what we thought they would like, only much, much, much, much stronger.

For this concert, all the solo songs were removed and the setlist was comprised entirely of their group songs, with none of the members pausing for individual breaks during the set. SUGA says:

——The setlist made us think, 'Will we really be able to do this?' or 'If we actually do this, we'll die!' (laughs). But it was our first in-person concert in two years . . . We got rid of all the fancy staging and effects and made the whole show concentrate on us seven from beginning to end. It was a gamble for us. Because during dance rehearsals we were saying things like, "Hey, can we really do all this?" or "We'll only know when we're onstage."

While the setlist was as ambitious as SUGA says it was, particularly in terms of how physically straining it would be, the ambition was also necessary, as SUGA explains:

——The point of this setlist was, "Let's put together a song made only of our biggest hits!"

I said it was the beginning of our new chapter, and in that moment, I really felt like it would be that.

A moment where I couldn't quite see what exactly it would be like but felt, 'There's going to be something more after this.'

—Jung Kook

Indeed, *BTS PERMISSION TO DANCE ON STAGE—LA* featured everything that was big and successful about BTS. It opened with "ON" and burned through "Burning Up (FIRE)," "Dope," and "DNA" before segueing into the recent hits "Boy With Luv," "Dynamite," and "Butter." This made way for a line of powerful numbers beginning with "I NEED U" to "IDOL" while in between these anchoring songs were cuts from the *BE* album. Ending with "Permission to Dance" as the final encore, the history of BTS from past to present would play out in the course of this single setlist. Jin explains it further:

———It really was a chronicle of BTS. Most concerts are about the most recent album. But this concert was all the hits we had saved up exploding at once (laughs). There were many in the audience who probably became fans through "Dynamite," "Butter," or "Permission to Dance." But to us, there are songs like "Dope," "Burning Up (FIRE)," "IDOL," or "FAKE LOVE." So we put all of those in as well and made a kind of title song setlist. It was that much more enjoyable for the audience, and a good way for fans who had just gotten to know us to learn more about our work.

There was some concern with whether they could successfully pull off such a list. But Jung Kook explains why they had no choice but to go with this approach:

———We wanted to give people the best possible show we can with the time and space that was given to us, and we especially wanted to show them the seven of us being onstage the whole time. We were worried. Even if the seven of us stood on that stage together, there was no way of predicting how much or little the audience would enjoy it.

Jung Kook needn't have worried—the response was explosive. Tickets for the four dates at the SoFi Stadium were immediately sold out, and from the moment they began the cheers and screams did not end. The gambit of having all seven of them onstage at the same time paid off, as they were able to put on a show of unrelenting energy that kept building on itself. SUGA speaks of the confidence he felt in this performance:

———You know how in the second half of the show, we're basically in full sprint from "Airplane pt.2" to "IDOL"? I even thought if we weren't able to do that part properly, there was no point in people seeing the show. The first half was more about the dancing, and the second half was about having fun with the audience. And that was the part we were most confident in. I think all our strong points come out there. No set lines of movement, just running around and putting out everything that we are on the stage. Then you end up with a wild kind of performance, and do things you didn't expect to do (laughs). I think it's parts like that that make our concerts so special.

The opening number was, again, "ON," the title song for *MAP OF THE SOUL : 7*. BTS were finally able to showcase the song's epic staging in front of a live audience. It felt like things were going back to normal for them, and they threw themselves into it. Jimin remembers how he felt when the concert began:

———You know that part in the opening number, "ON," where the LED screens come up and we go out onstage. We can see the audience's reaction from behind the screen. But on the first night, we were too keyed up to even take that in. All we could do as we got ready to go out was warm up and think of our choreography and lines of movement. When the concert actually began, we were actually taken aback. Because all throughout the pandemic, we had gotten used to only having the camera in front of us. But it was the second night when we could see the people from a crack between the LED screens. They were singing, screaming, waving their ARMY Bombs . . . That's when I thought, 'That's right, we're doing this performance so we get to see them.' And, 'We're back.'

To do an entire concert with all seven members onstage from beginning to end was an incredible endeavor, especially considering it was the first live concert experience in two years. But V knew that sometimes, joy could make one overcome physical limits:

——My leg was actually acting up right before the concerts. So I was really concerned. 'What if it gets worse,' 'What if it hurts again.' But once the concerts began, and I saw the fans, I was just . . . I was so happy. Really, I was so happy that hurting or not, I was flying through the air. I'd only see the happiness that was right in front of me, and I couldn't feel the slightest pain or any other emotion. And then I'd come back to the hotel and do physical therapy (laughs).

Still overwhelmed from that first in-person concert in two years, V continues:

——There's a part in "IDOL" where we run around a lot, and I really ran around in that part, all excited. I could spend all that happiness in joy. If virtual performances meant setting your expression and gestures to the camera, this concert was about putting all that down and beginning again from pure happiness. I didn't need to calculate anything in my movements, I could just be natural. The pandemic was really hard, but it made me appreciate how precious doing live performances was. It's important to keep in mind, always, that making albums and performing are precious experiences. Really, if I could do those concerts in my dreams again, I would.

Unlike V, j-hope tried hard to keep his emotions under control as he performed. He says that while he had craved to perform for a live audience once again, he focused more on putting on a show that the fans would be happy with.

———I also wanted to go, 'Eh, whatever! Let's enjoy ourselves!' (laughs). But I couldn't. This was a very meaningful performance for a very meaningful audience, and my first priority was to put on as perfect a show as possible. That was what I kept coming back to. I wanted to be more professional than ever before. So I was mostly thinking, 'Let's not get too excited, let's show a little re-straint in the first concert.'

j-hope adds:

———Honestly, if I didn't do that, I really would've lost control.

This is BTS. To give oneself to the happiness of having come through the pandemic and to the first concert on the other side to the point of transcending one's physical limit, while at the same time keeping one's tears in check to put on the best show possible for the fans. This com-bination of hot energy and ice-cold professionalism was enabling BTS to reach the next level.

What j-hope has to say about the UN experience both describes the path they had trod so far and their trailblazing attitude toward the future:

———In the end, the fact that we were given such an invitation at all was an incredible honor. But I still feel a bit embarrassed to ac-cept and overwhelmed. Because I'm an extremely ordinary person. Just a Gwangju native, with a very ordinary upbringing, so much so that all this took a while for me to accept. But to always be grateful for what I've been given is my motto and personal vibe, so whether I'm making music with BTS or going to the UN, I try to study up on my responsibilities as much as I possibly can on my level. I do have a sense of mission about my work, in the end.

Grammy Awards

Their concerts continued in 2022. *BTS PERMISSION TO DANCE ON STAGE—SEOUL*˙ was held on March 10, 12, and 13 and *BTS PERMISSION TO DANCE ON STAGE—LAS VEGAS*˙˙ on April 8, 9, 15, and 16 at the Allegiant Stadium. BTS was finally able to meet their Korean fans,[52] and the Seoul concerts were effectively a herald of the pandemic ending in Korea as well. TV programs began welcoming back live studio audiences, and artists restarted their tours. A new era dawned for BTS and other K-pop artists.

The 64th Annual Grammy Awards held on April 3, 2022, at the MGM Grand Garden Arena in Las Vegas had a different heft to it than the Grammy ceremonies that had come before. Originally scheduled for January 31, its date for welcoming its first live audience in two years was

---

52 This was two years and five months since BTS WORLD TOUR "LOVE YOURSELF: SPEAK YOURSELF" held in Jamsil Stadium on October 26, 27, and 29, 2019. However, because of another wave of COVID-19 infections, the audience was asked not to shout or cheer during the concerts.

delayed for two months with promises of putting on live performances. In the year before at the 63rd Annual Grammy Awards, BTS had contributed a video of their performing "Dynamite"* to the awards show, and they were scheduled to perform "Butter" live for this one. They were, for the second year in a row, nominated for Best Pop Duo/Group.

But just as they did in the 2021 AMAs that previous November when they won Artist of the Year, j-hope tried not to put too much meaning into awards:

———It was an unexpected award, and looking back, it does make me think, 'Wow, that was a big deal' . . . But to be honest, I try not to set too much store on prizes these days. Maybe I just believe that as long as I continue to work hard at and be grateful for what I do and what's given to me, meaningful rewards will follow in whatever form. And the fundamental reason for us winning awards is because of the love we receive, and that's possible because of our fans . . . I think awards are important to the extent that they let us know how much our fans love us.

Having transcended the compulsion to have to prove something to the world, BTS began searching for not goals that other people would be impressed by but inner values instead. j-hope's solo album *Jack In The Box* was perhaps a part of this process. To the BTS members, prizes would always be a big honor, but they tried not to find the meaning of their work in prizes. As RM humorously says about awards and accolades:

————It's not like the Grammys are our friend, or anything . . . (laughs). It's just that everyone keeps going, "Grammy, Grammy," but it's amazing that we were nominated at all. And who cares if we didn't win, anyway? I guess you can put it on a shelf and say, "I'm a Grammy-winning artist," for a few seconds (laughs).

In truth, BTS had hoped to win a Grammy in 2021. They were nominated for the first time for Best Pop Duo/Group Performance and Big Hit Entertainment had ordered a Grammy-shaped cake. This was par for the course for any label whose artist was nominated for a big award, but because of the pandemic, the members waited for the news in Korea and not the site of the awards themselves, and the busy goings-on of the Big Hit staff made them feel as nervous as everyone else about the results. The members even woke up at two in the morning to watch the ceremony. On the mood at that time, V says:

————We were basically thinking, 'It's okay if we don't win,' but on the day of the event itself, the people in the company kept getting our hopes up! (Laughs.) They were just bustling about and brought a cake, and we were like, 'Are we really going to win . . . ?' Everyone was in that room and just . . . (laughs).

In contrast, the mood for the 64th Annual Grammy Awards in 2022 could only be different, as BTS had to show up in person in Las Vegas where a huge entourage could not follow and pandemic measures kept the staff they could bring to a minimum. If anything, BTS could prepare for their stage in a calmer mood than usual. And having won Artist of the Year at the AMAs and performed *BTS PERMISSION TO DANCE ON STAGE—LA* and *BTS PERMISSION TO DANCE ON STAGE—SEOUL*, they had new priorities. Getting awards at award shows were happy occasions, but they could no longer be something to aspire to. Jung Kook explains what they intended to obtain as artists at the Grammys:

———It would've been nice to win a prize, of course, but I don't think we really focused on that. It was a valuable enough experience to have performed on that stage, and we were grateful to the fans for it. More than winning, I was thinking, 'I want to leave behind something meaningful through performance.' We were nervous about the award, of course. But honestly, it's satisfying enough to me to have performed there.

The problem was, this stage performance proved to be a logistical nightmare in itself. It was almost a BTS trademark at this point that every performance required absurd amounts of effort, and the Grammy stage was no different. j-hope and Jung Kook had both tested positive for COVID-19 before the ceremony and had entered quarantine in Korea and the US respectively—by the time they were out of it, they had only a single day to practice with the other members.

And the "Butter" choreography was to be the most difficult they had ever shown in any awards show. As it was eventually revealed, the center-piece of the choreography* is when the members gather in the center of the stage and take off their jackets at once so the sleeves weave into each other. There were other aspects of that performance that were difficult as well, but those could be overcome with effort. But this particular trick could still go wrong on the very night, and indeed, it kept going wrong right up to the final rehearsal.

The jacket trick wasn't the only problem. The "Butter" performance at the Grammys was as elaborate as a Broadway musical number where BTS pretended to be spies or burglars breaking into an art gallery. As it begins, Jin is sitting at a security console watching the members,[53] who eventually make their way to the stage.

Jung Kook enters the stage suspended from above, while V in the audience exchanges a few words with Olivia Rodrigo sitting next to him before presenting a card that he tosses to the stage, which Jung Kook ostensibly catches and inserts into a card reader whereupon all the members except Jin step onto the stage. The choreography involves avoiding security lasers while doing more card tricks until culminating in a big finish with all seven members and backup dancers.

Not only did they have to diverge far from the original "Butter" choreography but also execute magic tricks and do some character acting at the same time. There were so many elements that could go wrong that it had to have been nerve-wracking to prepare for. V, who took a critical point in the performance where he connects the skit in the beginning with the part where the song begins, said he whispered nothing into Olivia Rodrigo's ear and only pretended to say something. He has described how nervous he was in *Weverse Magazine*:

---

53 Jin had injured his left index finger and was post-surgery at the time, and he participated in the performance as much as he could under the circumstances.

I had the feeling I would mess up my timing to toss my card if I entered into an actual conversation. I kept counting off, 'One, two, three, four' in my head, waiting for the moment to toss it. I had in-ear monitors in both ears and couldn't really hear what Olivia Rodrigo was saying, either. I was really shaking, to be honest. We were so worried we couldn't pull off the jacket trick that it was all we could talk about right before we got on stage. We'd rehearsed it only that one time with all the members together just the day before, and that was the biggest worry.

BTS pulling off that Grammy Award performance was like watching a true *Mission: Impossible*–style series of highly choreographed moves. When V tossed his card and Jung Kook seemingly grabbed it out of thin air the cheering began, and the noise grew louder as the members made their way onto the stage. Then came the dance section where the members dodged laser beams and played card tricks. As tension mounted to a climax, they threw off their jackets.

Everyone knows what happened next: the jackets magically tied together. It was a most BTS of moments. Since their debut to this, the Grammy Awards stage, they had gone through good times and bad, but when they were performing, they always put their all into it. If God indeed existed, clearly BTS were blessed onstage—or more precisely, through determination and effort, they had flown as high as they could fly and touched the face of the divine.

Billboard named this performance the best of the evening, while *Rolling Stone* placed it at thirteenth in its list of greatest Grammy performances of all time. The approval of these two behemoths of American mainstream music journalism wasn't the be-all and end-all, but it was enough of a record of what BTS had managed to accomplish on that stage. SUGA says of that night and the American music market in general:

———Since the US is the biggest music market in the world, we were a little fearful at first. But looking back, I wonder, 'Why were we so intimidated?' Not to mention our goal now isn't to win awards but to be like other legendary artists and be working as BTS for as long as possible. There aren't really that many artists who have a very long golden era. But that doesn't mean the artists stop making music overnight or groups just disappear. We're thinking long and hard about how to be onstage for as long and as happily as we can.

INTRO : We're Now Going to Progress to Some Steps

One of the most memorable moments during the pandemic for BTS was appearing in *In the SOOP BTS ver.*,[54]* a television show where the members leave behind the city to spend a few days of rest in nature. BTS shot this show twice, in 2020 and 2021. The fact that they were shooting

---

54 As shown on JTBC and Weverse, with season one airing beginning August 19, 2020 (eight episodes), and season two airing beginning October 15, 2021 (four episodes). Both seasons are available on Weverse.

a show meant this was work, but there was something about this venture that made it different from the other things on their schedule. SUGA remembers the first *In the SOOP* recording:

———In a way, it was time for us to go on a trip together. Because we were preparing to discuss "Dynamite" and a host of other things. I have such great memories of that trip. We all made our meals together, talked, joked around. Because we knew it was so rare to have time like that together, none of us wanted to waste a second of it. So we tried to listen hard to what each other was saying at all times. The *In the SOOP* shoots require you to get up in the morning and think about what you're going to do that day. Then you're like, 'I've never had so much free time before, what do I do?' and then you think of something and spend all day doing that. I realized it was a wonderful thing to spend my days like that.

There were times when they lived in the dorm anxiously waiting for their debut, when they first appeared at the AMAs and their hands shook from nervousness, or when they were on their way up that they thought someday it would all come crashing down. And then, the pandemic happened. But through all that, BTS had lived through it and found their path, and SUGA had become the kind of person who enjoyed indulging in quiet days doing ordinary things with the other members.

Jimin brightens up when talking about *In the SOOP* and his feelings toward SUGA and the other members while making it:

———SUGA is normally pretty quiet and in his feelings, but *In the SOOP* brought him out of himself, as well as the other members . . . I don't know, I felt like, 'I'm so glad we are the people we are.' I was so grateful to all of them. We talked about our private struggles, some for the first time, and really listened to each other's stories.

Jimin's final comment on *In the SOOP* is essentially the meaning BTS members found within each other.

———We spent time together like real brothers.

On April 2, 2021, something big happened in the mainstream Korean music industry: a company called HYBE bought Ithaca Holdings, an American media company. Ithaca Holdings was established by Scooter Braun, who managed Ariana Grande and Justin Bieber, and the company in turned owned subsidiaries such as Scooter Braun Project and Big Machine Label Group. HYBE spent approximately 1 trillion won on its acquisition. And as anyone even remotely interested in K-pop can tell you, HYBE was actually the new name of Big Hit Entertainment since March 31, 2021.

The members of BTS had come from their different towns outside of Seoul to the capital city and debuted as an idol group of a small company, and they had reached heights no one would've imagined for them. They had performed on the Grammy Awards stage and released a forty-eight-track anthology album titled *Proof* commemorating the near-ten years since their debut. And while they grew, Big Hit Entertainment itself also became larger with every passing year. It acquired several companies, created an online platform called Weverse where fans could gather, and merged V Live into it.

As BTS transformed from complete outsider to a complete outlier that proved the exception to every rule in the industry, HYBE itself became an outlier of its own in the K-pop and Korean mainstream entertainment industry. BTS and HYBE were no longer marginal, but they were not as large as the mainstream, either. They were a world unto itself.

But beyond such earthly accomplishments was the truly special gift, the single greatest thing the members had gained from the group: each other. j-hope distills the true meaning of BTS as follows:

———We're basically family, if you think about it. I've seen more of them than my actual family these past ten years . . . If any of them feel sick or happy or sad, I immediately feel the same way. It just happened like that, all of a sudden. When they suffer, I want to be next to them, and when they rejoice, I want to laugh with them, and when they have worries, I want to listen to them . . . I think that's who we are to each other.

j-hope blew up the TIME magazine BTS cover[55] into a poster and had everyone in the group sign it before signing it himself and having it framed and hung in his living room. These seven strangers had come from all over the country to Seoul and become each other's family. Inside the most commercial system of the Korean music industry, where incredible amounts of capital, human resources, marketing, and technology converge, BTS—ironically enough—found a family in each other. The very first line of their very first album, "Intro : 2 COOL 4 SKOOL˙ (Feat. DJ Friz)" in *2 COOL 4 SKOOL*, proved prescient:

We're now going to progress to some steps

---

55 BTS became the first Korean music artists to be on the cover of *Time* magazine's global edition on October 22, 2018. *Time* praised BTS as next-generation leaders and interviewed them in an article titled "How BTS Is Taking Over the World."

This progress was marked not by amazing stats or prizes or other outside proof but in the growth of a community built around each other and their fans, a progress filled with joy and sadness and the future still to come. j-hope, who had come up from Gwangju to Seoul on Christmas Eve of 2010 with only a dream of becoming a recording artist, speaks of his hope for the future of BTS:

———Even now, our group, shall we say . . . We still put in a lot of effort. We don't give up, and thinking of our fans who're supporting us we're like, 'Let's try it, whatever it may be.' And that's scary, too. Because you can't help thinking it can all come crashing down someday. But we take great pride in each other. We've always tried our best, and we're continuing to try our best. I think that's worthy of some respect. And they all have their own thoughts, and they're all so kind (laughs). How did I ever get to meet such people . . . ! There may be moments where we don't quite connect, but we've always overcome that through communication that I'm just too blessed to have met them in this life. I always want to express my thanks to the other members, and we keep running ahead with the thought of, 'If ARMY can smile and rejoice, that is our ultimate happiness.'

Proof

ANTHOLOGY ALBUM
2022. 6. 10

TRACK

CD 1
01 Born Singer
02 No More Dream
03 N.O
04 Boy In Luv
05 Danger
06 I NEED U
07 RUN
08 Burning Up (FIRE)
09 Blood Sweat & Tears
10 Spring Day
11 DNA
12 FAKE LOVE
13 IDOL
14 Boy With Luv (Feat. Halsey)
15 ON
16 Dynamite
17 Life Goes On
18 Butter
19 Yet To Come
   (The Most Beautiful Moment)

CD 2
01 Run BTS
02 Intro : Persona
03 Stay
04 Moon
05 Jamais Vu
06 Trivia 轉 : Seesaw
07 BTS Cypher PT.3 : KILLER
   (Feat. Supreme Boi)
08 Outro : Ego
09 Her
10 Filter
11 Friends
12 Singularity
13 00:00 (Zero O'Clock)
14 Euphoria
15 Dimple